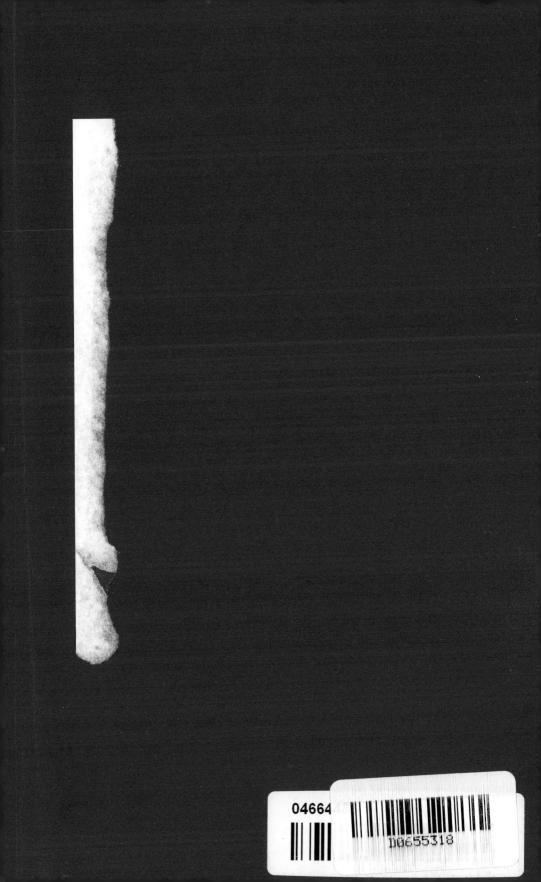

BOMBER FLIGHT BERLIN

www.**rbooks**.co.uk

Also by Mike Rossiter

Ark Royal
Sink the *Belgrano*
Target Basra

with Lieutenant Commander John Moffat
I Sank the *Bismarck*

BOMBER FLIGHT BERLIN

MIKE ROSSITER

BANTAM PRESS

LONDON • TORONTO • SYDNEY • AUCKLAND • JOHANNESBURG

TRANSWORLD PUBLISHERS
61–63 Uxbridge Road, London W5 5SA
A Random House Group Company
www.rbooks.co.uk

First published in Great Britain
in 2010 by Bantam Press
an imprint of Transworld Publishers

A CIP catalogue record for this book
is available from the British Library.

ISBNs 9780593065907 (cased)
9780593065891 (tpb)

Addresses for Random House Group Ltd companies outside the UK
can be found at: www.randomhouse.co.uk
The Random House Group Ltd Reg. No. 954009

The Random House Group Limited supports the Forest Stewardship
Council (FSC), the leading international forest-certification organization.
All our titles that are printed on Greenpeace-approved FSC-certified paper
carry the FSC logo. Our paper procurement policy can be found at
www.rbooks.co.uk/environment

Typeset in 12/16pt Times New Roman by
Falcon Oast Graphic Art Ltd.
Printed and bound in Great Britain by
Clays Ltd, Bungay, Suffolk

2 4 6 8 10 9 7 5 3 1

Mixed Sources
Product group from well-managed
forests and other controlled sources
www.fsc.org Cert no. TT-COC-2139
© 1996 Forest Stewardship Council
FSC

To my parents,
who survived the Blitz on London

CONTENTS

Acknowledgements	ix
Preface	1
Introduction: Days to Remember	7
1. The Tools of the Trade	17
2. The Skipper Gets Inspired	27
3. Into Uniform	39
4. The Shape of Things to Come	58
5. The Only Weapon	73
6. The Crew Meets Up	87
7. The Start of the Revolution	109
8. Harris Takes Over	124
9. Into Battle	139
10. The Winning Weapon	153
11. The Next Five Missions	168
12. Lucky C Charlie	186
13. Living Dangerously	202
14. Otherwise a quiet trip	216
15. Maximum Effort	225
16. The End of C Charlie	243

17. Leading the Way   254

18. The End Game   270

Conclusion: Reunion   280

Bibliography   291

Picture Acknowledgements   295

Index   297

ACKNOWLEDGEMENTS

It will be obvious that I could not have written this book without the assistance of Flight Lieutenant Geoff King DFC and I am grateful for the time that he spent talking to me and answering my questions. I was relatively ignorant of the history of Bomber Command in the Second World War and I would like to thank Adam Harcourt-Webster for his advice on how to approach this subject and for his initial suggestions of some key texts. Adam also provided very welcome assistance in tracking down the members of the bomber crew who, with Geoff King, form the basis of this book. Sadly, most of those crew members have now died, leaving few records of what they once did in the skies of Europe. Surviving relatives were pleased in most cases to give as much assistance as they could, and I must thank Laura Davis, Roy's wife, in the Isle of Man, who not only talked about her husband but also remembered the crew on leave in wartime Boston with great affection. Maureen Cole, William Burns, Ian Rodger and Peter Campbell in Kirkcudbright sent me what information they could find of

Robbie Burns, and Gwen Green in Toowoomba told me about Frank's early childhood on his father's farm and the difficulties that he had in adjusting to civilian life when he returned to Australia after the war. Fraser Laing in Canada also gave me some information about his father George.

I would like to thank the staff at the National Archives in Kew and Peter Elliot, the Senior Keeper at the RAF Museum Archives in Hendon, for their help in finding and reproducing files and documents for me.

I must also thank those whose work is so vital to my ability to write and publish these stories of ordinary people like Geoff King and George Laing who took part in one of the most horrific wars in history. The book would not exist without the work of my agent, Luigi Bonomi, and the people with whom I work at Transworld: my editor Simon Thorogood, production editor Vivien Garrett, picture editor Sheila Lee and copy-editor Brenda Updegraff. As ever, my wife, Anne, and my two sons, Max and Alex, put up with a great deal, and I am eternally grateful.

PREFACE

G eoff King, his pilot and skipper George Laing, and the five other members of the bomber crew whose story this is started their front-line service in September 1943. The war had ground on for four long years and over that time Bomber Command had grown in size and effectiveness. A year earlier just 178 four-engined bombers had been in service; now there were 740 of these aircraft. In the month that Geoff King first took off on a raid over Germany, Bomber Command dropped over 128,000 tons of high explosives on German cities. The crew started their operational tour at a critical time. They were just a few weeks away from being thrown into the massive campaign of raids against the German capital, Berlin. Many senior officers in the Royal Air Force believed that these unrelenting air raids on the centre of Nazi power might bring about the end of the war.

The leaders of Bomber Command supported a view that had gained a great deal of currency in the 1930s – that strategic bombing could win a war by creating such devastation that the people and the government of the bombed country would no longer have the will to continue the fight. This was based on a naïve analysis of the way that modern societies were held together and functioned, but it became such an article of faith that it prevented any deep analysis of just how bomber forces were going to achieve their strategic objectives.

The start of the war in 1939 quickly showed that creating a strategic bomber force required a great deal more thought and effort than had previously been imagined. Whether it was mounting daylight raids against German shipping, or carrying out leaflet-drops over German cities, or indeed the first night raids against Berlin, the casualties in aircraft and aircrew were out of all proportion to the damage inflicted against Germany. It became obvious that vital issues like training for long-range navigation at night or in bad weather, bombing accuracy, protection against fighter attack and the development of radio direction-finding aids had all been seriously neglected by the RAF.

The Blitz – the bombing of London and other cities like Coventry by the German Luftwaffe – created the most awesome destruction of populated areas ever seen in war and revealed to the world how deadly air raids were. It showed also that, despite the initial damage, the numbers of planes and the sheer weight of bombs needed to destroy a city or knock out a country permanently was much greater than that currently deployed by either Germany or Britain.

Rather than abandon the dream of a war-winning weapon, Bomber Command persisted, building more and bigger bombers, assembling an enormous fleet of aircraft. At the same time, technical innovations created a variety of techniques to transmit radio beams to keep the bombers on course and produced airborne radar to assist the bomb aimers in identifying their targets. The commander-in-chief of Bomber Command, Sir Arthur Harris, was determined to eradicate the weaknesses and failures that had bedevilled the bomber force in the first years of the war. Yet the modernization and expansion never entirely reduced the regular casualties that the Germans managed to inflict on every operation, and these meant that the odds were always against a bomber crew surviving a full tour of thirty missions.

The casualties, however, did not deter people like Geoff King, who was just one of the thousands who volunteered to join Bomber Command. Part of the attraction was the adventure of flight. The RAF was modern, at the cutting edge of technology, the aircraft were fast and impressive, and the men who flew in them were bold and glamorous. Bomber Command at the time was viewed by the population at large as the only service that was taking the war to the enemy's heartland; people believed that the bombers were making the Germans pay for the violence they had inflicted on the cities of Britain. Of this there was no doubt. The Blitz on London and Coventry had shocked the world, but the thousand-bomber raid on Cologne and the fire-raising raids on Hamburg that followed in July 1943 were far more severe than anything the Luftwaffe had been able to carry out.

Geoff King was a young man from a poor farm labourer's family in Essex, but the volunteers came from every country in the Commonwealth. In 57 Squadron, where Geoff and his crew first saw combat, almost a third of the airmen were from Canada. Geoff's crew had a Canadian, George Laing, as its skipper; a Scot, Robbie Burns, as its flight engineer; a Londoner, Vincent Day, as its wireless operator; a Welshman, Sidney Thomas, as rear gunner; and an Australian, Frank Green, in the mid-upper gun turret. Roy Davis, the navigator, from Manchester, had been to grammar school, while Geoff had left school at fourteen.

All of the crew, whatever their background and education, had come out of the lengthy training period with well-developed engineering and mathematical skills. These were necessary to operate and fly the advanced and complicated weapon that was a Lancaster bomber to a target many hundreds of miles away – yet these talents, which might have remained hidden for ever without the onset of war, were not enough. Germany invested as much in its air defences as Britain invested in its bomber force, and flying over occupied Europe to a target in Germany meant spending hours in constant danger of death or injury. Without the courage, and the considerable mental and physical strength, of the aircrews, the bomber offensive against Germany would have been impossible. Berlin was the best-defended target of all and the long bombing run over the spread-out city required exceptional fortitude and commitment. Geoff and his crew flew over this target ten times and were hit on several occasions, once having to return to their base with two engines out of action. The flight home, at a height within easy range of anti-aircraft fire, in bad weather, with the added fear of having to ditch in the North Sea, was a test of endurance. That night was the worst Christmas Eve that any of them could remember, but a week later, the aircraft repaired, they were once more flying through the shellbursts and searchlights over Berlin.

The raids on the German capital did not end the war. The defences were formidable and in the period from September 1943 to March 1944, German night fighters or anti-aircraft fire shot down around 1,500 heavy bombers, with the loss of almost 10,000 young aircrew. Geoff and his crew not only survived this endless storm of shells and bullets, but throughout their tour their performance as a bomber crew improved. They were getting to the target and coming closer to the aiming point. On their twenty-ninth mission they were selected to carry out a pinpoint raid on a German port in the Baltic, where they narrowly avoided being shot down by enemy fighters.

When, against all odds, their first tour was finished, the crew rejected the offer of a six-month rest from operations to spend time in training units. Whilst most aircrew grasped at the chance of a break from the relentless stress of mission after mission, Geoff, George and the rest of the crew had become so sure of their own abilities, so confident and trusting in each other that they preferred to stay together and continue to risk their lives over Germany rather than be split up.

Their next set of operations, as target-markers in 97 Squadron, involved a completely different set of dangers.

Flying in daylight against precision targets in France while the Allied armies stormed the beaches of Normandy was the culmination of the skills that they had honed in the previous six months flying over Berlin and other German cities. The D-Day landings marked the end of the dream that the bombers would defeat Germany single-handed, but Geoff and his crew continued to play a key role in the war, preventing the build-up of German reinforcements and then targeting the sites that were launching V1 'buzz' bombs against London.

Out of the 125,000 aircrew who served in Bomber Command in the war, 55,500 died and another 8,403 were seriously wounded. Only 24 per cent of the aircrew in Bomber Command survived death, injury or capture. In the face of these statistics, what Geoff and his crew did in their two tours of operations was truly remarkable. They were ordinary young men who faced the threat of death over Germany on more than fifty long, stressful operations, and they showed skill and courage of a very high order. These missions took place over just twelve months, but they never forgot their frightening, heart-stopping experiences over Berlin and other targets, nor the comrades they shared it with. That bond has remained with them to the grave.

The tale of Geoff, George and the others has been pieced together from a written memoir, remembered anecdotes and a few sparse contemporary records, and it deserves to be told. Sadly, in a few more years none of the men who carried out these or similar missions will be alive to tell their own stories.

Introduction

DAYS TO REMEMBER

Turning right from the long, sweeping turn-off at junction 7 on the M11 motorway takes you on to a wide, little-used dual carriageway. It runs south of Stansted airport, from where, in 1944, United States B-26 bombers took off to attack German positions on the beaches of Normandy. Now twin-engined Airbus and Boeing jets, glinting in the sun, fly overhead on their way to cities in Europe and beyond. Further, and the road offers exits for quaintly named towns and villages that have lain for centuries in the gentle Essex countryside.

On the outskirts of one small market town, with narrow streets and old cottages with ornate rendered walls, lives Geoff King, now in his late eighties, less healthy and less mobile than he would like to be. Still with an active mind, he sits in his conservatory observing the rich variety of wild birds that flock to his country garden. Occasionally he studies the books, maps and photographs of a former life that surround his desk. A flight lieutenant in the Royal Air Force, awarded the Distinguished Flying Cross, Geoff King is never far from the memories of a short period, almost seventy years ago, when death sat on his shoulder. In just twelve months, Geoff formed a vital, rock-solid bond with six other airmen. It became the most fundamental aspect of their existence, and was to remain with them in some form for the rest of their lives.

On the evening of 23 September 1943, at East Kirkby air base in Lincolnshire, Geoff sat in the second 'dickie seat' in the cockpit of a Lancaster bomber, call sign E Edward. The aircraft's four Rolls-Royce Merlin engines – the same engines that had powered the Spitfire and Hurricane fighters in the Battle of Britain in 1940 – their twelve cylinders firing noisily but not yet delivering their massive 1,400 horsepower, sent vibrations along the wings and through the whole airframe. The cockpit was crowded with levers and dials, and the smell of metal, hot oil and high-octane petrol filled the fuselage, mingling with the exhausts from the procession of Lancasters in front of them.

It was four years into the Second World War. British and US forces had defeated the Axis armies of Germany and Italy in North Africa and had invaded southern Italy. There was heavy fighting with the German army as the Allies tried to advance up the Italian peninsula; the German army was also engaged in a dreadful, blood-soaked conflict with the Red Army in Russia. The United States Army Air Force (USAAF) had established bases in England, Stansted among them, and their big B-17 and

B-21 bombers had started to launch daylight raids on targets in Germany, but had suffered heavy casualties. The Royal Air Force had assembled in Bomber Command a force of 650 front-line heavy bombers that were conducting a continuous campaign of night raids on German cities and towns.

Lancaster E Edward, part of the complement of 57 Squadron, was just another aircraft on the latest raid on a German town, but for the crew it was highly significant. None of them had ever flown on an active mission before. In the pilot's seat to the left of Geoff was Flight Lieutenant George Laing, the 'Skipper', a tall, slim Canadian with piercing blue eyes and a wicked smile. He had a blunt, no-nonsense approach to flying and to serving in the RAF that had already aroused the ire of some members of the squadron's hierarchy. George was keeping the big bomber on its course around the perimeter track of the airfield. It needed a deft hand on the throttles to prevent the large main wheels, which he could not see from the pilot's seat, from running off the concrete and becoming stuck in the muddy grass at its edge. The RAF training manual called on the captain of a bomber 'to make firm decisions in any emergency, and show calm determination throughout the operation, keeping in constant touch with all members of his crew. By leadership and courage he must earn the admiration of his crew, and by his flying skill, their confidence and respect.'

Directly behind the Skipper, shielded by a curtain, was Flight Lieutenant Roy Davis, 'Curly', from Manchester. Short, with dark curly hair, quiet and precise, Curly was the navigator, in Bomber Command's eyes the most important member of the crew. According to the manual he must 'prepare a flight plan and give accurate and frequent instructions regarding speed, height and course to the pilot throughout the mission, and must insist that they are obeyed in spite of external distractions. At all times he should know his position and be able to calculate the time of arrival at prescribed turning points, and rendezvous.'

Behind Curly, again on the left-hand side of the fuselage, sat the wireless operator, Warrant Officer First Class Vincent Day. 'Vin', a Londoner, was the shortest member of the crew and after a few drinks the life and soul of the party. The wireless operator had to keep watch on all the radio frequencies in use and monitor the transmissions from Base, Bomber Command, and on some missions from the Pathfinder aircraft leading the attack. All information had to be passed on quickly to the pilot, navigator and other members of the crew affected by it. The manual also said, ominously, that the wireless operator 'plays an invaluable part in safety when ditching becomes inevitable'. This was true. The transmission of a signal containing the accurate position of a downed crew was sometimes the key factor in their being saved from a freezing death in the North Sea.

Further aft, past the thick main spar that crossed the fuselage at thigh height, was the mid-upper gunner's position, a clear Plexiglas turret fitted with two .303-inch calibre machine guns that rose out of the top of the fuselage. The turret was occupied by Warrant Officer First Class Frank Green, 'Flash', an Australian and so, like the

Skipper, a long way from home. He was a long-distance runner, lean, quiet and patient. He was responsible for 'maintaining a continuous vigilant lookout for enemy aircraft throughout the operation, and in the airfield circuit and en route to and from his target must warn the pilot of any collision which is imminent.'

There was another gunner in the Lancaster, sitting cramped in a turret in the tail of the plane, with four machine guns pointing to the rear. The loneliest position of all, it was crewed by Pilot Officer Sidney 'Tommy' Thomas from Wales. 'Tommy' was the oldest member of the crew and was married – a rarity amongst front-line aircrew, many of whom were barely out of their teens. His was an uncomfortable position in many ways. It was very cold, hardly affected by the Lancaster's heating system, so every rear gunner was given an electrically heated flying suit. The position was also the most vulnerable to air attack, and bore the main weight and responsibility of defending the rest of the crew against enemy night fighters. His duty was 'to keep continuous watch throughout the mission, and when in the target area keep a strict lookout for hostile fighters, and not allow his attention to be distracted by the conflagration beneath him.'

Geoff King, or 'Kingy' as the Skipper called him, was the air bomber, popularly known as the bomb aimer, whose position after take-off was lying in the nose of the aircraft looking down and forward. Gentle and fresh-faced, Geoff was quiet and precise. His job was to operate the bombsight and give instructions to the pilot over the target area to ensure that the bomb load was dropped accurately on the planned aiming point, ignoring whatever explosions and anti-aircraft fire they might seem to be flying towards. The bomb aimer was also required to operate the forward gun turret, which was situated above the clear blister that housed the bombsight and on which were mounted two machine guns.

Finally, sitting to Geoff's right was the flight engineer, Warrant Officer Robert Burns. 'Jock', as he was inevitably called, was a stolid engineer from Kirkcudbright in Scotland with a distinctive burr to his voice and a warm but dry sense of humour. He had to have an understanding of all the mechanical details of the airframe and the engines, and was responsible for logging and monitoring fuel consumption, operating fuel transfers in flight, observing oil temperatures and pressures, supercharger settings and engine-power output. He had to have the knowledge and skill to carry out repairs in flight where possible. 'Essentially the pilot's assistant, he has to be able to fly the plane when necessary, and, over the target, by keeping a careful lookout on the starboard side of the cockpit, give immeasurable assistance to the Pilot and greatly relieve his mental strain.'

So the Lancaster, with seven souls on board, moved round the perimeter track, getting closer and closer to the end of the runway and its own take-off. The Skipper alternately advanced the throttles for the engines on one wing and then the other to manoeuvre the aircraft round the airfield, Jock anxiously checking engine temperature and oil pressure. The gunners checked their safety catches and the hydraulic power to their turrets. Everyone checked their intercoms, the radios, the navigation aids, ammunition, oxygen bottles, signal lamps, fuel load, oil and coolant. All this had already been checked that morning by the aircraft's ground crew, the engine mechanics, airframe riggers and armourers. It had been signed for by the Skipper, checked and tested again in the morning's air test, then checked yet again. Curly looked at his charts and rehearsed once more the heading and the flight times. Geoff went over in his head the target indicators and the geography of the approach to the target German city that he had been given at the briefing.

The Skipper focused on the aircraft ahead and on that part of the perimeter track that he could see from his position 20 feet above the concrete. He spoke on the intercom to each crew member in turn, then went through the take-off checklist with Jock: compass, air-speed indicator, heaters on, trim tabs on the elevator set, the rest neutral, master-engine fuel cocks on, selector cocks to no. 2 tank, booster pumps set, radiator flaps open, flaps set to 15 degrees. Now it was time to wait for a green light to flash on, then he could release the brakes and push all four throttles forward, port levers slightly in advance to counter the Lancaster's tendency to swing to port because of the rotation of its propellers. The noise of the engines rose to a roar and increased in pitch. The vibrations become more severe, and the Lancaster, carrying nearly 2,000 gallons of petrol, 4,000 lb of high explosive and hundreds of small incendiary bombs, rolled along the runway and strained to reach its take-off speed of 105 m.p.h.

The heart rate of every member of the crew increased.

As the tail wheel rose from the concrete now speeding beneath Tommy's turret, they all knew that they were at the point of no return. A slight mistake by the Skipper, an engine failure now, would end in their utter destruction, a livid, white-hot fireball and a thick column of black smoke marking the deaths of seven attractive, intelligent and highly trained young men.

On this particular late-summer evening, however, there were many emotions circulating through the hearts and minds of Geoff King, the Skipper and the crew. They had come together from many parts of Britain and her empire, and had known and flown with each other for several weeks. The awful tumult of war had enabled each of them to escape the limits of his background, education and geography, and to realize ambitions that earlier in his life would simply have been laughed aside. They had volunteered, and had been encouraged, in Bomber Command's constant search for new men, fresh blood. They had been well trained by men who knew what they were going to face over the skies of Germany, and the training had been intensive, drilling into them day after day the routines, the checklists, the calculations that would ensure that they could carry out their jobs and stay alive. They had got to know each other, learned to recognize each other's voices over the intercom, acquired a sense of how each man worked. But they had never flown over enemy territory and faced the guns of the German soldiers and airmen who wanted to kill them. This, they knew, was the one big test that would reveal whether their training had been good enough, whether deep inside themselves they were good enough to carry out the mission without letting themselves and their fellow crew members down. As the Lancaster's four big propellers hauled it into the sky and the Skipper raised the landing gear and retracted the flaps, and Curly read out the first heading of the night, the seven young men aboard E Edward were about to realize their lifetime's ambition: to be on active service in Bomber Command. They were also about to find out the truth about themselves.

1

THE TOOLS OF THE TRADE

Geoff King was born in January 1922, in a small hamlet in the parish of Berden, north-west Essex. Rural life in England had changed little since Constable painted his idyllic pastoral landscapes in this area a hundred years earlier. The cottage in which Geoff lived was built with beam-and-plaster walls, a thatched roof and brick floors laid over the earth. It had a small living room, a parlour and a tiny kitchen in a lean-to at the back. Upstairs there were two small bedrooms under the eaves. Water was drawn from a well and light was provided by oil lamps. It was dark and bleak.

The cottage was part of a small row attached to Peyton Hall Farm. It was an isolated life, and Geoff's sole companion was his younger sister Nan, but the farm was a marvellous place to explore and grow up. Opposite their cottage was a thatched, five-bay cart lodge with a large wagon bay at one end, and the massive wooden timbers of the building were a perfect climbing frame. Leading from the cart lodge was a gravel road which passed by the side of the horse pond, where the farm horses would stop to drink at the end of the working day. Here Geoff and Nan would spend hours with jam jars on the hunt for red-breasted sticklebacks and minnows, or early spring tadpoles. Another pond, sourced from a deep well in the fields, kept watercress beds topped up throughout the year, and both pond and well were out of bounds for the small children because they were deep and dangerous.

The meadows surrounding the family's cottage were a glorious sight in spring and summer, filled with wild flowers, yellow cowslips and primroses mingling with pale blue harebells. The hedgerows with their giant elm trees also contained a profusion of wild flowers, and a nearby wood was carpeted with bluebells and daffodils. The fields and woodland teemed with wildlife – foxes, rabbits, field mice – and a love of nature remains with Geoff to this day.

Geoff's father and grandfather had both fought for Britain – his father, in the Essex regiment, had taken part in the Battle of the Somme in 1916, and his grandfather, a former quartermaster sergeant, had fought in the Boer War at the relief of Mafeking in 1900 and then seen action a couple of years later in Afghanistan on the North-West Frontier. Both men were now employed as horse-keepers at Peyton Hall Farm. Life was dominated by labour. Every day at four in the morning the two men would wake, go out to the stable to groom the horses and harness them up for the working day, which would begin an hour later. They would then work until the light faded. Lunch was taken in the fields – the top of a home-baked cottage loaf and a piece of hard, strong cheese, a big slice of home-made fruit cake, all wrapped in greaseproof paper in a straw shoulder bag. A First World War army canteen was filled with unsweetened black tea.

There was little in the way of mechanization; all the work on the farm was carried out by manual labour with the assistance of the great Shire horses. Two of these magnificent animals would be harnessed up to a single-furrow wooden-beam plough and, Geoff's father walking behind, the thick earth would turn over clean and fresh as the horses pulled, their breath turning to frosty clouds in the cold morning air. It took ages, but the field would look magnificent with its dead straight furrows. Next came the horse-drawn harrows to break up the sods, then the seed drills.

Opening up the field for harvesting also demanded extremely hard work. To prevent the horse-drawn binder from damaging the crop, a 5-foot swathe was cut around the edge of the field by Geoff's father and grandfather using hand-held scythes. They would take it in turns to scythe down the wheat and tie it into loose sheaves; it would take days. As Geoff grew older this labour was eased as the farm acquired a small binder that could be pulled around the edge of the fields. This took just a few hours, greatly reducing the risk of the weather turning in the middle of the harvest and ruining the crop.

When the fields were cut the sheaves would be stood in stooks. These would be left in the fields for a few days for the grain and straw to dry, before being loaded on to horse-drawn carts and taken to the yard where the stacks were being built. Geoff would sometimes be allowed to lead the horses if there were not too many gates to negotiate. The animals sent hot gusts of breath over his head. Calm, bid-dable beasts, they towered above the little boy and could have hurled him into the air if they had wanted. In the stackyard the sheaves were built up into stacks, side by side, with enough space for the threshing machines to be placed between them. Then Geoff's father and grandfather would thatch them to keep the rain off the grain before it was threshed. Threshing was done by a machine hitched up to a steam traction engine – a fascinating monster to a young boy. It hissed and puffed on its great iron wheels, smoke pouring from its funnel, its brass gleaming, the smell of hot oil and coaldust mingling with the animal smells of the farmyard. Geoff was intrigued by this exotic machine and the sliding pistons, flywheels and pulleys that drove the thresher.

At the age of five it was time for school, which meant a walk every day to the little church school in Berden, 2½ miles away. Geoff's mother took him halfway there and he walked the rest of the way in the company of other chil-dren, across fields and along muddy paths, one day losing his wellington boots in the thick mud of a farmyard gate-way. The walk to school passed another hamlet, Little London, home to another set of grandparents, and there Geoff, and later his sister Nan too, stopped for a slice of bread with sweet condensed milk poured over it, or sprinkled with very moist brown sugar.

The winter of 1927 was a severe one. It started snowing in December and continued for days and days. The small rural community quickly became isolated as the snow deepened in the fields and thick drifts blocked the lanes and pathways. Ice formed on the inside of the bedroom windows and people huddled round their coal-burning ranges for warmth, wrapped in their thickest jumpers and overcoats. When food started to run out Geoff's father and the other men from the farm started to cut their way through the deep snowdrifts and, after several days, managed to clear a way to the grocer's shop in Manuden, the nearest village. Geoff rode the horse and cart as it forced its way through the deep, sparkling snow that had blanketed the normal contours of the countryside. The drifts stood high above the banks at the sides of the lane and, despite their efforts to clear it, in places the snow still reached the wheel hubs of the cart, nearly touching the chest of the great horse. At the store the cart was loaded with fresh bread and other food, then the men and their young companion struggled back to their beleaguered families.

Every farm had its orchard, and another time-honoured occupation for small children was scrumping – the illicit gathering of fallen fruit, or, if they were daring enough, fruit still hanging on the tree. The farm had a large Victoria plum tree and, close by, a pear tree that produced sweet Williams pears. The plums ripened first, and the two small children would make their silent, and they hoped secret, attack on the fruit. They walked along a deep ditch between the stackyard and the orchard, then from their hiding place crept under the hedge on the bank and crawled hurriedly to the fruit trees. After stuffing what fruit they could into every pocket and inside their jumpers, they crawled into a large drainpipe that ran under a track leading into the stackyard, where they ate as much fruit as they could cram into their stomachs. Geoff later discovered that every raid they made was gleefully observed by the farmer and his family.

Nothing remains the same, and the charmed young life in this rural backwater wasn't immune to change. One day when Geoff was seven a large biplane – he has no idea what type – flew low over the village while giving an aerial display at nearby Bishop's Stortford. It was the first aeroplane that he ever saw. Impressive and magical, it was also a harbinger of things to come. Barely eleven years later, so profound had been the changes in technology and circumstances that there was nobody in Britain who wasn't conscious of and apprehensive about aircraft flying above them. On a more immediate and personal level, the plane also seemed to mark a new phase, for a short while later Geoff found himself moving home. His family had been rescued from the rural squalor of their small cottage and given a modern council house with three bedrooms and electricity, water and gas laid on. This new row of houses had been built in the village of Manuden, which had around 600 inhabitants. Geoff found the local school more rigorous and demanding than his previous one, and initially it was a shock, but he was keen to learn and soon started to do well.

The most exciting thing that happened, however, was the stuff of childhood dreams. At the age of eight Geoff was asked to work in the village grocery store. His parents had to get permission from the local education authority in Saffron Walden and after a medical he was issued with a small red booklet that allowed him to work part-time. He was paid 5 shillings – 25 pence in today's money – plus a quarter of a pound of sweets a week!

The grocer's sold everything from pins to motorcycles and supplied all the local hamlets around the village. It also housed the post office and had the only public telephone in the village. Geoff prepared the orders of tea, sugar, dried fruit, biscuits, cheese and anything else that the customers ordered and delivered them on his bike. At the back of the shop was a baker's, making fresh bread and cakes, and at the side was the coalyard, where coal and coke would be shovelled into sacks weighing a hundredweight or half a hundredweight. Deliveries were still made by horse-drawn vehicles, the bread taken out daily in a small two-wheeled van and the coal weekly on the back of a four-wheeled cart.

The bakery in particular was a source of lasting memories for Geoff. The smell of the baked dough and the taste of freshly cut ham in a hot 'huffer' – a type of roll, which they made from pieces of dough from the offcuts of the loaves – he considered to be without equal. His love of tasty food never left him and his familiarity with baking gave him a useful point of contact with the cooks and caterers he was to meet in his service life.

At the age of fourteen he left school with basic qualifications in Elementary Education and was offered a three-year apprenticeship at Millars in Bishop's Stortford, a company that manufactured heavy plant and machinery for the construction industry. Clocking in each day at seven, with an hour for lunch and a morning and afternoon teabreak, he started working in the machine shop, learning to cut screw threads and operate capstan lathes to very fine tolerances, and then moved on to the drawing office. In retrospect, it was a key moment in Geoff's life. It was now that he made the final transition from an old, timeless, rural England to a modern, industrial life and, unbeknown to him at the time, it provided him with the skills that later would put him in the nose of a Lancaster bomber.

A year later, however, it might all have ended for ever. In August 1937 Geoff was cycling to work with a colleague. At a crossroads in the town, not far from the Millars factory, a car hit both of them. Geoff's workmate was merely bruised, but Geoff was carried along by the car for 100 yards before falling off the wing on to the road. Unconscious, he was taken to Rye House Hospital, where he was found to have a depressed fracture of the skull. Lying in a darkened room, he was kept on the danger list for over a week before he recovered sufficiently to be moved to a general ward. It was an anxious and worrying time for his parents, but eventually he was allowed home. He spent the next month recuperating, but when he returned to work he found that he had not properly recovered. His balance was affected and he had sudden headaches and nosebleeds.

Rightly concerned, Geoff's GP sent him to Harley Street for an examination by the eminent surgeon Lord Horder, a consultant to the Royal Family. His diagnosis was succinct and unhesitating. An operation was needed to open up

Geoff's skull and remove the pressure on his brain, and there was not a moment to lose. This, however, was in the days before the National Health Service, so the costs of the operation would naturally fall to the insurance company of the driver who had careered into Geoff and his friend. The company objected to the expense, so once more Geoff took the train to Liverpool Street Station and made his way across town to Wimpole Street to see the insurance company's own doctor, then on for a second opinion to the London Hospital to see a neural consultant. Neither could argue with the original diagnosis, so Geoff went back into hospital to await the operation. Any sort of surgery then was, of course, more dangerous than it is today, and there were no antibiotics, but in Lord Horder's opinion Geoff had no choice. Entering the hospital, it was impossible for him not to feel anxious about what the future might hold.

The operation, however, had a happy outcome and eventually Geoff returned to work at Millars. He was told that he would have an area of vulnerability in his skull for the rest of his life and that he should never play sports or become involved in any other activity that might result in a blow to the head. Nevertheless, he continued to play tennis and ride his bike, and of course nobody could foresee what was going to happen in a few years' time.

In Millars it was time for Geoff to try his hand at the thread-cutting machine in the workshop. The machines were all driven by pulleys from an overhead drive shaft that ran the length of the factory, and this particular machine was right at the end of the shaft, where the rough forge castings were stored. It was roofed but otherwise open to the elements, even in winter. Sometimes the wind and snow blew in, but Geoff continued to work to extreme tolerances, despite being bundled up in overcoats, mufflers and mittens. This was before computers had transformed machinery; the most precise and accurate equipment was still manufactured by workmen using their own skill and craftsmanship, honed by years of apprenticeship. When Geoff was able to produce flawless work in the screw-cutters, he was allowed to start training on centre and turret lathes, making round- and square-sectioned screw threads and eventually graduating to work on large centre lathes making components for the various jigs used on the assembly line in the factory. All the cutting tools that he used were his responsibility and he kept them sharp and accurate, grinding and forming them so that he could work to tolerances of 1,000th of an inch. He took considerable pride in his developing craftsmanship, and he was growing up. With the prospects of finishing his apprenticeship, and the rising demand for skilled craftsmen in the car and air-craft factories springing up in Luton and other towns just a few miles from London, the future looked good.

2

THE SKIPPER GETS INSPIRED

George Laing was born 3,000 miles away from the sleepy hollow of Berden, in another small town, Durban, Manitoba, in the great prairies of Canada. His parents, Scottish immigrants, had led a peripatetic life. His father, Charles, had immigrated to Canada from Scotland in 1912, but at the outbreak of the First World War in 1914 he had enlisted in the armed forces. Charles Laing fought, like Geoff's father, in the Battle of the Somme, and was affected by a German poison-gas attack, but he recovered and continued to fight in the army until the Armistice. He travelled back to Scotland and in Edinburgh met and married his wife, Elizabeth, with whom he returned to Canada in 1919, intending to settle down in the new country.

The Laings lived first in Alberta, where Charles worked for a construction company building a dam on the Bow

River, but he suffered continual health problems as a consequence of the gas attack in the war. He had to face the fact that he was no longer fit enough to work in a physically demanding industry like civil engineering, so he decided to move further east. The family legend is that he and Elizabeth reached Winnipeg and took a train along the Swan River Valley to the end of the line. There, in the small town of Durban, they decided to set up a general store. They were in the heart of the flat wheatfields of Canada, which alternately baked in the hot prairie summer or lay buried under thick snow in the extremely cold winters, but where the large, shallow alluvial lakes offered good duck shooting. Here, in November 1922, George was born.

As a young child George was seriously ill with peritonitis and spent many months in hospital, away from his family. There were moments when his parents feared for his life. When he finally left hospital he spent a long time convalescing at home, where he was doted on not only by his sisters but also by the young women who worked for his mother in the store's bakery and the neighbouring women who came to shop and gossip. This early familiarity with the opposite sex was sometimes later used to explain away George's fatal charm and attraction for the girls that he met in London and in Boston in Lincolnshire.

Tragedy struck his life when he was seven years old, when the injuries that his father had suffered in the war finally killed him. From then on he had to help his mother run the business, serving in the store, fetching and carrying, but still keeping abreast of the lessons that he attended in the small, four-roomed schoolhouse in the town.

George was a determined, forceful boy for his age and played in the local curling and ice-hockey teams. Canadians often say that ice hockey is a fight where a game broke out, and one day George thought he had been badly fouled by one of the players. The dispute simmered, then at the end of the game it flared up and George sprang to attack the older boy, who had added insult to injury. The boy, a neighbour, alarmed by George's anger, fled with George in pursuit. They ran over the frozen ground, their boots crunching the snow, their breath, hanging in the ice-cold air, growing harsher by the minute. They ran and ran until the older boy was exhausted and stumbled to a halt. He fell to the ground and said, 'George, I'm finished. Let's go home.' George stood there, also tired and exhausted, his heart thudding, his chest bursting so that he felt he didn't have the energy to raise a finger. They sat down together, every breath burning their lungs, until they had recovered and then they walked home. George never forgot this quarrel and how, when he was at the limits of his physical endurance, his anger had suddenly seemed pointless.

Life during the 1920s and 1930s could be harsh. The great Depression had cut grain prices to the bone and in the hamlet of Durban there was high unemployment, the farmers struggling to break even and hold their creditors at bay. Many feared homelessness and starvation. The store that George's mother owned and ran was a central part of the small community, not only socially but economically as well. The banks and the seed companies to which the local farmers were indebted were remote, and indifferent to the fate of Elizabeth Laing's friends and neighbours, but she knew that life was desperate for some of them. The community in which George grew up was self-sufficient, a farming community that still retained some vestiges of the pioneering spirit of the first settlers, and Elizabeth made some efforts to create a cooperative based around her village store. She extended loans and lines of credit for many of the goods that she stocked – not only for food but also for farm tools and even concentrated hog food – so that the struggling smallholders could keep their heads above water. Many years later, when George made a return visit to the area, some neighbouring farmers still remembered the role that the village store and George's mother had played during the Depression.

Although life could be hard, particularly in the deep winter, there were touring carnivals and spring and summer barn dances in the village. These were the high point of the social life of the area, with a local band put together from anyone who could play the piano, the banjo or the fiddle, and they were attended by whole families from the surrounding farms and settlements. The youngest children would fall asleep on the hay in the barn, while the adults and adolescent children would keep on dancing until the sun rose early in the morning.

The community was remote, almost 350 miles from the state capital, Winnipeg, and it wasn't until George was sixteen that he made his first journey there, to join the crowds at the civic ceremonies greeting King George VI and Queen Elizabeth on their state visit to Canada.

George stayed at the village school for all his schooling, even for the classes leading up to the matriculation examinations, which he would take when he was eighteen, but he was developing a desire to get away from the Swan River Valley to discover what opportunities lay in the wider world. These ambitions were fuelled by one of his schoolmasters, who came from the neighbouring town of Reston. In 1934, when George was twelve years old, a boy from Reston named Archie Guthrie travelled by train and cargo boat to the UK, where he joined the Royal Air Force. He stayed in touch with his home town, writing the occasional piece about his experiences for the local newspaper which George's teacher would read out to the class. George was intrigued and fascinated by these tales of the journey across the Atlantic and news of life in the RAF, where Guthrie learned to fly and was eventually promoted to the rank of squadron leader in 9 Squadron. Part of Bomber Command, he flew one of the most modern bombers then in service, the twin-engined Vickers Wellington. George later believed that it was these stories that whetted his own appetite for flying and fuelled his desire to join the Royal Canadian Air Force.

Guthrie's adventures were certainly a powerful influence. George had heard the stories of his father's experience in France during the First World War and had witnessed first-hand the long illness caused by a German gas attack in the trenches. Every year on 11 November, with the other boys from his school, he had lined up along the main street of Durban for the small service of remembrance held by the local Veterans Association. Nevertheless, when he was told as he sat at his school desk that war had once more been declared by Britain and France against Germany, he felt only a rushing sense of excitement – a realization that now he too would be able to travel, and that at least maybe here was his chance to learn to fly.

But at the age of sixteen he was still too young, so for the next two years he and his friends sat in the classroom in their small prairie school while thousands of miles away young men just a few years older sat at the controls of some of the world's fastest aircraft, fighting an heroic life-or-death battle.

On 18 December 1939, twenty-four Wellington bombers flew on a mission to attack German shipping, searching the estuary of the Jade and the Schillig approaches, then flying on to the port of Wilhelmshaven. They saw three large warships moored there, but didn't attack them for fear of damaging parts of the town. On their approach to the port the Wellingtons were attacked by a large group of single- and twin-engined German fighters, and during this aerial battle, which lasted for forty minutes, twelve of the bombers were shot down. One of those fatally hit planes was flown by Squadron Leader Archie Guthrie. The death of their local flying legend was announced in the Reston paper and came as a shock to many. But the news did not alter George's ambition one iota. If anything, the gallant death of the squadron leader merely fuelled his dreams of joining the air force.

He had to wait, impatiently, for another sixteen months, until in April 1941 he had passed his eighteenth birthday and had finally completed his last matriculation exam. The very next day he once more made the long drive to

Winnipeg and presented himself to the Royal Canadian Air Force recruitment officer. In 1939 the governments of Canada, Great Britain, Australia, New Zealand and South Africa had created the British Commonwealth Air Training Plan. Under this international scheme, the Canadian government established a flight-training programme that would eventually train over 25,000 Canadians as pilots, as well as thousands of others from the UK, Australia and a host of other countries. Half of all the aircrews for the Commonwealth, and others who had escaped from occupied Europe, went through this training scheme in Canada. George was going to be one of the 167,000 students who went through the plan. Impressed with the young man's zeal but uncertain of his academic ability, the recruiting officer pointed out that he would need to know what grades George had achieved in his exams before he could sign him up for the training programme. George was told that he could enlist now and return in two months' time when his results were available. He raised his right hand and swore allegiance to the King, then made the long drive from Winnipeg back to Durban.

Two months later a letter arrived saying that he had been accepted as a recruit into the Air Training Plan and instructing him to attend his initial training camp at Brandon, Manitoba. Before he left his home town he was offered a free haircut by the Durban barber and his curly hair was cropped in an approved military short back and sides. When he arrived at the training camp he was lined up with the other recruits for a haircut and he left the camp barber completely bald.

George's stay at that camp was short; he was then sent with most of the others to Paulson in Manitoba, then on to a posting at No. 10 Training Squadron at a town called Dauphin. Through all that time he and the other recruits were put on guard duty, standing around apparently immobile aircraft on a shift system of two hours on and two hours off, armed with rifles but no ammunition. The pointless, arbitrary absurdities of military bureaucracy didn't perturb George, however. For the first time in his life he was mixing with people from all walks of life, not only young men from every province of Canada but also some of the thousands of volunteers from the United States who had made their way to Canada to fight for Britain. Talking to boys from Hudson Bay in the far north, or from Atlanta, Georgia, George couldn't believe his luck. It was as though the whole world was opening up to him.

The first selection for pilot training was carried out at an Initial Training School, where there were classes in navigation, aeronautics and engineering, and several hours where the students were tested on a Link trainer – a flight simulator that allowed the instructors to make some assessment of a candidate's physical coordination. George made no secret of the fact that his ambition was to be the best pilot in the world, and he was selected to start on a pilot training course.

His lessons were given by civilian trainers in a Tiger Moth aircraft, a single-engined biplane. Old-fashioned and quaint compared with a modern fighter, none the less it seemed to George, as he recalled later, a big enough aeroplane for a novice, and certainly faster than a Fordson tractor or the old Buick that he had driven around Durban. George may not have been the best pilot in the world, but he was good, with quick reflexes and excellent hand–eye coordination. Flying came naturally to him and he was allowed to go solo after just six hours of tuition in the Tiger Moth. Once in the air he felt in his element. Flying solo at the age of eighteen was a remarkable realization of the ambition he had held since he was twelve years old. He sometimes wondered at his good fortune as he flew over the flat prairies and lakes of Manitoba, the roads stretching to the horizon, the wheatfields in high summer spread out beneath him, dotted with farmhouses and barns. He felt like the king of the world!

The elementary training course took roughly eight weeks, at the end of which a pilot should have had a minimum of fifty hours' flight time, although George clocked up close to a hundred. This prepared the trainee pilots for the next stage – tuition on twin-engined aircraft at a Service Flying Training School. The greatest demand at this stage in the war was for bomber crews and George was happy with this.

His multi-engined flying was done on a Cessna Crane, a small five-passenger aircraft known as the 'Bamboo Wonder' because of its wooden frame and canvas-covered fuselage. It was considered fragile and unsuitable for aero-batics of any sort. So concerned were the instructors about this that George and the other tyro pilots were shown an uncovered airframe and warned not to indulge in any risky manoeuvres. Although not particularly stable when flying on one engine, the Crane was a relatively safe and docile aircraft – but any mistake in aviation can have severe consequences, and a cadet was killed on the course at Yorkton while George was there.

He stayed at Yorkton for sixteen weeks, putting in almost 200 hours on the twin-engined aircraft. There was a lot of pressure to perform well at cross-country navigation and night-flying exercises, and the training could be arduous, with three-hour solo flights and stressful night-time formation flying. Towards the end of the course George was taken up by an instructor who, at a random point in the flight, pulled back on the throttles and announced, 'Forced landing! Where are you going to put her down?' George had to have the right answer. He once said later that a decisive attitude was essential for a pilot. 'Make your first decision your last one. If the field you have selected to land in turns out to be ploughed, don't suddenly change your mind – it'll be too late. Focus on what you have to do and deal with it.'

The ground tuition was also packed with more theory of flight, navigation and also weapons instruction. It was hard and demanding, but the atmosphere was relaxed and informal. One of George's instructors had been born in Durban and still had family there. He had even attended the same small local school as George, so they often made the journey home together on a forty-eight-hour pass. He was on first-name terms with some of the other instructors, who were only a year or so older than him and enjoyed a friendly relationship with their pupils.

George was considered a good pilot, always graded above average by his instructors, and he had no difficulties passing out of the course. His one potential problem came when he had a collision with another aircraft while he was taxiing his Crane to a hangar. The wingtip of the parked plane, another Crane, was badly crumpled. He was ordered to the commanding officer's quarters and feared that this would be the end of his flying career.

He remembers standing in front of his CO trying not to show that he was sick to his stomach at the prospect of being kicked off the course. He stood there for what seemed to him a very long time while the officer just stared into space. Then, to George's alarm, the officer slowly undid the fly buttons of his trousers. He took off his spectacles, breathed on the lenses, then pulled his shirt-tail out through his flies and polished them. He held his spectacles up to the light then, satisfied that they were spotless, readjusted his dress. Turning to George, he said, 'Son, you have learned one very important thing. When you damage government property, make sure it's too expensive for them to claim it out of your wages. That's all.'

Cadets came and went in rapid succession through the Flying School at Yorkton and to the commanding officer they were usually an anonymous sea of bright young faces, but at the passing-out parade he remembered George's name – a fact that was proudly remarked upon by Elizabeth Laing, who had come to watch her son receive his pilot's wings. She assumed that it was because George had been particularly brilliant, and he never told her the real reason.

Like all the other cadets at the Flying School, George was now due to be posted abroad and was given two weeks' leave before the journey overseas. This gave him the opportunity to return home to say goodbye to his friends from the hockey team and to many of the girls he used to dance with at the long summer barn dances. He was now a tall, handsome man with a strong, blue-eyed gaze and a wicked smile. In his pilot's uniform he cut a dashing figure, attracting admiring looks wherever he went, with the added glamour of a young man about to go off to war.

Elizabeth went with him to Winnipeg, from where he was to take a train to Halifax in Nova Scotia to board the troop ship. It was not an easy journey for her to make. She had seen the tragedy that war could bring to families, and she had watched her husband Charles suffer and die a young man from the injuries that he had received in the trenches of the First World War. Now her son was about to leave to fight in another European war and the fear that this might be the last she ever saw of him could not be suppressed. When they reached Winnipeg she told George that she would not wait for him to board his train, but would instead say goodbye and return home. It was, she told him, better for her to leave him, rather than to wait and see him leave her. As she left her young son and made her lone journey back to Durban, her thoughts must have been full of sadness and apprehension.

3

INTO UNIFORM

While the young George Laing had been impatiently working his way through school in Manitoba, Geoff had been continuing his apprenticeship at Millars engineering factory in Bishop's Stortford. There had been an almost inevitable build-up to war over the past year, a steady background drumbeat of political tension with Germany and Italy, constantly referred to in the newspapers and on the radio. Gas masks had been issued, and various types of shelter to protect against bombs and falling masonry from the anticipated air raids had been offered to the public to erect in their back gardens, while communal ones were dug in parks, factories and schools.

The threat of war had never intruded urgently enough to interrupt the normal routine of work and home life, however. Geoff continued to arrive at the factory gates at seven every morning, played tennis at the local tennis club or went out cycling at weekends. If he thought about the future, he assumed that he would eventually qualify as a skilled engineer and look for a well-paid, secure job. Even when Germany invaded Poland and Prime Minister Neville Chamberlain made his quiet, almost sorrowful broadcast on 3 September announcing the start of another war with Germany, life in Bishop's Stortford and the family council house continued just the same. For Geoff's father there were still the horses to harness up and a harvest to get in over the next few days.

On reflection many years later, Geoff could not explain why, on a bright sunny morning a few days after the declaration of war, his life took one of those dramatic shifts in direction that sometimes affect the most level-headed and down-to-earth people. It was early, just a few minutes before clocking-in time, and Geoff was on his bike approaching the main gates of the factory. For the first time he heard the slightly chilling sound of the air-raid sirens that had been installed above police and fire stations to warn people to make for the shelters. He got off his bike, wondering what to do, when a burst of sound and fury erupted over his head. Three very low-flying Hurricane fighters hurtled in a V shape directly above him, the whistling of their propellers and the great rushing noise of their turbo-charged Rolls-Royce Merlin engines filling his eardrums. Then they were gone, their exhausts rapidly fading into the distance. Geoff was rooted to the spot, transfixed, as his eyes followed the fighters until they disappeared behind the rooftops. He had never seen anything so fast and so purposeful; it was a sight that was utterly stirring. That flight of Hurricanes, gleaming in the morning sun, was like an epiphany, and in that instant Geoff knew that he was going to join the Royal Air Force.

Not long after this he wrote to the Air Ministry Recruitment Office. He had no wish – nor indeed any belief that he would be able – to qualify as a pilot or aircrew; his sole desire was to exercise his skills on equipment that was more exciting, more advanced, more potent than the machinery he was building at Millars. The bureaucracy for handling volunteers and recruits was slow, but eventually, after several months, Geoff was told to present himself for an interview and a physical examination. In April 1940, at the Caxton Hall in Cambridge, he joined hundreds of other volunteers – a mixture of young and not so young, some who had a burning desire to fly, others who simply preferred to exercise some choice about what they did in the war rather than wait for the lottery of conscription.

While he was waiting, the recruitment officer appeared from a cubbyhole and started walking up and down the rows of volunteers, calling out Geoff's name. He held in his hand a letter from Geoff's employers, Millars. They had written to the Recruitment Office asking that Geoff be refused admission into the air force on the grounds that the work he was performing at Millars was essential to the war effort. Many occupations in the mines, in factories, on the railways and in the docks were 'reserved occupations', meaning workers in them were exempt from mobilization into the armed forces. The recruiting officer looked at Geoff and said, 'Son, this is one of the finest references that you are ever likely to get.' The choice was Geoff's.

'What,' asked the recruiting officer, 'do you really want to do?'

'If I wanted to stay in a factory in Bishop's Stortford, I wouldn't have come here today,' Geoff replied.

From then on, with such a glowing recommendation from his employers, his recruitment was a formality. A very short interview and a brief oral test of his engineering knowledge, and he was signed up as a direct-entry fitter. Such was the shortage of mechanics in the RAF that Geoff was told he was required immediately and that very same morning, before he had time to think or change his mind, he was drafted to an aero-engine course at Cardington, in Bedfordshire, where just a few years previously the giant airships R100 and R101 had been built and berthed. In a brief telegram to his mother before he got on the train, he asked her to tell his employers he was not coming back and to forward a change of clothing, a toothbrush and a razor to RAF Cardington. In just a few hours his life had once more taken a radical change of course. The next day he swore the oath of allegiance to the King, had a medical and dental inspection (which resulted in the extraction of a tooth on the spot) and was issued with his uniform.

A few days later Geoff was once more on a train, bound this time for Morecambe, the holiday resort in Lancashire, and his first RAF unit, N Flight No. 5 Squadron. For the next few weeks he was billeted in a seaside boarding house run by two elderly sisters, who treated the eighteen-year-old boy as one of the family. This was the only good thing about this posting, for the induction period was intensely tedious. The RAF might well have been short of skilled craftsmen, but knowledge of drill and parades, physical training and respect for spit and polish were also called for. After a sense of discipline had been drummed into him and he had learned the right way to Blanco his webbing belt and shoulder straps and obtain a glass-like sheen on the toecaps of his service boots, Geoff was finally sent to RAF St Athan, near Barry in Wales. This at last was what he had been taken into the Royal Air Force for – a course on the maintenance and repair of aero engines.

One of the first practical exercises he had to undertake in the first few days was to file a metal cube about 2 inches square to within a thousandth of an inch on all surfaces. Coming to grips with aero engines started with taking apart and reassembling a motorbike engine, then moving on to an engine called a de Havilland Gipsy and an air-cooled radial Bristol Pegasus, and then a water-cooled Rolls-Royce Kestrel, cousin to the Merlin that powered the Hurricanes that had blasted over Bishop's Stortford. Both the Pegasus and the Kestrel were complicated, advanced pieces of machinery with thousands of moving parts. The Kestrel would run at over 3,000 r.p.m. and deliver 650 horsepower. Becoming an engine mechanic meant developing an intimate knowledge of the electrical and ignition systems, the carburettors, the airscrew gearing, coolant pumps and filters, and the instrumentation that fed temperature and oil pressure into the cockpit. Over the previous five years there had been big advances in the power and sophistication of piston engines, and Geoff was now at the cutting edge of mechanical engineering. But he also had to become familiar with safety procedures in

the hangars and on the airfields, the correct drill for starting various engines, airfield signals and taxiing procedures.
He had to absorb a great deal of information very quickly,
particularly when, halfway through the course, the wartime
need for people like Geoff had become so great that its
duration was cut from twenty-four weeks to eighteen.

The wider war also had an impact on the camp in Barry.
The German army, after launching a well-planned and
successful airborne and maritime invasion of Norway and
Denmark in April 1940, had invaded Holland, Belgium
and Luxembourg in May, and then France, occupying
Paris on 14 June. It was the sixth European capital to fall
under Nazi rule in nine months. RAF St Athan saw an
influx of French aircrew, many of whom had flown into
England with their aircraft after the French government
had capitulated. Nearby was a camp for girls who had
volunteered for the Women's Land Army, an auxiliary
organization that drafted women as labour on Britain's
farms. Geoff and some of the other cadets on his course
had been in the habit of sneaking into the camp to spend a
few hours in some female company. The French pilots
quickly scouted this out, but they proved too attractive for
the virtue of some of the young women, and too careless
of the rules, so the camp was quickly placed out of bounds
to any male visitors of whatever nationality.

A deadlier encroachment was felt when a German
bomber made a daylight raid on the base and a stick of
bombs fell across St Athan, destroying the living quarters
in the barracks. Fortunately, Geoff was in a workshop a
quarter of a mile away and nobody was hurt. There was

a lot of damage, however, and everybody's bunks were moved to the hangars, which were noisy, cold, and very difficult to get to sleep in. Some of the men, Geoff included, bunked down unofficially in the adjoining air-raid shelters. The next detail was to supplement the air-raid defences by digging slit trenches all over the base, during the course of which the cadets discovered that under 4 inches of topsoil was a thick layer of bedrock. They all lost a lot of weight, recalls Geoff. The work on the slit trenches was finished just in time for him, along with the rest on his course, to be posted to their various first operational units. As a qualified flight mechanic (Engines), he was sent to No. 1 Air Armament School at Manby, near Louth, not far from the coast in Lincolnshire. Manby was a training station for Bomber Command, with two separate flights training aircrew in either bombing or aerial gunnery.

Bomber Command was one of the two great commands – the other was Fighter Command – that had been created by the Royal Air Force in 1937 as a way of managing an expanding organization. The division was a response to the threat of German rearmament, which included plans for the Luftwaffe (the German air force) to have a front-line strength of 3,420 aircraft by the end of 1939. Originally the British government intended to spend equal sums re-equipping both commands with modern aircraft, but in fact more money had been spent on Hurricane and Spitfire fighters than on bombers. Fighters were cheaper to build, they were smaller and had only one engine, and because they required only a single crew member to fly them, the manpower to expand Fighter Command was easier to find and less costly. The decision had not been purely economic, however. The development of radar meant that fighters had a better chance of successfully intercepting a wave of attacking bombers, so it seemed intelligent to strengthen fighter defence against the strategic bomber.

The close victory of Fighter Command against the Luftwaffe during the Battle of Britain in 1940 was the result of this far-sighted decision, but Bomber Command had not been totally neglected. In 1938 the air staff had proposed that the command 'should be a force at least comparable in striking power with those components of the strongest foreign air force that is capable of attacking this country and our sea borne trade.' When war broke out, Bomber Command had fifty-five squadrons, which totalled 920 aircraft. This impressive number was still way below the alleged strength of the Luftwaffe; furthermore, once allowances were made for training squadrons and reserves, and some squadrons that had been sent to France, only 352 aircraft were actually available from bases in the UK, and some of these lacked properly trained crews.

The bomber force was composed of five different types of aircraft, some of which were outdated and unsuitable for front-line service. The most modern was the Vickers Wellington, a twin-engined, long-range night bomber that could carry a load of 4,500lb of bombs, deliver them to a target 1,250 miles away and return to base. It was introduced into service in 1938 and was highly innovative in its design, using a type of construction that gave the fuselage considerable strength and proved later to be able to survive extensive damage from anti-aircraft fire and enemy fighters.

The Hampden, built by Handley Page, was equally modern and also entered squadron service in 1938. It could carry a similar bomb load to the Wellington, but had been designed to be fast and manoeuvrable and so carried less defensive armament. The design had also sacrificed crew comfort – the accommodation for the pilot, navigator/ bomb aimer, radio operator and rear gunner was so cramped that the plane was nicknamed the 'Flying Suitcase'.

The third of these modern twin-engined bombers was the Bristol Blenheim, which had originally been designed not as a warplane but as a fast passenger liner. When it first flew in 1935 its speed of 260 m.p.h. made it faster than any fighter currently in service with the RAF, but the extra equipment needed for it to carry out its role as a daytime bomber reduced its operational speed, and its bomb load of 1,200 lb was also not that effective.

The main heavy bomber in service in 1939 was the Armstrong Whitworth Whitley, again with two engines, but this aircraft could carry a bomb load of 7,000lb to a height of 26,000 feet and could reach targets 1,500 miles away.

Finally there was the Fairey Battle, a single-engined air- craft with a crew of three and a 1,000lb bomb load. With a single rearward-firing machine gun, it was in practice un- defended, with a slow speed.

Aviation was a fast-moving technology in the late 1930s and all these bombers were, by 1939, too slow and too poorly armed to defend themselves against the modern fighters by then in service, in particular the German Messerschmitt Bf 109 (Me 109), which was fitted with cannon that fired destructive heavy shells. The bombers in the RAF unfortunately also had other faults that were exposed by front-line service. The Whitley was designed initially without flaps – the devices on the edge of the wings that help provide extra lift at low speed. In order to compensate for this lack, and to keep the take-off and landing speed low, the wings were built with a high angle of incidence. This meant that in level flight the Whitley had a nose-down attitude, which caused a lot of drag, eating into its fuel efficiency and its speed. Various engines were fitted to different models of the aeroplane, but it could never succeed in maintaining height with one engine out of action. The Whitley was designed to operate at high altitude, but it was badly affected by icing conditions and became unstable in bad weather. Various de-icing devices were fitted, but none solved the problem. Four Whitleys of 10 Squadron faced severe icing conditions over the Frisian Islands and, despite running their de-icing equipment, anti-icing spray and utilizing hot-air intakes, one aircraft fell from 16,000 feet to 4,000 feet in an uncontrollable flat spin.

In September 1940, when Geoff King arrived, RAF Manby had a complement of all these aircraft as well as examples of other obsolete planes that had been supplied to the RAF in the pre-war years. Bomber Command's training flight, located on the southern side of the base, had an array of Fairey Battles, Hampdens, Whitleys and Blenheims in which the observers, who acted as navigators/bomb aimers, received their training. The

Battles were also used as towing aircraft for the targets used to train the air gunners. The planes would occasionally receive a stray bullet on these exercises, and the job of piloting the tugs was never popular.

Parked on the other side of the aerodrome, where the gunnery courses were held, were such exotic aircraft as the Handley Page Harrow and the Boulton Paul Overstrand, a biplane. Despite the latter's First World War appearance, it was first delivered to the RAF in 1934. It was the first RAF plane to have an enclosed hydraulic-operated gun turret, and it was this feature that was used at Manby for the introductory training of gunners. An Overstrand fell apart in mid-air in the middle of 1940, and the example at Manby was strictly limited to ground training. The Harrow was a high-winged, twin-engined monoplane with a fixed undercarriage. The one at Manby never flew in Geoff's time there, but they served as transport aircraft up until 1945.

The Gunnery Flight was being equipped with Wellingtons, the new mainstay of Bomber Command, because they could be used to train several gunners at the same time, and Geoff started to work on these machines straight away. They were powered by the MkVII Bristol Pegasus radial engine, a very reliable power plant. Daily maintenance consisted of checking the oil and coolant, looking for leaks and making sure that the engine ran at the right revs after start-up. This last was known as the magneto check, because the engine relied on a rotating magnet in a coil to produce a spark for the sparkplug; any error in the timing could make the engine run erratically and cause a loss of power. Other work could entail the entire replacement and dismantling of the engine, which was a lengthy job. Maintenance checks were an important part of life on the unit; a Form 700 had to be signed by the engineer and countersigned by the pilot before the aircraft was allowed even to start taxiing for take-off.

The senior staff on the base encouraged engineers to fly on the Wellingtons to give them a better understanding of the aircrews' concerns. Geoff's first flight was with a pilot called Sergeant Sloman, a member of the Polish air-force-in-exile, whom Geoff remembers as being an enormous bear of a man but very well mannered. Sloman hated the Germans and would much rather have been flying in a front-line bomber squadron. Geoff sat behind him as he taxied the Wellington around the perimeter, took off and flew out over the North Sea where the gunnery firing range was situated. For over an hour the aircraft vibrated to the bursts of machine-gun fire from the gun turrets and the smell of cordite filled the fuselage. After the exercise, Sloman turned the bomber for home. Manby and the surrounding area were now covered in a thick bank of fog, making it impossible to land. Sloman made several attempts to penetrate the fog, but it was too thick so he gave up. On the ground, flight control was becoming anxious and fired signal flares every time they heard the sound of the Wellington struggling to make an approach. Eventually the noise of the engines receded, leaving the onlookers to ponder the fate of the plane and the passengers and crew.

The Wellington flew inland for some miles, but the fog

was widespread. Geoff could see that they were flying slightly north of west and knew that the fuel load they had taken on board was not sufficient for a very long diversion. He found himself wondering if his first flight would be his last, but there was little he could do. Eventually the fog eased and Sloman put the aircraft down for a perfect landing at a base some miles further west. When they got back to base, Geoff was told that there had been grave doubts about the ability of the Wellington to find anywhere to land.

A few weeks later Geoff was standing outside one of the hangars on the base with some of the other mechanics. A Hampden bomber was at the end of the runway, its engines running at full revs, and as it started its take-off roll Geoff and his companions turned to watch, as most people on an air base do. The Hampden rose into the air, its undercarriage was raised, then it turned and started to bank on to its heading. The aircraft had just reached about 1,000 feet and was turning when there was a blinding flash and the whole plane disappeared in a red ball of flame. The blast hit the bystanders a second later, as bits of wreckage were already falling to the ground. The Hampden had been carrying an experimental mine and it was assumed that the pressure fuse had been incorrectly set. This was the first fatal incident that Geoff had witnessed. No matter how many more he saw, they never ceased to shock him. The sudden destruction of a plane and the death of its crew was a dreadful reminder of one's own vulnerability.

Even on the ground, vigilance was essential. The Wellington's Pegasus engines would sometimes refuse to start, despite the sparkplugs firing, and this could lead to a sudden explosion in the air intake. If this happened, fast action was essential – the fitter, provided he was able to reach, would quickly ram a fire blanket or even a large cloth into the engine to smother the flames. In one incident that Geoff witnessed, a Wellington was starting its engines when a fire broke out. The fire quickly spread to the wing, while the crew and the trainee gunners on board desperately evacuated the plane before the fabric-covered fuselage ignited as well.

The only time that Geoff tried to stop an engine fire, he stuffed a canvas engine cover into the intake but the engine suddenly caught and started to run. The propeller snagged one of the cords on the cover and whipped it out of the intake, knocking Geoff into the path of the propeller. He managed to hang on to the cowling and drop behind the propeller, but a few weeks later he saw someone else suffer the gory end that he had narrowly avoided. An airman was cycling along on the perimeter road around the airfield when a Blenheim bomber came in to land. The pilot had misjudged the approach and was far too low. One of the propellers hit the airman, flinging blood and pieces of his torso in a lurid arc. It was a sight that made people physically sick, and Geoff was shaken by the incident for several days.

There were other mishaps. An ex-coastal command pilot took up a Wellington on a familiarization flight but forgot to lower the landing gear when he attempted to land. He executed a perfect belly-landing and the crew climbed out unhurt, but both engines were ruined and the fuselage needed a rebuild. Then an autogiro had just started to take off when a Wellington pilot opened his throttles to taxi and the autogiro was picked up by the stream of air from the propellers and hurled into the air, landing in a heap of wreckage. All these accidents were caused by poor safety procedures and a lack of training – the results of a massive expansion of the RAF ranks with personnel from all walks of life, people who were still attempting, in many cases, to get to grips with the discipline demanded by the art of flying. It was unforgiving of those who made mistakes.

Geoff's real introduction to the rigours of flight occurred later in his tour of duty at Manby, and it came about indirectly, because of the conflict between the discipline of the pre-war regular air force officers and the newer influx of volunteers who expected something different. The station commander, Group Captain Ivens, was known as Ivan the Terrible, and he and his station warrant officer, WO Killian, followed the regulations to the letter. Every week there was a station parade at which uniforms had to be immaculate and the men were expected to be perfectly groomed. There was considerable resentment at this. A section of Hurricane fighters had been posted to Manby to help protect North Sea coastal shipping, and many of the engineering and ground staff who had to be responsible for this flight as well as their normal aircraft were on duty from 06.30 until 22.30. At the station parade one week, some men were disciplined for being poorly turned out. At the following week's parade the entire base personnel were assembled in full uniform to salute the raising of the flag. As soon as the lanyard was pulled, a large pair of Women's Auxiliary Air Force (WAAF) knickers unfurled and started fluttering from the top of the flagpole while a wave of laughter swept the parade ground. Apoplectic with fury, the station commander demanded to know who had perpetrated the outrage. He was met with a stony silence. He then announced that the whole camp was confined to barracks for seven days, there would be a colour parade every day, and after normal working hours all personnel, including the WAAFs, would march round the perimeter road in parade dress. This would continue until the culprit confessed. It was clearly an outrageous punishment and would be extremely onerous on everybody. The punishment started, but within a few days the station commander was replaced.

The new station CO was Wing Commander George Stainforth, who came with an illustrious flying pedigree and was a complete change, transforming the atmosphere overnight. Stainforth had flown the precursor of the Spitfire, the Supermarine S.6B seaplane, when it won the Schneider Trophy in 1929 and again in 1931, and he had also held the world air speed record in the same plane, becoming the first man to exceed 400 m.p.h. He liked to keep his flying hand in by taking up many of the aircraft on their air test after they had been repaired in the hangars. A Wellington had suffered some damage as a result of an accident, and its fuselage, which was covered with fabric, had had a section replaced. This was then painted with a cellulose liquid that caused the fabric to stiffen. Stainforth walked into the hangar and approached Geoff, telling him to get his parachute because he was going to take him up for a spin. Basking in the attention of the charismatic CO, the young fitter rushed to board the Wellington and took his seat in the wireless operator's station behind the wing commander and the senior rigger, Flight Sergeant 'Chalky' White.

The Wellington took off and gained height. At 6,000 feet, Stainforth started to put it through some aerobatics, corkscrewing dives, and at one point Geoff, struggling to keep his breakfast down, thought that the plane was going to be made to loop the loop. The manoeuvres continued, with Stainforth throwing the aircraft all over the sky, when with a bang the newly repaired fabric on the fuselage ripped away and the aircraft was filled with a roaring rush of air. Everything that wasn't secured began to be sucked out of the Wellington's now exposed framework. A bolt of fear went through Geoff and he sat rigid, holding the framework of the radio operator's table in a grip of death. Stainforth turned round and Geoff saw rather than heard his shouted 'Are you all right, lad?' He didn't reply – the noise was so intense he thought he would never be heard, and it was hard for him to get his breath in the rushing air. To add to his fears, the aircraft started to pitch in an alarming fashion. Both the wing commander in the left-hand seat and the rigger next to him were now desperately struggling with the controls, trying to hold the plane steady. The torn fabric had been whipped back in the slipstream and had caught around the tail plane, where it was creating enormous drag and jamming the elevators. A less experienced pilot would probably have been unable to save the situation, but Stainforth, with White adding his strength, managed to keep the aircraft level, reduce its speed and gently manoeuvre it to a safe but bumpy landing. Everyone on the base had come out to watch.

Geoff almost fell out of the plane. He thought he was lucky to be alive. Stainforth put his hand on his shoulder, beamed at him and said, 'Well lad, you've had your first bit of airborne excitement today!' And with that he walked off, his parachute over his shoulder.

The frightening experience that Geoff had gone through at the hands of the new station commander, feeling that the fuselage of the Wellington was disintegrating around him, did not have any adverse effect. On the contrary, he was deeply impressed by Stainforth's calmness and the skill with which he had mastered the situation. The heroic image of the wing commander grappling with the controls remains with him to this day. After this Geoff began to do as many test flights as possible in the repaired Wellingtons. The boy who left school at fourteen had wanted to fly and, if he could, be at the controls of his own aeroplane and on 14 June 1941 he volunteered for aircrew training. After a few weeks he was called before the selection board, which was chaired by Stainforth. The wing commander obviously thought that someone who volunteered for flying duties after the experience he had suffered at his hands was the right sort of material, and Geoff King was one of the four selected.

Stainforth didn't stay long at Manby after this. He was posted to the Middle East, and there he was shot down and killed in 1942 while piloting a Beaufighter against the German Afrika Korps.

Geoff was enormously proud at having got through the selection board. Before he was posted to his aircrew training unit he was asked if he would care to be released to work in an aircraft factory, as there was a dreadful shortage of skilled workers in this vital industry. He immediately declined. The prospect of training to become a pilot was priceless.

4

THE SHAPE OF THINGS TO COME

Geoff King spent nineteen months in the Royal Air Force training as a mechanic and serving at Manby. Those months, between April 1940 and November 1941, saw Germany achieve absolute domination of continental Europe, leaving Britain isolated. Geoff couldn't escape that overriding sense of crisis and vulnerability that gripped the population. British cities were bombed and set on fire by the Luftwaffe. It was a demonstration of the awful effect of air power which had long been anticipated but which still horrified the world. What Geoff and many others were less aware of, however, was that in this same period Bomber Command was going through crisis after crisis on the way to becoming a far more potent weapon of war – one that would send him, and thousands like him, on nightly raids over Germany to wreak destruction still undreamt of in 1940.

The Luftwaffe was first to take centre stage in this bloody drama. On Saturday, 24 August 1940 its bombers launched attacks on front-line RAF fighter bases at Hornchurch, North Weald, Lympne and Manston. Manston and Lympne were both put out of action for several days. Attacks on fighter bases had been a constant German strategy since the beginning of July, part of an overall plan to destroy the Royal Air Force before the planned invasion of Britain, and they were increasing in intensity and effectiveness. Great aerial battles took place daily over the south of England, and, as well as these day-light raids by twin-engined bombers like the Heinkel 111 and Dornier 17, Junkers dive bombers attacked shipping in the English Channel, and the ports of Dover and Chatham were bombed. Daylight raids attempted to target factories, like the Saunders-Roe aircraft works at Southampton, and the rolling mills and refineries producing aluminium for the aircraft industry.

Late in the afternoon of that Saturday, a beautiful late summer's day, a raid on the London docks took place, and bombs fell on the City of London, one of which damaged St Giles' Church, Cripplegate. Later that same night a large force of German bombers, almost 100, headed for their targets on the Medway and the Thames. The Shorts Brothers aircraft factory at Rochester and an oil-storage depot at Thameshaven were to be destroyed.

Navigation at night was always a difficult task, par-ticularly for navigators whose aircraft could travel several miles in the minutes it took to make observations, calculate wind speed and direction, and then attempt to work out a position. The Germans had developed a system of radio beams, called Knickebein, that could be picked up by their aircraft, enabling the navigators to work out where they were in relation to the target. However, it did not always work and had been subjected to interference by deliberate transmissions from Britain. On the night of 24 August the fleet of German bombers flew over their intended targets and instead found another one a few miles to the west. For the first time in the war, bombs fell on shops and offices in Oxford Street and Finsbury and on the working-class homes of Stepney, Bethnal Green and East Ham.

Prime Minster Winston Churchill ordered Bomber Command to make a retaliatory raid on Berlin, which was organized and carried out the next night, 25 August. A fleet of eighty-eight bombers – twin-engined Wellingtons and Hampdens, the latter flying at the limit of their range – flew to Berlin armed with 250lb high-explosive bombs and incendiaries. Their targets were the railway stations in the capital and the huge German air ministry at its centre. The weather that night was not in their favour. The pilots found that they were flying into strong headwinds, using up their fuel, and their navigators had to make tense calculations about possible alternative landing sites on their return. There was thick cloud over Berlin and the navigators/observers dropped their bombs based on their dead-reckoning position – that is, when their calculation of flying time and speed over the ground suggested they might be over the target. The commanding officer of 5 Group Bomber Command, who had supplied the Hampden aircraft, thought it unlikely that more than a dozen bombs actually landed on Berlin.

The attacks on the capital cities of Britain and Germany had taken place at a critical point in the German attempt to defeat the Royal Air Force and establish dominance of the air over the UK. After the French government's capitulation on 25 June 1940, German plans for the invasion of Britain had been drawn up based on the experience of their successful campaigns in Poland, Norway, Holland and France. It was by now a well-tried formula: annihilation of the enemy air force, followed by the rapid advance of German armies backed by powerful direct air support acting as a highly mobile artillery. The effectiveness of these tactics in France had taken even the German high command by surprise. The only difference now was that the RAF was the largest air force they had encountered so far in their assault on Europe and it would naturally take longer to subdue.

On 12 June Field Marshal Keitel of the German general staff had issued a directive to the effect that Germany's failure to command the sea could be compensated for by air superiority. The landings on Britain were to be treated as a powerful river crossing, with the Luftwaffe playing its normal role – in other words, destroying the RAF. In the first place the fighter defences to the south of a line between London and Gloucester were to be attacked and destroyed by a series of daylight raids, after which the offensive would roll further north. Meanwhile, as part of the same plan, a day-and-night bombing offensive would be waged against the British aircraft industry. The forces in France that would be devoted to this campaign were around 840 long-range bombers (twin-engined aircraft like the Heinkel 111 and the Dornier 17); 280 Junkers 87 'Stuka' dive bombers, which had been so effective in paralysing the French army; 760 single-engined Me 109 fighters; and 220 twin-engined fighters, Me 110s.

Starting on 17 July, bombing attacks on the coastal ports and Channel shipping by dive bombers had begun, accompanied by raids of small formations of bombers, around ten or twelve planes in each, escorted by larger numbers of fighters. Their targets were still confined to the south coast and the primary intention was to bring the RAF into combat in order to start the process of attrition.

The full-scale offensive against the RAF was to begin in mid-August. Before this date, things had not gone as smoothly as the German high command had hoped. The German fighter forces found themselves seriously split. The Me 110 was proving to be vulnerable to the RAF's Spitfires and Hurricanes, and it too needed protection. Meanwhile, the Me 109s were being forced to stay close to the bombers instead of providing top cover and attacking the formations of British fighters as they rose to meet the attack.

On 13 August the main campaign started, and on that day 485 bombers and 1,000 fighters carried out missions over the southern part of Britain. In the following days the scale of attack on the south of England was extremely heavy, with air battles fought daily over the countryside of Kent and Sussex, while bomber attacks on ports, shipping and the aircraft industry continued day and night. By 19 August, when five days of bad weather imposed a hiatus in the campaign, there was no sign of the RAF being broken. When the weather improved, the raids started to hit targets closer to London, thus adding to the problems of the pilots of the Me 109s which were at the limit of their range.

By the time the Wellingtons and Hampdens dropped a few bombs on Berlin on 25 August, the German campaign had been running for over two months and the daily raids of Luftwaffe bombers and their fighter escorts were still being intercepted by squadrons of Hurricanes and Spitfires. Between 23 and 31 August, Germany lost 197 fighters and 139 bombers, and it was clear that the RAF, whatever its own losses – and they were serious – was still unbeaten. The creation of the hoped-for conditions for the invasion of Britain could not possibly be brought about by pursuing the original plan to achieve German air superiority.

In Germany's victories over Poland and Holland, those governments had capitulated after bombing raids on their main centres of population, and Denmark had done so at the mere threat of an attack. If the Royal Air Force could not be defeated, then it might be possible to force the British government to deal with Germany by bombing London. On 2 September Hitler gave an order to the Luftwaffe that London and other large cities in Britain should be attacked by day and by night. Two days later he announced the change of policy in public at a nurses' rally, dressing it up as a justified retaliation for the attacks on Berlin the previous week:

When the British air force drops two or three or four thousand kilograms of bombs, then we will in one night drop four hundred thousand kilograms. When they declare that they will increase their attacks on our cities, then we will raze their cities to the ground. We will stop the handiwork of these night air pirates, so help us God.

On the afternoon of 7 September, a warm, sunny Saturday, this policy was put into play when 372 bombers, escorted by single- and twin-engined fighters, attacked the docks in London's East End and the densely packed houses surrounding them. At around five o'clock in the evening the docks were set on fire by incendiaries dropped by the first wave of bombers. Onlookers could see the enemy aircraft circling the target area, in formation, as the thick white smoke from the spreading blaze poured into the sky. From all over London fire engines sped to the area. As night fell, the flames gave a lurid, flickering red cast to the giant columns of smoke that were visible from 20 miles away.

The incendiaries set fire to the Surrey Docks on the south side of the river, where 250 acres of timber were stored. A. P. Herbert, then a young petty officer in the Royal Navy Auxiliary Thames Patrol, set out in his motorboat from Hammersmith and headed down the Thames. The fires were like the light of day, and as he passed under Tower Bridge into the Pool of London, packed with barges and cargo steamers, the air grew thick with smoke and heat, with sparks and burning fragments whirled around in hot gusts. Rounding the bend in the river at Limehouse, he saw 'a stupendous spectacle. Half a mile or more of the Surrey shore was burning. The wind was westerly, and the smoke and flames swept across the river.' With a wet towel wrapped across his face, he pressed on. 'The scene was like a lake in Hell. Burning barges were drifting everywhere. We could hear the hiss and roar of the conflagration, a formidable noise, but we could not see it, so dense was the smoke.' Throughout the docks, different warehouses poured out their individual contribution to the giant column of flames and smoke. Thick black smoke from burning rubber and paint threatened to asphyxiate anyone it engulfed, while burning pepper stung the eyes and throat for miles around.

In air-raid shelters, in back gardens and open spaces, people sat and listened, fearful, some distraught, as the bombs fell, smashing homes to rubble and matchwood, flinging bricks and wooden beams high in the air, the explosions coming heart-stoppingly near then receding, but never ending. Firemen, air-raid wardens, nurses, doctors and hundreds of other civilian volunteers were caught, and sometimes killed, in the destruction that spread over the east of the city.

Later that night a second wave of 255 bombers flew over the burning East End of London and dropped more bombs and incendiaries. In the morning the streets were littered with rubble and broken glass, brick dust and plaster, mingled with soot from the fires as hundreds of fire hoses sprayed water over burning and smouldering wreckage. That morning there were nineteen huge fires still burning, and scores of others surrounded by exhausted firemen and their fire engines. There were almost 1,000 small fires, some of which were left to burn themselves out. In that night 430 people had died and 1,600 had been seriously injured, while thousands more were left homeless.

The next night, Sunday the 8th, thousands of civilians headed with whatever bedding and possessions they could carry to wherever they thought they would be safe. Hundreds went to the underground station at Liverpool Street, seeking shelter deep below the city. They hammered and banged on the gates until they were opened, then took shelter on the platforms. That evening, just after eight o'clock, more bombers dropped their loads on the city and another 400 or more Londoners were killed, more houses blown up and more fires started. On 9 September 220 planes attacked during the day, and on the 15th another 123 bombers flew over London during the day and 230 more arrived to drop their bombs and incendiaries at night.

The Luftwaffe continued to make London its main target; on every day for the rest of the month there were raids by bomber forces varying in strength from 35 to 260 aircraft, while every night between 60 and 260 planes struck the city.

The Germans continued to lose aircraft in the daytime raids. Between 7 and 15 September they lost 99 fighters and 199 bombers, so by October the raids started to be conducted solely at night. On the night of 9 October, with a full moon, another massive raid took place: 487 bombers carrying 386 tons of high explosives and 70,000 incendiary bombs hammered London in a bid to produce political pressure on the government for negotiations. But the effects of the bombing, although deadly, hugely stressful and frightening for a population forced to spend its nights in air-raid shelters listening to the anti-aircraft guns and the crash of exploding bombs, were too widespread to bring about the anticipated paralysis. A huge metropolis like London could absorb and adapt to the damage. Moreover, the expected collapse of morale did not occur. By November the opportunity to launch an invasion across the English Channel had been lost, and Reichsmarschall Hermann Goering, head of the Luftwaffe, dictated another shift in bombing policy. In what was now clearly a war of attrition, it was important to prevent Britain replacing the arms she had lost in the evacuation of France and further building up her armed forces. The new plan presented to the Luftwaffe based in Occupied France called for the sustained bombing of London and also for attacks on the industrial areas of Coventry, Birmingham and Wolverhampton.

The Germans had developed two new methods of radio direction to replace the Knickebein system used in the initial raids on London and the south of England, and receivers for one of these methods, the X-beams, had been fitted to a unit of Heinkel 111 bombers – the Kampfgeschwader 100 (KG 100) – which was specially trained in its use. This unit would precede the main attacking force and drop incendiary bombs on the target, creating large fires so that the following bombers would have a clearly marked aiming point. The X-beam system had yet to be used in combat, but it was planned to test it for the first time in the raid on Coventry. On 14 November the Heinkel aircraft of KG 100 took off from their airfield at Vannes in Brittany and flew to Coventry. The raid was to be carried out by a force of 469 bombers, carrying 420 tons of high explosives and large quantities of incendiaries.

Coventry was a small city, with an official population of around 230,000, but this had been swollen by an influx of people taking jobs in its factories, which were working flat out for the war effort, making aircraft engines, cars and munitions. Daimler was producing armoured gun turrets for tanks, and Alvis and Morris Motors were producing aircraft engines. In all, there were over thirty important factories and workshops producing for the armed forces.

The lead Heinkels of KG 100 arrived over the town at 19.20 to drop their flares and incendiary bombs. Coventry had been hit before, with small raids beginning in August that year; so far, 176 people had been killed in seventeen raids. This raid, however, was starting earlier than usual, and it began with the slow descent of parachute flares spreading a flat white light, emitting trails of sparks like a giant firework – something that the air-raid wardens on duty had never seen before. The volume of incendiary bombs was also much greater than in any previous raid and soon the fire services were unable to respond. The centre of Coventry was uncontrollably ablaze.

The fire-fighting effort was also badly affected by the high-explosive bombs that started to fall on the city at around nine in the evening. Water mains were ruptured, streets were blocked by piles of rubble and rescuers were attempting to find survivors in the wrecked houses and to extinguish the fires under the rain of explosives. The original plan for the raid had been to target Coventry, Birmingham and Wolverhampton. British intelligence, however, had intercepted some signals that suggested Wolverhampton would be hit, so anti-aircraft defences had been rushed to that city. German aerial reconnaissance had revealed the strengthening of Wolverhampton's defences, so that raid was cancelled, but it left Coventry's anti-aircraft emplacements depleted. By around midnight the thirty-six guns, all that were available to defend Coventry, started to run out of ammunition. The crowded old city centre was completely ablaze; everything was burning, including the cathedral. Shops, houses, schools and hospitals were all blasted by the bombs and several factories, including those of Daimler and Alvis, were severely damaged. When the raid finished at six in the morning complete areas of the city had been totally devastated. In whole neighbourhoods all that remained of streets of terraced houses were a few external walls. The buildings were gutted, pavements and roads covered by piles of blasted rubble. The destruction encompassed almost 50,000 houses – more than a third of the housing stock of the city – and 554 people had been killed. Over half of the municipal buses were wrecked and most of the telephone lines were put out of action. The main railway lines passing through the city were blocked and 100 acres of the city centre lay in smoking ruins.

Such a concentrated attack on such a small target had a completely different impact from that of the Blitz on London. In the days immediately after the bombing people fled the town at night for fear of another raid. The local council and emergency services seemed dazed and unable to provide any assistance to the thousands of people, homeless, stunned by the ferocity of the experience that they had lived through, and desperate for food and shelter. There was a moment when the government feared that Coventry would collapse as a functioning community. But the feeling of fear and helplessness did not last for long. Within a fortnight factories were working again, shops had opened, even if half wrecked, and the clear-up had begun. Reporters found that the mood of the people had reverted to a wry optimism and a desire for retaliation against Germany.

As 1940 drew to a close, the Luftwaffe brought its X-beams into service on a raid against London. On 29 December the Heinkels of KG 100 were directed along a line running north-west–south-east over an aiming point along Charing Cross Road at the junction with Tottenham Court Road. There was, however, a fresh south-westerly wind and the first incendiary marker bombs to be dropped drifted and landed to the east, close to St Paul's Cathedral. The other bombers, following on obediently, dropped their loads on the markers. The incendiaries started fires that threatened to engulf St Paul's as they spread through the old, closely packed streets of the City of London. The attack was called off after two hours because of very bad weather at the German airfields in northern France, but the City continued to burn. Eight of its historic Wren churches were destroyed and 160 people died that night.

By December, London had ceased to be a main nightly target as the focus slowly shifted to Liverpool and other major ports such as Plymouth, Bristol, Swansea, Cardiff and Hull. By April 1941 the German campaign against Greece and preparations for the invasion of Crete were under way, and many of their bombers and fighters were also being relocated to the east in readiness for the attack on Russia. However, in a final farewell, the two biggest raids so far in the war were directed at London. In the first, on 10 May, 550 aircraft – a number achieved by bombers making two or even three trips from airfields in France and Belgium – carrying 708 tons of bombs and 86,700 incendiaries, caused enormous damage in Greater London. Three nights later the raid was repeated.

By the end of May 1941 the programme for defeating Britain from the air had overrun its time. Britain was either going to succumb to the stranglehold on her shipping exerted by the U-boats and Atlantic raiders, or capitulate after the defeat of Russia. By the time the Luftwaffe abandoned its aerial onslaught, cities and ports around the country had been subjected to the most intense and consistent bombardment ever seen so far in the history of war. Over 20,000 civilians in London alone were dead, and more than a million houses had been destroyed or damaged. The Luftwaffe had first tried to defeat the Royal Air Force, then attempted mass bomber raids that would force Churchill and his government to sue for peace, and finally sought to destroy from the air the means by which Britain could rearm and resupply itself. The strategy had failed. Britain, it seemed, had survived a threat that was as bad as any posed by the Spanish Armada, or Napoleon, and newspapers and the cinema were eager to draw these parallels. The 'Boys in Blue' – the young men in RAF uniforms – were the heroes of the hour and Geoff had never been so certain that joining the air force had been the right thing to do. On one of his leaves he was selected by the RAF for a series of propaganda photos that showed him in his uniform while his family gathered in the harvest. He had come a long way from the farm cottage, and he intended to go much further.

5

THE ONLY WEAPON

Although neither of them knew it, Geoff King's elation at being accepted for aircrew training coincided with George Laing finally achieving his ambition of joining the Commonwealth Air Training Plan in Manitoba. Geoff, of course, had far more experience of life in the Royal Air Force than George, but both of them were ignorant of what Bomber Command's record had been in the war so far, or what they might be expected to do once they became qualified aircrew.

The effects of war were far more obvious to Geoff in the UK. While he was on the ground staff at Manby, a German bomber had made a daylight raid on the air base, flying directly over the watchtower. The machine gunner stationed on it had a clear field of fire at the bomber and it crashed in a field just outside the perimeter. Geoff had been one of the first people there and it had been a tragic sight – the twisted aluminium of the aircraft, its cooling engines still ticking as the metal contracted, the smell of fuel and oil, and the dead crew, apparently no older than Geoff himself. They were the first dead bodies he had ever seen, and the fact that they were the enemy did not seem to be that important. He had heard the German bombers flying overhead on their way to attack Hull and other towns in the Midlands. Other than this, his knowledge of the course of the war had, like George's, been confined to news bulletins and newspapers, with their reports of the dreadful destruction of London and other British cities, and the retaliation by British bombers against German industry. They had no idea of the arduous conditions faced by the bomber crews during the first months of the war, nor any notion of the extent to which Bomber Command's pre-war plans and strategy were pitilessly exposed in the conflict with Germany. Eventually the lessons that were learned would form part of their training, but the start of Britain's air war, although less spectacular than the German Blitz on England, cost the lives of hundreds of aircrew.

During 1937 the British chiefs of staff of the armed forces had drawn up a plan that outlined the tasks of the various services, the navy, army and air force, in the event of a war with Germany. In the view of the air staff, the most effective targets for the RAF's bombers were the major industrial areas of the Ruhr that provided the muscle of Germany's power, producing 70–80 per cent of her coal supplies and around 75 per cent of her iron and steel output. If these targets could be attacked before Germany had a chance to establish proper defences, then a crippling blow might be struck at the very beginning of the conflict.

Political considerations didn't favour this 'first-strike' option, as it would be called today. The British and French governments did not want to be the first to launch an aerial attack that might be seen as an unethical assault on civilians or non-military targets and which would hand Hitler a propaganda advantage in neutral countries. Shortly before the outbreak of war there had been an exchange of letters between the governments of Britain, Germany, France and the United States, in which President Roosevelt had sought to extract commitments from the warring parties to eschew the bombing of civilians. The French government also believed that an aggressive air attack launched against Germany would lead to German retaliation against them at a time when their air defence network was unprepared; this view was shared by some senior staff in the Royal Air Force. French military doctrine also held that their air force ought to be used primarily in a tactical role, in support of their ground forces. The plans for attacks on the Ruhr were therefore shelved and alternative military targets were considered instead.

After close examination, this was not such a simple task as it at first seemed. The important consideration was the commitment that Britain had given to avoid targeting civilians. Military camps and aerodromes were not thought to be strategically worthwhile targets. The bombers would be vulnerable as they made their way deep into enemy territory and the success of their attack would require extremely accurate and timely information about the size and location of the enemy forces targeted. By their very nature, troops or aircraft could move quickly, and there would be little point in attacking an empty barracks or encampment. Dockyards were likely to be heavily defended and were usually close to towns and civilian houses. By a process of elimination, the conclusion was drawn that the only valid military target for the RAF was the German navy.

Operations were carried out against German warships on the very first day of the war, but locating ships at sea proved to be extremely difficult. The problem was the time that elapsed between the first sighting of the enemy and a strike force reaching the position where the target was expected to be. A warship travelling at 20 knots might be more than 60 miles away from its last reported position. This difficulty was less serious than the vulnerability of Bomber Command's aircraft to fighter attack, which quickly resulted in severe casualties. On 3 September 1939 a force of eighteen Hampdens and nine Wellingtons was sent to attack ships of the German fleet that had been observed off the coast of Denmark. They failed to find them. The next day a Blenheim located three battleships, two at anchor off Brunsbüttel and one near Wilhelmshaven in the company of four destroyers. Later identification suggested that the warship in Wilhelmshaven was in fact a cruiser. Fifteen Blenheims were sent to attack it, with the four destroyers as an alternative target. Fourteen Wellingtons were directed to attack the two battleships at Brunsbüttel. Only three of the fifteen Blenheims located the cruiser, which turned out to be *Admiral Scheer*. They made a low-level attack, from below 500 feet, and four bombs hit the ship but failed to explode. One of the Blenheims crashed on the deck of another cruiser, *Emden*, which was moored near to *Scheer*. In all, five of these fifteen Blenheims failed to return to base and it was assumed that they had been shot down, or had got lost and been forced to ditch. Of the fourteen Wellingtons, most turned back because of bad weather, though a section of three reached Brunsbüttel. The leader bombed a warship, but the other two of the section were never seen again; they were also presumed to have been shot down. One of the Wellingtons was believed to have bombed Esbjerg in neutral Holland in mistake for Brunsbüttel. In total, seven aircraft out of twenty-nine were lost.

On 29 September twelve Hampdens attacked two destroyers near Heligoland, two small islands 50 miles off the coast of Germany. Five aircraft were shot down by German fighters for a loss of two Me 109s. The destroyers were undamaged.

In October and November searches were carried out for German warships but no contact was made, although aircraft were lost because of low cloud and storms, or through poor navigation. In December the disappointing results of this initial campaign caused the War Cabinet to call for a more energetic policy. They resolved to instruct Bomber Command to put more aircraft into the air and launch a major attack against the German navy.

On 13 December a British submarine reported sighting two pocket battleships, two cruisers and two battlecruisers in the middle of the North Sea and Bomber Command was alerted to hunt them down and attack them. The next day a force of twelve Wellingtons spotted one of the battleships and a cruiser steering for the mouth of the Elbe, but the bombers had themselves been spotted and were attacked by German fighters. This time the German pilots did not abandon their attack and five of the Wellingtons failed to return, while a sixth crashed on landing back at their airfield.

On the 18th another major mission was launched by twenty-four Wellingtons at Wilhelmshaven, where three large warships – a *Scharnhorst*-class heavy cruiser, a pocket battleship and a light cruiser – had been observed moored at the quay. However, the formation of bombers was attacked for forty-five minutes by Me 109s and 110s; twelve of the twenty-four Wellingtons were shot down. This, of course, was the raid in which George Laing's Canadian hero, Archie Guthrie, was killed. Bomber Command's analysis was that the enemy had picked up the Wellingtons' radio transmissions almost as soon as they took off, with the result that the German fighters had been in the air waiting for them.

A casualty rate of 50 per cent was an extraordinarily heavy price and the Air Ministry called a halt to these sorts of raids until the Wellingtons could be fitted with self-sealing petrol tanks and better armour plating. In fact, the most important lesson, as the RAF recognized, had been that the heavy bombers of the time could not be safely used by day. The firepower of their turrets, which had in any case proved not particularly effective, did not compensate for their slow speed, lack of manoeuvrability and their many blind spots. The only advantage was, to quote a report of the time:

> The fact that this lesson was driven home before the land campaign opened properly had a decisive effect on the build-up of the British bomber forces. If these aircraft had been used by day in the campaigns over the Low Countries and Germany, their numbers would have been so reduced as to severely retard the conclusion of the air war.

The first phase of Bomber Command's operations was in fact a costly failure.

Apart from the campaign against German maritime targets, Bomber Command was engaged in an extensive programme of propaganda leafleting over German cities in the first six months of the war. Bundles of leaflets and newspapers were dropped at night, usually from Whitley bombers. As the weather got worse with the approach of winter, the crews started to suffer from their aircrafts' susceptibility to icing up and from their poor heating and lack of an oxygen supply. The raids, given the code name Nickel, also started to reveal how difficult it was to navigate over long distances at night. In some early raids propaganda leaflets were dropped over Denmark in error, and in one seven Whitleys took off for Berlin but only one of these aircraft actually reached the target, the rest returning to their base because of bad weather. On 18 October six aircraft were despatched to drop leaflets on Hamburg, Bremen and Hanover. Three were successful, although one of these had to make a forced landing in France on the return flight. The other three could not locate their targets and again brought their loads of leaflets back to base.

A report on a propaganda raid by four Whitleys on the night of 27 October vividly illustrates how arduous these missions were. One aircraft had been ordered to drop leaflets over Frankfurt:

> The outside air temperature was −26°C and the tube used to eject the leaflets was so badly frozen it was hard to move into position. The navigator, the crewmember responsible for dropping the leaflets, lost consciousness temporarily as a result of his efforts. On the return journey at 17,000 feet some of the crew lost consciousness because of the cold. The starboard engine caught fire and the Whitley immediately started to lose height, the air speed indicator froze up, and the aircraft went into a dive probably because of the six inches of ice on the wings.

The plane was falling on an even keel when ice was seen protruding from the cowling of the port engine and that engine then also stopped. The order to bale out was given, but two members of the crew were unconscious, so the pilot attempted to land the plane, flying through the tops of trees and into a field. The crew were remarkably unharmed, and after putting out the fire in the starboard engine they got back into the fuselage for shelter and fell asleep till morning.

On another Whitley on the same mission:

the cockpit heating system was useless and some members of the crew butted their heads against the floor and the navigation table to feel some form of pain other than the awful feeling of frost bite and lack of oxygen. The crew reported that they felt incapable of cohesion of thought or action and the rear gunner could not have resisted any fighter attack. In any case his vision was totally obscured by ice on the turret.

The official report summing up the propaganda flights carried out over the winter of 1939–40 remarked, with typical understatement, 'the courage and fortitude of the crews on these operations went largely unrecognised'.

The difficulties, and the casualties, experienced on these various types of mission in the first months of the war suggests that even if the policy of striking the Ruhr with a knock-out blow had ever been attempted, it was unlikely to have had anywhere near the desired effect.

When the Germans invaded Denmark and Norway, then launched their assault on Holland, Belgium and France in May 1940, French aversion to any strike on German territory vanished and once more the plans to take the war to Germany with a bombing assault on its industrial base were considered. The rapid advance of the German army through Belgium and Holland, however, led to demands from the British general staff for the bomber force to be used against advancing columns of German troops and to destroy road and rail bottlenecks to halt the invading army's progress.

The air staff pointed out that they could not accept that

the bombers could do anything decisive other than impose some sort of delay, but given the extremely serious strategic situation, they could only attempt what they were asked. The commander-in-chief of Bomber Command, Air Chief Marshal Sir Charles Portal, who had been appointed on 4 April, protested strongly about this demand. He wrote that there would be losses of up to 50 per cent in the proposed operations and he had serious doubts whether the results would justify such casualties. He was proved right. On 12 May, nine Blenheim bombers made an attack on German columns on the Maastricht–Tongres road. Only two of them returned to base. The Belgians asked for an attack on two bridges over the Albert Canal, so five Fairey Battles, the single-engined light bombers, flew with volunteer crews in an attempt to destroy the bridges and deny them to the advancing German forces. Only one of these planes returned. Twenty-four Blenheims were sent on a diversionary raid at the same time and ten of these were shot down. Similar attacks were made on bridges, roads and German armoured columns on 13 and 14 May, but with equally heavy losses. Out of 109 aircraft despatched by the RAF, at least 49 were destroyed. Flying at low level, in broad daylight, the German fighters – more than 100 m.p.h. faster, far more manoeuvrable and armed with heavier cannon – dominated the skies over France and cut the British bomber formations to pieces. Three days later, twelve Blenheims were attacked by a group of Me 109 fighters and eleven of the bombers were shot down. This annihilation made the chiefs of staff abandon the use of the medium bombers – the Fairey Battles and Blenheims – by day, until the desperate circumstances of the encirclement of the British Expeditionary Force on 20 May caused this ruling to be suspended. From then on, until the evacuation of Dunkirk from 26 May to 4 June, some daylight attacks continued, but the bomber force mainly attempted to attack communications and troop concentrations by night.

The Luftwaffe's bombing of Rotterdam on 14 May, and the heavy civilian casualties this caused, removed any lingering concerns about bombing targets in Germany. With Bomber Command arguing that the best way to slow down the German advance was to cripple the armed forces' industrial infrastructure, the War Cabinet approved a raid to target the synthetic oil industry in the Ruhr. Carried out on the night of 15 May, this was the first strategic bombing operation of the war and seventy-eight aircraft took part. On 17 May forty-eight Hampdens and twenty-four Whitleys were sent to attack refineries at Hamburg and Bremen. According to intelligence reports, oil refineries were set alight, two barracks and two merchant ships were destroyed.

Apart from a short period when the heavy bombers were used to support the embattled armies in France, the night-bombing campaign against the oil industry and communications centres continued throughout May and June 1940. In 430 sorties, a total of 535 tons of high explosives was dropped on oil facilities alone. There were some indications that these raids were causing significant damage. On 17 June crews reported that fires were blazing in a plant at Gelsenkirchen, and that fires at Homburg had spread into one large conflagration which blazed fiercely for twenty minutes then turned to a thick column of smoke that rose 2,000 feet into the air.

At the time there was no independent verification of these claims. Aircraft were not fitted with target cameras and reconnaissance flights were often not available. German authorities did produce damage reports, and the one produced by Luftgaus (air districts) XII and XIII, the authorities responsible for the areas around Wiesbaden and Nuremberg, showed that in May and June between 60 and 70 per cent of the bombs dropped landed in open country, about 10 per cent hit a military or industrial target and the rest struck residential areas. The report, of course, was not made available to the British until the end of the war in 1945, but at the time some senior staff in Bomber Command had their doubts about the accuracy of the bombing effort at night. This stemmed primarily from the known problems of navigation, and it seemed legitimate to ask how, given that so many of the crews on the 'Nickel' operations had returned after failing to locate their target, similar crews, flying aircraft armed with bombs, had apparently had such success. Air Chief Marshal Portal was one of those harbouring doubts. It was to take more than a year before the truth was known.

The immediate demands on Bomber Command and its heavy bombers were to assist in the reduction of the air attacks on Great Britain, which meant targeting the German aircraft industry, the airframe assembly plants and aluminium producers. But there was a tendency to assume that Bomber Command could be used to solve any and all problems facing the chiefs of staff. There were calls for further attacks on railway marshalling yards and on the German canal system, such as the destruction of the important waterway the Dortmund–Ems Canal. The medium bombers were to focus on enemy-occupied aerodromes, then a week later enemy ports and shipping became the primary targets. After further discussions, the air staff decided that up until now the impact of many of the attacks on German targets had been dissipated because they had been too dispersed. They called for concentration, telling Portal that the first-priority targets were five airframe factories and five aircraft equipment depots. They suggested that 140 bombs of 500lb should be aimed at each to ensure its destruction.

Portal thought that this overly detailed prescription had gone too far and that the truth about Bomber Command's abilities needed to be communicated to the senior staff of the Royal Air Force and the Ministry. In a reply to the air staff he wrote:

> of the ten first priority targets only three could be found with any certainty in moonlight by the average crew. Most of the targets are so far to the east as to allow little time for finding them and returning by day break, or for searching for an alternative target. Almost all these targets are isolated, so that all bombs which missed the actual target would do no damage and cause the minimum disturbance.

Portal continued this attack in a letter to the deputy chief of the air staff, saying:

in the bomber command we have the one directly offensive weapon in the whole of our armoury, the one means by which we can undermine the morale of a large part of the enemy people, shake their faith in the enemy regime and at the same time and with the same bombs dislocate the major part of their heavy industry, much of their chemical industry and a good part of their oil production.

His words made little immediate difference. As the Battle of Britain got under way and preparations for Operation Sea Lion, the German invasion of Britain, became more apparent, there was increased emphasis from the War Cabinet on targets whose destruction could immediately improve the safety of Britain, including factories and the assemblies of troop-carrying barges. Portal, however, had seen the limitations of Bomber Command, its aircraft and crews, and believed he knew what was needed. His opportunity to effect a change came in October 1940 when he was promoted to become chief of the air staff.

6

THE CREW MEETS UP

George Laing made his farewells to his mother at Winnipeg, then the next day, with hundreds of other volunteers for the war in Europe, took the train to Halifax in Nova Scotia. It was November 1942, and he would see Christmas away from home for the first time.

Coming from the farmlands of Manitoba, George had never seen a ship as large as the one that he and thousands of others were forming up in ranks to get on board. The process took hours as an endless stream of men walked up the gangways and disappeared into the enormous hull. Looking around him, George thought that the whole of Canada was preparing to embark. The ship, *Queen Elizabeth*, weighed 84,000 tons and was actually the largest vessel afloat; she was to remain so for over thirty years. Built for the lucrative Atlantic crossing, *Queen Elizabeth* had never gone into passenger service; instead, in 1940 she had been requisitioned by the British government and converted into a troop ship. Even as a passenger liner, with luxurious state rooms and suites in first class, the great ship could comfortably take 8,000 passengers, but as a troop ship her accommodation almost doubled. The capacity of her lifeboats remained the same – a catastrophe in waiting, which, were it to happen, would far exceed the death toll of *Titanic*. *Queen Elizabeth*, however, if not unsinkable, was considered immune from U-boat attack by virtue of her high speed; she was able to maintain an average of 25 knots across the Atlantic. This was far in excess of the average speed of the convoys then crossing back and forth between Canada and the UK, so the liner sailed alone.

The great high sides of the ship towered above George as he stood on the quayside, Her black hull and lofty promenade decks painted in battleship grey seemed larger than any building he had seen in Winnipeg. Once he had boarded, however, he found his horizons considerably reduced. A first-class state room designed for one wealthy passenger now accommodated sixteen sergeant pilots, with all their kitbags stowed in the bathroom. The bunks were only about 8 inches apart and with all of them occupied it was practically impossible to move. One sergeant came up with the idea that the cabin operate on a shift system, allowing half to sleep while the others ate and stayed out of the cabin. With main meals served every twelve hours, the rota worked well enough.

Queen Elizabeth was escorted by aircraft on anti-submarine patrol for a few miles out of Halifax before gathering speed under the steam from her twelve boilers and crossing the Atlantic in just three and a half days. The biggest lake George had ever seen was about 6 miles across. As he said later, the Atlantic looked awful big.

They docked at Greenock on the Clyde. George and his companions were disembarked via a landing craft and once more put on a train, this time for Bournemouth, the sedate resort on the south coast. It was a tough journey, long and with no food or water available. At their destination they were billeted in an apartment block on the sea front, where at last they were given a solid meal of steak and potatoes in a basement bowling avenue doing duty as a dining room. The promenade was cold and blustery, the English Channel grey and windswept beyond. It was a bleak outlook, with the beaches mined, protected by thick rusting coils of barbed wire, and concrete pillboxes dotted along the front. The food was good and there was lots of it, but every day there was a parade and a route march led by a British officer and the Canadians were unenthusiastic, gradually sneaking on to the passing trams or quickly disappearing down a side street to find a pub. Their stay in Bournemouth was short, however. Ten days later they were posted to their various RAF Advanced Flying Units and George found himself on the way to 18 AFU at RAF Church Lawford near Rugby.

Instruction here was on another twin-engined trainer, the Airspeed Oxford, known as the 'Oxbox', a heavier aircraft with a much higher sink rate than the Cranes that George had flown in Canada. It was intended to give the pilot an idea of the 'feel' of a plane with similar characteristics to the bigger operational aircraft they would be going on to fly. George was expected to show continued improvement in his skill as a pilot and gain experience in flying long cross-country trips at night and in adverse weather.

The training regime was rigorous and tiring, with up to five training flights a day. Night training in particular could be tense. George put on a mask for these flights. Similar to a welder's helmet, it was fitted with red-coloured glass in the eye piece. The cockpit windows were tinted green so that it would appear that he was flying on a pitch-dark night with only the instruments in the cabin visible. Take-offs, landings and cross-country routes would be flown under these conditions, with the instructor in the right-hand seat ready to intervene at the slightest sign of an error! The mask device was also used for instruction in Beam Approach blind-landing signals, which would, via a series of faster or slower beeps, audibly guide a pilot to a point 600 feet over the threshold of the runway. The instructor would remain mute next to him until the sweat broke out on George's forehead, at which point the instructor would take the controls. Whipping off the mask, George would see that he was just 15 feet above the runway – a scary sight, but it taught him confidence, firstly in his machine and in the signals, which would get you down and give you a fighting chance, then in his own flying skills and, most importantly, in his own judgement. The instructors knew that, where George was heading, doubt or lack of confidence would be fatal.

Once he had mastered these exercises, there was more training, this time in real night flying. RAF bases were fitted with low-output radio beacons that transmitted a two-letter identification signal in Morse code and dim red visual beacons known as 'pundits'. These were designed to assist returning aircraft at night. Often George would be set the task of flying a 300-mile course around three or four air bases, relying on memorized compass headings and the identification codes of the airfields. He found it extremely stressful to come to the end of a twenty-minute leg of one of these flights and have to wait expectantly for a signal to appear in his headphones, then strain his eyes for the pulsing dim red beacon.

The instructors were not impatient to let their charges go solo. They were not there to weed out failures, although they would be ruthless if they thought someone was not making the grade. Their aim was to make sure that the men had absorbed everything they needed to become safe and effective pilots, versed in the skills and techniques of flying in extreme conditions with an engine failure on take-off, or any other emergency they could conjure up during a training flight. When George was allowed to go solo, he discovered that being the only occupant of a cockpit at night, buffeted by winds and rain, on a triangular course over unfamiliar country, could be one of the loneliest experiences on earth. On a real mission, of course, there would be six other crew members in the plane, all looking to him to get them home. Perhaps, thought George, lonely as it was, being on your own might be easier.

George got on well with his instructor, who had been to Canada and liked the country and its people. As George and he were both sergeants, they could eat and drink together in the same mess. The class division between officers and 'other ranks' was both a source of amazement and distasteful to George and most of his fellow Canadian volunteers. In any case, the officers and some of the other British instructors were a very different breed in George's eyes. He didn't think they ever understood Canadians and how they thought. 'If we didn't like something,' he said, 'we told them, but for the British the word of an officer was the word of God.' They bitterly resented their group captain, who George felt was still fighting the First World War. 'His coat was about six inches from the floor for keeping his horse dry if he was on horseback, and he raised so much Cain with the Canadians that there was almost a rebellion. We felt we hadn't volunteered for any of his type of bull-shit.' The officer was quickly replaced.

The mood of the Canadians should have been accurately gauged from their first few days at the unit in Church Lawford. All the men were formed up on church parade on Sunday, with the Canadians, including their officers, not knowing what to expect. George realized that there was only one service and it was Church of England. The sergeant major called out, 'Fall out the Catholic and the Jew,' and, George remembered, at a stroke all 126 Canadians made a right turn and quick-marched off the parade ground. 'We had Jews and Catholics with us, but we were not going to let them be singled out. It was done without any prior arrangement – it was spontaneous. And that's the type of behaviour that the British could not tolerate. But they never put us on church parade again.'

George passed out of the AFU rated by his instructors as 'above average'. He was pleased, but of course believed deep down that he deserved it. He was a pilot, a natural one and a damned good one at that; he couldn't wait to start flying in the war. First, however, he had to go on another course, at an Operational Training Unit (OTU). There was still more to learn, and he was posted to No. 29 OTU at RAF North Luffenham.

Geoff King's first stop on his hopeful route to becoming a pilot was in a bastion of English class and privilege, the suburb of St John's Wood in London. At the start of the war the Royal Air Force had taken over Lord's cricket ground, and the Long Room in the MCC Pavilion, with its portraits of glorious cricketers long past, was the scene of examinations in maths, physics and English – subjects that stretched Geoff's abilities – and there were daily drill sessions in the outfield. Then it was on to Brighton, where there were more examinations in further maths, basic navigation, and law, punctuated by intervals of drunken revelry in a dive called Sherrie's Bar, which attracted airmen and women of easy virtue in great numbers, and became so notorious that it was finally put out of bounds by the authorities. Next came a spell at No. 6 Initial Training Wing at Aberystwyth, where Geoff met and became seriously attached to a beautiful young woman with gorgeous black hair, Eleanor. It was a glorious summer, and the couple would walk along the cliff path into Clanach Bay, or climb Constitution Hill for a view of a glorious sunset. Geoff and Eleanor vowed to get married. Despite these intense distractions, he passed his course at Aberystwyth and was now considered competent to become a pilot, navigator or bomb aimer.

Geoff's pilot training took place at No. 7 Elementary Flying Training School at Desford, just outside Leicester, where, like George, he got into the cockpit of a Tiger Moth biplane. Flying was a revelation, with the noise of the engine whipping past in the slipstream, the smell of hot oil and exhaust, and an exhilarating view; it was a completely different experience from flying in the fuselage of a Wellington bomber. In control of an aeroplane at last, even under the watchful eye of an instructor, Geoff could not help but think of the recent visit he had made to his home to see his father, grandfather and sister still working on the farm, stacking hay, leading out the horses as they had done for a generation. Now here he was, at the controls of an aeroplane, 1,000 feet high, with a golden summer countryside drowsing beneath him. The war had transformed his life beyond his imagination.

The course was rigorous, with instruction in the principles of aerodynamics, cockpit procedure, engineering and maintenance. Many of these subjects were extensions of the courses that Geoff had already taken and presented no obstacle. There was one serious problem, however, and that was a slight lack of coordination. Whether it was to do with the accident and operation that he had had when he was sixteen, he didn't know; but despite every encouragement from his instructor, Geoff seemed unable to land. After twelve hours in the air, which was all that the course provided for, he was told that it wasn't safe to allow him to go solo. There was no appeal. His dream of being a pilot was not going to be fulfilled. As some consolation, there were plenty of others in the same situation. One pupil in Geoff's class who had been allowed to go solo landed his Tiger Moth on the roof of one of the hangars. He was brought down with just some minor injuries, but his aircraft was still perched on top of the building when Geoff left Desford to await reclassification.

In March 1942, the rapid introduction of new heavy, four-engined bombers had begun to place an extra load on the RAF's training organization. The aircraft now coming off the production lines – Stirlings, Halifaxes and Lancasters – had a mid-upper gun turret, so needed an extra gunner. Moreover, the drive for more accurate bombing was placing greater demands on the observers, who carried out the roles of both navigator and bomb aimer in the twin-engined Wellingtons and Hampdens. It was felt that the observer could not become accustomed quickly enough to the night vision required to guide the pilot on to the target, so the observer's job and the training for it were split into two: navigator and air bomber, or bomb aimer as it became known. It had been the practice to train two pilots for the big new bombers, but this put a severe strain on the pilot instructors, so the policy was abolished and there was now to be only one pilot in the cockpit, with either the bomb aimer or the flight engineer given sufficient training to fly the aircraft in an emergency. It was on one of these new courses that Geoff was sent to Dumfries, for training as a bomb aimer.

The course required a grasp on Geoff's part of some fairly advanced theory, particularly the mathematical formulae for calculating the trajectories of different bombs and bullets, launched at different angles and speeds. He also had to learn about the variety of fuses and many types of signal cartridges and flares that were in use. Lectures were carried out within a programme of flying exercises, practice bombing and gunnery. They flew over a bombing range on the north side of the Solway Firth, dropping 7lb practice smoke bombs. Sometimes the bombing exercise was combined with a long cross-country navigation trip and other bombing ranges were used. Early navigation exercises were made up mainly of map-reading and basic dead reckoning. The course and air speed were calculated using smoke floats dropped into the sea; the pilot was told to approach the smoke from several directions so that the bomb aimer could assess the wind drift with the aid of the wire graticules of the bomb sight, and then use a hand-held Dalton computer – a specialized slide rule – to work out the true course and speed of the aircraft. Once the wind speed and direction had been observed, it was possible to calculate the resultant true ground speed – information vital not only for reaching a desired target, but for calculating where to release the bombs so that they would hit their target.

Most of the cross-country exercises took around two or three hours, similar to those flown by George, but these were solely a test of the bomb aimer's skills and his night vision. Infra-red transmitters would be placed on a prominent building in a town that was designated as a target. Once this had been identified by the bomb aimer, the aircraft would carry out a normal bombing run and a camera would record the point at which the bomb-release button had been pressed. On their return the film would be analysed for accuracy.

When he completed the course at Dumfries on 27 January 1943, Geoff was placed at the head of the class and as a result he was given a commission as a pilot officer. He had expected to be promoted to flight sergeant and had already bought the sergeant's stripes to sew on to his leading airman's uniform.

I can remember the warrant officer coming up to me while I was walking back to the mess and giving me the news of my success. I was extremely proud. I had always harboured a bit of regret that I had not been able to get through the pilot training and this bit of success and recognition gave a well-needed boost to my self-confidence.

Geoff returned home once more, this time to show off his officer's uniform and his wings. While he was in Manuden another rail travel warrant arrived in the post. He was to report to No. 29 Operational Training Unit, RAF North Luffenham.

No one knows the real meaning or importance of events in their lives until much later, if they ever do. At the time that Geoff received his orders, he was still inwardly smarting at being deprived of the chance to fly his own aircraft. He knew that he would have to fly under the command of someone who had been given that opportunity and he hoped that his future pilot would deserve his wings. It would be unbearable to fly with someone who did not command Geoff's respect in his ability or his character.

Whether this foreboding unconsciously had any influence
on Geoff he is not sure, but looking back now over almost
seventy years he finds it remarkable that the future course
of his life hung on an extremely slim thread.

He caught his train at King's Cross by a matter of
seconds and, pushing along the crowded corridor with his
kitbag, found a single seat in a crowded compartment and
managed to grab it. The train was already moving, rattling
and clanking, with smoke curling past the blackout
windows. Geoff settled down to a long, slow journey,
loosened his overcoat and pulled out his *Daily Mirror*. It
was his favourite newspaper. He liked the cartoons, particularly the comic strip *Jane*, featuring a long-legged
blonde who somehow always seemed to keep some shreds
of clothing on. He also preferred the *Mirror*'s stance, which
was loud and critical of the government, the 'brass hats',
bureaucrats and 'bullshit'. The paper was popular with the
forces and its criticisms often stung the government, which
had once threatened it with closure.

After an hour or so the train made one of its frequent
stops and a young man in RAF uniform entered the
carriage to take another empty seat, heaving his kitbag into
the luggage rack above him. He too took out a copy of the
Mirror. Geoff could see that he was a pilot officer, a
navigator, and after a while they struck up a conversation,
first about the news and then quickly, when they both
realized they were headed for North Luffenham, about
their experience of the RAF, their courses and their past.
Roy Davis, a dark, curly-haired young man, was from
Manchester, a grammar-school boy who had left school at

eighteen to work for ICI, the chemical giant. He had been especially good at maths and physics, and would have gone on to university if his parents had been able to afford it. As it was, he had been working on special materials for aircraft and had decided, despite his job being a reserved occupation, to join the air force. Like Geoff, he had a sweetheart, a young girl called Laura who had worked at ICI as a lab assistant. They had been romantically attached for three years and hoped eventually to get married.

The two young men enjoyed each other's company and Geoff thought that Roy was probably a pretty good navigator. They met up again that night, when for the first time in Geoff's three years in the RAF he was able to stroll into an officers' mess and be greeted by the bar steward. He felt that in some way he had arrived.

The next day all the new arrivals were assembled in one of the aircraft hangars. Crew selection in Bomber Command was an apparently chaotic process. There was no interference from senior officers; instead, all the prospective new aircrew were assembled in a hangar and were expected to sort themselves out into crews for their next phase of training. George Laing was there with George Dobbin, a friend from Basswood, Manitoba, with whom he had gone through the whole training programme. Dobbin could not believe his eyes when he saw how the process was going to work. He said to Laing, 'I've been to horse sales that were better done than this.' So he sat in a corner and refused to pick out a crew: 'Whoever's left over are my crew.'

George Laing thought this was an extreme reaction and

started looking round but, like almost everyone else, he knew very few people and those he did know were all pilots anyway. Then he spotted a couple of young officers leaning against a wall ignoring the proceedings.

Geoff and Roy Davis had spotted each other in the crowd and had started talking. They had got on well together the previous day, and there was an unspoken understanding between them that they were good at what they did and that they were the key components of a bomber crew, the people who were able to make a mission a success or a failure. Geoff is adamant that, as they leaned aginst the wall of the hangar, with all the hubbub going on around them, George approached them and said, 'Well, you sons of bitches, you're the last – I guess you'll be flying with me.'

George tells a different story. He thinks he was approached by them and that they asked him if he had a bomb aimer and a navigator. He replied that he didn't and they said, 'Well, we would like to fly with you.' George said that was OK and they then asked what about a radio operator and a rear gunner?

'I haven't the foggiest,' said George. He indicated a gaggle at the far side of the hangar. 'They're British – why don't you go and talk to them and get a couple more guys?' Off they went and came back with Sidney Thomas, a Welsh rear gunner, and Vincent Day, a Cockney wireless operator.

Geoff thinks that these two other members of the crew weren't rounded up until the next day, but however they were thrown together, by the start of their first training flight on a Wellington bomber, George Laing, the Skipper, Roy 'Curly' Davis, Sidney 'Tommy' Thomas, Vincent 'Vin' Day and Geoff 'Kingy' King were a ready-formed crew, or so they hoped.

More day and night flying exercises followed, stretching their skills at navigation, practice bombing and fighter affiliation exercises. Geoff at least had flown on a Wellington before, as had some of the others, but this was a completely new experience for George. These same aircraft had flown on active service over Germany. They were starting to be replaced in serious numbers by the new four-engined heavies, but they were still a formidable aircraft for a novice, with engines delivering 3,000 horsepower compared to the 700 of the Airspeed Oxford George had flown at the Advanced Flying Unit. They were used mainly on daylight navigation exercises and were designed to introduce bomber crews to the tactics needed to confound fighter attacks. Mock attacks by fighters could take place at any time during the exercise. The front and rear gun turrets were fitted with cine cameras that would run when the guns were fired and would give the instructors some indication of how good the gunners' aim was and how fast their reactions were as the attack developed. It provided hard evidence for the crews in training of just how much the gunners had to be on their toes, and how hard it was to evade an attack from a determined fighter pilot. In preparation for their later assignment to a bomber group, during the night training exercises they were also given experience in searchlight-avoidance drills.

As a crew they were still relatively unknown to each

other. None of them really knew how good a pilot George was, and he had no idea how good they were at their various trades. The navigation exercises were valuable, and Curly seemed good, but they were not as rigorous as a lengthy trip into unknown weather over the North Sea towards a target in Germany. The gunners were competent, but would they freeze in fear when confronted by a German fighter blasting cannon shells at them? As for the bomb aimer, they found high-level bombing a mixture of art and science that called for the utmost cooperation and rapport between Geoff and the Skipper. Once a bomb was released, it continued forward at the same speed and in the same path relative to the ground as that of the aircraft. As it fell to earth, each different bomb developed a different speed and trajectory, altering the time it took to fall, which the bomb aimer had to take into account when setting up the bombsight. It could take a bomb thirty seconds to fall, so Geoff had to press the release 'tit' while he was still a mile or more from the target. To be spot on, he had to learn to anticipate the target touching the crosshairs of the bombsight by his own reaction time. This took practice, and more practice. For his part, the Skipper knew that the bomb aimer's settings were only of use if the plane was kept dead level, at the same speed and height as the figures set up on the bombsight. This took great skill and effort, and bomb aimer and pilot had to blend their skills as delicately as musicians in a duet. But however much they practised, how would they behave when the searchlights were searching for them, and the German flak was sending shrapnel whistling through the fuselage?

The Skipper had an easy-going, devil-may-care attitude, but it partly hid a thoughtful, very serious side. He insisted that his crew maintain proper radio and intercom procedure during the flight, so that idle chatter was kept to a minimum and everyone in the aircraft knew immediately who it was who was speaking. He also told them that they had to keep their knowledge up to date of all the emergency procedures for all the crew positions on board the aircraft. This meant that they had to put in some extra work and training in their off-duty hours, but again George insisted on it and he would brook no opposition. He was in charge, and everybody was going to know it.

Despite this, or perhaps because of it, they found themselves beginning to work together very effectively during the training missions. One exercise, designed to test their coordination, took place in a hangar divided into separate cubicles. Each cubicle had workspaces for a crew, with the pilot and bomb aimer on a raised dais. Engine noises filled the hangar so that the crew had to communicate via intercom. They were tested with sudden information from the instructors telling them of mechanical problems, weather changes, last-minute instructions from base over the radio and so on. Two large clocks were set up in the hangar to run slightly faster than real time, so calculations required by a change in wind speed, loss of an engine or an alternative target had to be made slightly faster than normal. It was a good test of coordination and showed how quickly chaos could take over if strict procedures were abandoned.

Geoff was also trained to be the emergency pilot, which was done using a Link flight simulator. The small mock-up of a cockpit was gimballed so that it could move dynamically like a real aeroplane and respond authentically to the controls. The instructor was in a separate unit with his own controls and could present the pupil with a sudden problem such as loss of speed or control, or a frightening stall from which it required split-second coordination to recover. The course consisted of a complete pilot's training procedure from take-off to landing, together with all the emergency drills. Geoff wondered whether he might have been able to qualify as a pilot if he had been able to spend a similar amount of time on the Link during his initial pilot training. Given his failure then, he also wondered how he would fare if he suddenly had to take over the controls of a bomber in the middle of a mission.

Almost a third of the pilots on the training course were Canadians, far from home. Some, like the Skipper, were happy to go and see the sights of London when they had a weekend leave, hoping their charm and the glamour of their uniform would bring them some female company and a good time. It invariably did, though sometimes at the cost of a wicked hangover and an empty wallet. Others were truly homesick. One, George Kain, a friend of the Skipper's, struck up a friendship with Geoff, who discovered that he had grown up on a wheat farm in the prairies of Saskatchewan. Geoff invited him home when they both had a weekend leave and he was happy to accept. To Geoff's surprise, the Canadian started to get seriously involved in the life of the farm at Berden. Whenever he got the chance, Kain would make his way there and throw himself into the work, rising at 4.30 in the morning to start harnessing up the horses, labouring alongside Geoff's father and the other hands, scything, stacking sheaves and doing whatever else was necessary to bring the harvest home. Their friendship prospered and they were eventually sent to the same squadron, where George Kain often suggested to Geoff that he should transfer crews and come to fly with him.

This time of training saw crews continually on the move. From North Luffenham the Skipper and his crew transferred to RAF Bruntingthorpe in Leicestershire, which had a tarmac runway, for more night and day training, then at the end of June they were told to report to the 1660 Heavy Conversion Unit based at RAF Swinderby in Lincolnshire. Here they were introduced to the Manchester, a twin-engined heavy bomber, designed in the late 1930s to carry a 9,000lb bomb load at over 300 m.p.h. By the time Geoff and the Skipper were flying them at Swinderby they had been withdrawn from front-line service because the plane had been dogged by problems. Perhaps the most fundamental was that it had been designed around a Rolls-Royce engine called the Vulture, a massive, 1,400-horsepower engine that drove an enormous propeller. The Vulture had twenty-four cylinders mounted in a cruciform shape and it often ran hot, burning out the ignition leads and cracking the bearing webs.

The Manchester was difficult to fly with only one engine, struggling to maintain any height but, despite all this, the Skipper loved it. It had power and was fast – he often likened it to the Mosquito in its speed and handling. The Manchester, however, not only had unreliable engines but its undercarriage was weak and its hydraulic system prone to failure. Geoff noticed one problem on his first exercise. The power supply to the bomb-release gear was weak and often failed. The bomb doors could be opened by a compressed air bottle and then the practice load had to be manually jettisoned from the cockpit after going around again, but there was always the nagging worry that there had been a hang-up, and nobody wanted to land with a bomb still in the plane, even a practice one.

After a few hours on the Manchester, they were introduced to the plane that had succeeded it, the Lancaster. Avro's chief designer, Roy Chadwick, realizing that the Manchester was a doomed design, had gone back to the drawing board, increased the wingspan of his plane and replaced the two Vultures with four Merlin engines. It was a transformation that produced an elegant swan from an ugly duckling. The Lancaster had greater speed and lifting capacity, and could fly much higher than the other four-engined bombers then in service, the Stirling and the Halifax. As the war progressed, the Lancaster was to become the backbone of Bomber Command.

It didn't take long for the Skipper to become familiar with the aircraft. He did a circuit with an instructor and was told, 'You've got the hang of it, Laing. Away you go and do it on your own.' As they got used to the aircraft they would shortly be going into war in, the crew was expanded by another two members, Frank 'Flash' Green and Robert 'Jock' Burns. Flash Green was an Australian, the eldest son of a family of eight children raised on a dairy farm run by his father in Victoria. He was quiet, and far from home like the Skipper. He had joined the Royal Australian Air Force when he was eighteen years old and was going to be their mid-upper gunner. Jock had been brought up in Kirkcudbright and had tried to join the RAF at the outbreak of war, but had been turned down because of his lack of education, having left school at fourteen. However, three months later he was accepted and went on to complete a taxing course in mechanical engineering at RAF Locking, qualifying as a flight engineer. His knowledge of various aero engines, including the Merlin, was as comprehensive as Geoff's, who had of course spent months repairing and maintaining them, but Jock had to have at his fingertips a knowledge of the Lancaster's fuel system, its electrical circuits and its hydraulics, and had to be able to intervene quickly if there was a problem with any one of them.

Towards the end of their training at Swinderby the exercises became even more intense, with night take-off and landing carrying a full load of fuel and dummy bombs, long cross-country flights with night-fighter and searchlight-battery affiliation exercises. Then there were three night exercises over the Irish Sea, combining bombing on an island bombing range and mine-laying exercises in open water.

Finally, on 1 September 1943, Geoff was promoted to flying officer and his training, and that of the rest of the Skipper's crew, was over. It was the culmination of a long, extremely rigorous process that had taken Geoff a year and nine months, the Skipper slightly longer, and the rest of the crew around the same amount of time. Not far short of fourteen years had gone into the training of one Lancaster bomber crew, and the odds were that they would have just a 35 per cent chance of surviving ten missions. Their instructors in the Operational Training Units and the Heavy Conversion Units had all been experienced aircrew who had survived thirty missions, and they had poured every ounce of their knowledge and experience into the minds and reflexes of their young charges. They hoped it would be enough for them to beat the odds, to come through the gunfire and night fighters over Germany as they themselves had done. Geoff, George and the rest of the crew hoped so too. There was no guarantee.

7

THE START OF THE REVOLUTION

To understand the type of battle Geoff, George and the rest of the crew were about to enter into, it is useful to understand Britain's greater air strategy. Even before the crew had begun their training, changes were afoot that would shape their experiences and define the sort of missions they would be asked to carry out. In October 1940 it had been possible for Bomber Command to turn its mind to a continuation of the attack on Germany and, with the promotion of Portal to the position of commander-in-chief of the RAF, there was a powerful advocate for this strategy. When he took up his post as chief of the air staff that October he proposed the adoption of tactics that would focus the bomber resources on a single target. For too long they had been frittered away in penny packets and he urged his successor as head of Bomber Command, Sir Richard Peirse, to adopt this strategy. A primary target should be selected, advised Portal, in a large, populous area and a heavy concentration of bombs should be delivered upon it. This would probably ensure the destruction of the target selected, a gasworks or a power station, and there would also be the considerable secondary effects from bombs dropped round the target damaging houses, water mains and other facilities.

Yet his was still a voice in the wilderness. The strategic bombing of Germany that had started on 15 May with the night attacks on oil and railway targets in the Ruhr was based on a combination of hope and illusion that they could somehow find their targets and hit them. Before the war it had been assumed that in daylight bombers would be able to drop bombs on average within 300 yards of the target. Even on this assumption, it was obvious that there would be a considerable spread of bombs and in order to damage a target effectively a large number would need to be used. The Air Ministry planners still unaccountably worked on the basis that the accuracy of bombing would be no different from that of pre-war daytime exercises whether carried out by day or at night.

Portal was more realistic, and the evidence to justify his fears about the effectiveness of his bombers slowly, like storm clouds on the horizon, started to gather. By Christmas Eve of 1940, Gelsenkirchen, the location of two of Germany's vital synthetic oil-production plants, had been attacked. One plant was targeted by 162 aircraft which dropped a total of 159 tons of high explosive. The other received the weight of 103 tons of high explosives from 134 bombers. An earlier analysis in June 1940 had made the assessment that Gelsenkirchen and plants at two other cities, Homburg and Wanne-Eickel, were 'exceptionally vulnerable to air attack. A dozen direct hits with 250lb or 500lb should put them out of action for months.'

After the final raid on 23 December, a daylight photographic reconnaissance flight brought back evidence that both Gelsenkirchen's oil plants were still working – neither appeared to have suffered any significant damage. The report and analysis were given to the air staff shortly after Christmas and it doubtless came as no surprise to Portal. It seems that a realistic view of the utility of bombing, however, was still not being absorbed by the War Cabinet or the chiefs of staff. On 15 January another bombing directive was issued, in which Portal was told that 'the sole primary aim of your bomber offensive, until further orders, should be the destruction of the German synthetic oil plants'.

Lobbying for the continued targeting of oil production in Germany was spearheaded by Geoffrey Lloyd MP, who chaired the Parliamentary Committee on the German Oil Position. Based on clearly rather inaccurate intelligence, one of their reports assumed that the attacks on the synthetic oil plants up to 4 October had reduced their output by 15 per cent and that this could be further worsened if the bombing were kept up. There were seventeen of these oil plants altogether and the complete destruction of the nine largest, the Committee urged, would reduce Germany's internal production of oil by about 80 per cent.

Operations against industrial towns and cities in Germany continued, but in April 1941 air staff studies started to reveal that the average night aiming error was far

greater than the 300 yards they had assumed it to be in daylight. The average distance from the target was more likely
to be as much as 1,000 yards. It turned out subsequently
that even this figure was wildly optimistic, but none the less
it did imply that oil industry targets, or any specific
industrial sites, were practically invulnerable. The logical
view that Portal had to explain to the civil servants and
politicians was that 'the most suitable object from the
economic point of view is not worth pursuing if it is not
tactically attainable'. In the absence of moonlight, the only
target that could be hit with any certainty at night was a
large industrial town. What Portal was advocating, in fact,
was a policy of area bombing, not because he wanted to,
but because with the current state of his force he could do
nothing else.

Portal still believed that the bomber force was an
effective weapon, but that it could only be so if it could
undertake massive attacks on large targets. With this in
view, he had been agitating for a much enlarged bomber
force, and for serious devotion of its efforts to area attacks.
However, the prime minister had also been harbouring
doubts and was coming to different conclusions. Churchill
and the War Cabinet were faced with very serious demands
from both the navy and the army for increases in resources,
and in particular for extra air reinforcements for the battle
in the Atlantic and for the war in North Africa and the
Mediterranean. Portal was not going to be given carte
blanche to build up his forces without some hard questions
being asked.

The prime minister's chief scientific adviser, Professor

Frederick Lindemann, later Lord Cherwell, was an advocate of air power and in order, so he thought, to help Portal, suggested to the air staff that photographs of the aiming point taken when bombs were released might usefully be examined to clarify what actually was happening on the raids over Germany. The investigation, which was carried out by a civil servant, D. M. Butt of the War Cabinet secretariat, looked at 650 photos taken between 2 June and 25 July. It was a small and limited sample from 6,100 sorties carried out in the period, because Bomber Command had allowed itself to be influenced by concerns expressed at squadron level, where it was felt that the camera was an official spy and that its use might demoralize the crews, so only a few aircraft were fitted with one.

The results produced by Mr Butt as a result of his survey were devastating. He reported that of those aircraft that reached the vicinity of their targets, only one in three was releasing its bombs within 5 miles. This was the average, but the results varied according to weather conditions. In full moonlight, two attackers in five got their bombs within 5 miles of the target, but in thick haze that ratio dropped to one in fifteen! The location of the target was also a factor. Over the Ruhr, because of widespread smoke pollution from the region's heavy industry, only one aircraft in ten came within 5 miles of its target. These were, of course, only the results for crews that claimed actually to have attacked the target; alarmingly, only two thirds of the crews on all these sorties fell into this group. Boiled down, it meant that fewer than a quarter of the bombers on any given raid dropped their bombs within 5 miles of the target. As Butt pointed out, except with a city as large as Berlin, much of the area in the 5-mile radius of a target would be open countryside.

The greater percentage of Bomber Command's effort was completely wasted and had been since the beginning of the war. Naturally, these conclusions caused consternation amongst the most senior officers in Bomber Command and they also became of deep concern to Churchill. In September 1941 Portal produced a planning document for the prime minister and his staff that argued that, if Bomber Command were to achieve decisive results in its war over Germany, then an estimated 4,000 heavy bombers were required and they would need to mount an intensive campaign for a period of six months.

Churchill brought Portal up sharply in his reply.

It is very disputable whether bombing by itself will be a decisive factor in the present war. On the contrary all that we have learnt since the war began shows that its effects both physical and moral are greatly exaggerated ... in calculating the number of bombers necessary to achieve hypothetical and indefinite tasks it should be noted that only a quarter of our bombs hit the targets.

Portal knew that Bomber Command could not continue on the same path. The Butt Report had been far more damaging than even he, Portal, with his realistic assessments, could possibly have envisaged. In his reply he could only admit that things needed to improve: 'Much more must be done to improve the accuracy of our night bombing. I regard this as perhaps the greatest of the operational problems confronting us at the present time.' Then, in order to regain the initiative with Churchill and to move the argument on, he listed all the things he was trying to introduce. There was the prospect of special crews who would be trained in navigation to lead the bombers to their target; the introduction of radio navigation systems, which were already in development but had not yet been tested on operations; and the delivery of the much more powerful heavy bombers, which were already starting to leave the factories.

Sadly for Portal, the storm was not yet over. The sudden realization that much of the bomber effort was wasted had also raised questions about the leadership of Bomber Command, in particular its commanding officer, Sir Richard Peirse. He had tried to argue away the Butt Report, which had not endeared him to either Portal or Churchill. But Bomber Command was now about to experience a calamitous three months, when confidence in it sank to a very low ebb.

The Germans had started to improve and build up their air defences, which were now becoming highly effective. The raids on Germany on 15 May 1940 had come as a shock to Luftwaffe chief Goering and had revealed how ineffective German anti-aircraft artillery was. A decision was made to set up a night-fighter force and a unit of the twin-engined Me 110 fighters was put under the command of Major Wolfgang Falck, who set about developing tactics and organization.

It was obvious to the Luftwaffe that, if there was going to be a night-bomber offensive by Britain, the main target would be the Ruhr, not only because it was the powerhouse of the German economy, but for the more prosaic reason that it was the area of Germany within easy range of British bombers at the time. Three regions of the Ruhr were cleared of anti-aircraft batteries so that the night fighters would be free to roam in them safe from friendly fire. The planes were controlled from the ground by radio and were directed to British bombers that had been located by searchlight. Their first operations achieved some success and more aircraft were sent to the new night-fighter organizations. By April 1941 a new command had been created, under the leadership of General Josef Kammhuber, and became known as XII Fliegerkorps (air corps). Twin-engined Junkers 88s were also equipped for night fighting and these formed a second unit, alongside the Me 110 group already in existence.

Two other developments in the initial phases of the creation of the night-fighter force also combined to make the Luftwaffe a formidable opponent. Together they were to be responsible for the majority of the deaths suffered by the crews of Bomber Command.

The Germans had developed radar prior to the start of war, but Kammhuber himself did not have much idea about its use. Anti-aircraft radar sets existed in the form of large parabolic aerials that could be directed on to a target. At first this equipment was used by flak regiments to assist their target-finding. The Luftwaffe, however, sent some expert signals companies to Kammhuber and, under their guidance, he set up the first preliminary chain of radar-guided night-fighter zones. Soon a chain of these giant round aerials stretched along the coasts of Holland and Germany.

Three night-fighter zones were set up in the neighbour-hood of the Zuider Zee and the Rhine estuary, in the path of RAF bombers flying to the Ruhr. The zones were 90 kilometres in length and 20 kilometres in depth, and each was occupied by a searchlight battalion and two of the radar installations. One of the radar sets would track a night fighter in the zone, while the other would track the targets. The target-tracking radar was linked to a master searchlight that controlled a searchlight cone, while the ground control room would direct the fighter. Soon other zones – or boxes, as the RAF referred to them – were added near Kiel and Bremen.

Soon another more powerful radar was put into pro-duction. These aerials, some 10 metres in diameter, had a range of 60 kilometres. The boxes were enlarged to take advantage of this greater coverage of airspace and the plotting rooms could monitor the location of the bomber and the fighter, then direct the pilot to a successful inter-ception. The giant radar also came with increased definition, so the location of the target was much more precise. Construction of the radar sites continued so that there was a chain of them from the Baltic to the French coast. The lines of boxes were placed in front of the search-light zones and the pilots were encouraged to attempt an interception first under radar direction, and if that failed, to follow the target into the searchlight zones. By March

1941 the boxes had been extended to cover the whole of the Ruhr and around 160 night fighters were normally operating at any one time. This system was beginning to raise the stakes for Bomber Command and, as the losses increased, it threw into sharp relief the new research that showed how little damage the British campaign was inflicting on Germany.

In the first two weeks of August 1941, 107 RAF bombers were lost. In September, 76 aircraft failed to return and another 62 crashed in England because of damage caused by anti-aircraft fire or fighter aircraft. In October, 108 aircraft were missing or crashed, and in November, 37 aircraft out of just 400 sorties were lost. On the night of 7/8 November, Air Vice Marshal Peirse ordered 392 aircraft, a record number, to take part in bombing attacks on Berlin, Cologne and Mannheim. The weather was particularly poor over the North Sea on the route to Berlin, and the weather forecasts given at the briefings meant that amongst the crews detailed for the raid there was considerable anxiety and depression at the prospect of the night's work. Of the 169 bombers that headed for the German capital, fewer than half reached their target. Those that did caused negligible damage. Eleven people were killed and fourteen injured, and the German damage report listed damage to just one industrial building, a gas holder, thirty houses, two railway buildings and two offices. Against this damage, however, had to be set the casualties suffered by the RAF bombers. Twenty-one aircraft were shot down, with their crew of eighty-one airmen dying – a loss of over 12 per cent of the force. Overall that night, thirty-seven aircraft were lost. The operation seemed to some observers to be a desperate effort by Peirse to shore up his reputation. There had been considerable opposition to the raid on Berlin; in fact, the head of 5 Group had been allowed to withdraw his bombers from the raid and instead to target Cologne. But the results did not deter Peirse.

Another bold initiative, the first mass raid on a German town, was ordered for 16 December 1941, on Mannheim-Ludwigshafen, two towns adjacent to each other on opposite banks of the Rhine and along the River Neckar. Together they formed one of the biggest inland ports in Europe, the base of a large chemical industry built around the giant IG Farben, whose factories and refineries stretched along the bank of the Rhine in Ludwigshafen. The original operation order was issued on 4 December and its stated intention was to 'cause the maximum possible destruction in a selected German town'. Originally, the plan was to mount a raid of 200 bombers, but by the 16th the weather forecast had forced this figure to be cut to 160.

There was another innovation in the bombing policy associated with this raid. Only one aiming point was specified for each town, and 3 Group was detailed to set aside fourteen aircraft which would carry the maximum load of small 4lb incendiary bombs to make the initial fire-raising attack. These aircraft were to be flown by the most experienced crews available in the group and they were to act as a pathfinder force, although the policy to create such a thing had not yet been articulated. Peirse was following

Portal's strategy for success to the letter. A steady stream of attacking bombers was planned for this raid, so that it would have the maximum debilitating impact on the defenders and the sheltering civilians, while still allowing the last of the bombers enough time to make their return journey under cover of darkness.

The first aircraft on the target dropped their bombs at 19.45 and the remainder of the sixty-one Wellingtons continued to attack the town until 03.30 the next morning. Only fourteen failed to bomb the target. The thirty-five Whitleys of 4 Group arrived at 21.45. Then came 5 Group's Hampdens, twenty-nine of which were over the target from 22.50 to 02.10, followed by another wave of Whitleys from 02.00 to 02.55. Only two Whitleys failed to bomb the target, while nine Hampdens were unsuccessful. Even the inadequate Blenheims were pressed into service, with nine being sent, but they suffered the worst casualties. Only three of them found the target and of these one made a forced landing on its return. Two of the others crashed in England and one was missing. Out of a total of 160 aircraft, then, 103 bombed Mannheim-Ludwigshafen with 89 tons of high-explosive bombs and 13,586 4lb incendiaries. Ten aircraft were lost, including those that crashed on their return to base.

The damage caused was more impressive than on previous raids on German towns. The bomber crews reported that as many as twenty-five fires were burning when they arrived over the target and that the blaze could be seen 35 miles away. The German authorities reported that there was a 25 per cent loss of production at the Lanz machine works, complete loss of production at the Erbar sugar factory, plus other damage to high-tension cables, to the main railway station and signals, and to water mains; this last prevented prompt action in fighting the initial fires that led to larger outbreaks. Some damage was reported to a ship- and machinery-construction company, including to a turning shop with the destruction of eight lathes and some loss of production. However, railway traffic was fully restored next day, 17 December, and the oil-storage tanks at the German–American Petroleum company were untouched.

This relative success was not enough, however. British losses were still around 10 per cent of the total number of aircraft that attacked the target. Moreover, the large losses that had occurred on the raid on Berlin in November had come to the attention of Churchill and he voiced his criticisms over a dinner with Peirse at Chequers, the prime minister's country retreat, and asked for a report, saying, 'There is no particular point at this time in bombing Berlin. The losses sustained were most grievous. We cannot afford losses on that scale ... Losses which are acceptable in a battle or for some decisive military objective ought not to be incurred merely as a matter of routine.'

It was now the duty of both Fighter Command and Bomber Command to re-gather their strength for the spring.

Portal was most concerned about this latest development in Churchill's attitude towards the bomber offensive. He was even more worried when he saw the draft of the report that Peirse had drawn up before it was sent to the chiefs of staff and to Churchill. Many of the losses had been caused by extremely bad weather over the North Sea and by the unforeseen headwinds on the return journey. This combination of factors had severely affected the endurance of many of the bombers and on the return journey a significant number had been lost because of lack of fuel. Portal rejected the report and asked for clarification, in particular of why the mission had been allowed to go ahead in the light of such a poor weather forecast. The reply was not particularly satisfactory. Peirse said, 'We were all aware of the possibility of severe icing up to 15,000 feet, over the North Sea, but it was not expected that the mass of clouds would extend to 18,000 feet, nor that cloud would be generated over western Germany. These two factors must be regarded as contributing to our loss.'

He then went on to say that the quality of the crews he was receiving, and their lack of experience in long-range flying, was a continual problem: 'An investigation of the amount of fuel left in the tanks after the operation has shown that for pilots who understood how to run their engines economically, the amount of fuel carried was sufficient.' This rather begs the question whether it was sufficient for those who could not manage their engines efficiently and what fate was envisaged for them. However, the statement that was the most damning in Portal's eyes – and would have been in Churchill's if he had ever seen it – was, 'Further very accurate anti-aircraft fire was reported over Berlin. A loss of at least ten percent cannot therefore be regarded as unusual or unexpected.'

Portal knew that in fact it should have been unusual, and certainly not expected.

In just four months, almost the whole front line of Bomber Command had been wiped out. A calculation was made that for every German civilian killed, a costly and highly trained RAF airman also died. The losses, and the concern expressed by the prime minister, had brought matters to a head. The complacent attitude of the head of Bomber Command to the level of attrition being experienced by his squadrons was insupportable. Portal had lost any confidence in the continued reign of Sir Richard Peirse. Shortly he was ousted and replaced.

There were several radical changes in the pipeline for Bomber Command: the new four-engined heavy bombers, a greater emphasis on efficiency and navigation, and the provision of modern technology to guide the bombers to their targets. The most profound innovation, though, was none of these. It was the replacement of Sir Richard Peirse with a new leader. Air Marshal Sir Arthur Harris would take over the command and the mission. Like Portal, he was a true believer in air power and he would run Bomber Command in the unrelenting belief that it was the winning weapon.

8

HARRIS TAKES OVER

Harris took up the position as commander-in-chief at Bomber Command on 23 April 1942, at a time when its purpose and effectiveness were under intense scrutiny from all quarters. The press and the population at large were happy to celebrate the attacks on German cities, buoyed up by the belief that at last the Germans were getting a taste of their own medicine, and that Berlin and the Ruhr were suffering the same night-time assaults as Coventry or London. The War Cabinet and the senior staff at the Air Ministry, however, knew that casualties had started to rise and that the raids were nowhere near as effective as the propaganda stories suggested. Amongst the senior officers at group level, morale had started to worsen. It was essential for Harris to show that things were being turned around so that Bomber Command might once more press ahead with its plans for a much larger force able to destroy the heart of Europe.

Harris wrote later that the problems facing Bomber Command could be surmounted only by intensive research, continual experiment and unshakeable resolution. Nine days before he took command, the Air Ministry had issued a directive that called on Bomber Command to 'focus attacks on the morale of the enemy civil population and in particular of the industrial workers'. This was to be done by destroying, mainly through incendiary attacks, first of all four large cities in the Ruhr and then, as opportunity offered, fourteen other cities in northern, central and southern Germany.

In an interview for a newsreel shortly after he took over, Harris said, 'There are some people who say that bombing cannot win the war. My reply is that it has never been tried yet. We shall see.'

The first great aid to improving the performance of Bomber Command was the introduction of an electronic method of guiding bombers to their target. This was similar to the Luftwaffe's Knickebein system, which had been used fairly successfully in attacks on British cities during the Blitz. Harris had poured scorn on it at the time, but could not deny that there was a need for a similar system in Bomber Command. The British system was called Gee, and it utilized a set of radio pulses transmitted from three stations in the UK. A receiver installed on the bomber would pick up the transmissions, which would appear as lines on a cathode-ray tube installed above the navigator's table. The navigator could compare the three lines with a grid marked over a map of Europe and use this to plot his position. Gee had been developed during 1941 and trialed over Wales in February 1942. Initially there had been very high expectations of the new system. The Air Ministry expected that it would enable aircaft to drop bombs on a target completely obscured by clouds, thus increasing the number of operational nights every month. Some Air Ministry analysts suggested that if Essen – situated in the Ruhr and home to the industrial giant Krupps – were bombed using Gee, then around 47 per cent of the bombs would find the target, even with ten tenths cloud (i.e. complete cover), and that the system should therefore not only be seen as an aid to more precise navigating, but also regarded as a blind-bombing device.

Gee was tested on various missions and was found in practice to have several limitations. Its range was only about 400 miles, and at the height at which the bombers had to operate to avoid flak its accuracy was only around 4 miles. It was still necessary to make some positive visual identification of the target, but in the Ruhr, obscured by the thick haze from its industries, it was nearly always impossible to identify particular towns, let alone specific factories like the Krupps works. However, use of the system did show a big increase in the proportion of aircraft reaching the vicinity of the target.

Bomber Command was given an opportunity to show what it could do in good visibility when a raid was launched against the Renault factory at Billancourt, just outside Paris, on 3 March 1942. Intelligence estimated that the plant was producing around 100 tanks, 200 lorries and a variety of engines a month for the German armed forces.

The French workforce lived in close proximity to the factory, so it was stressed that the attack should be as precise as possible, minimizing casualties amongst a civilian population who, under the Occupation, had little choice about where they worked and what the factory produced.

On the night of the attack the weather was clear and there was a full moon – perfect conditions for accurate bombing. On this raid a new target-marking method known as Shaker was to be employed. It had been developed with the idea that it could be used in conjunction with Gee, although none of the aircraft taking part in this raid was fitted with the Gee system. So that the bombers could identify the aiming point as accurately as possible, it was planned that an advance group of bombers, flown by experienced and skilled crews, would illuminate the target by dropping flares over it. A second wave of bombers armed with incendiaries would then attempt to identify the precise aiming point of the target and unload their munitions, raising fires that would then act as an aiming point for the rest of the bombers, which were armed with high explosives.

The entire raid was completed in an hour and fifty minutes, with on average a bomber passing over the target every thirty seconds. In all 470 tons of bombs were dropped on the factory. The attack was initially hailed as a remarkable success and in fact, compared to past raids on German cities, the accuracy was a vast improvement, with some squadrons getting all their bombs on the target and with a very high concentration around the aiming point.

The factory ceased production for two months; however, there had still been heavy casualties amongst the French population. The target had been well illuminated and lightly defended, but even so it was an example of what might be achieved with better navigation and a more planned, organized attack. With the addition of the new technical aids to navigation in the pipeline, there was real cause for optimism.

Gee was given its first real test a few days after the attack on the Renault factory when, on the night of 8 March, 211 aircraft were sent to bomb Essen and the Krupps works. Seventy-four of the bombers were fitted with Gee receivers and there were high hopes of success. The weather over the target was good, apart from the normal smoke haze at ground level.

The raid lasted for two hours, but the photographic evidence showed that no real damage was done to the main target area. Analysis of the bombing photograph showed that, although the flare-laying was more or less satisfactory, to use Harris's words, the main incendiary force did not arrive until the flares were out. They then scattered their incendiaries over a wide area and the resulting fires attracted the bombers of the main force. Another problem was that, in the conditions of haze over the target, the light from the illuminating flares was dissipated so that it was difficult to identify any detail on the ground.

Over the next three months there were eleven more raids on Essen using Gee, including one of 956 aircraft. On most of these raids the Shaker technique was used, and on 10 March a variation known as Sampson was also employed.

The Sampson method abandoned the use of illuminating flares; instead the Gee aircraft dropped loads of 25lb incendiary bombs to start fires and create a beacon for the main force. This method again proved to be inadequate, and no damage was caused to the Krupps works.

The whole area of the Ruhr was difficult for pilots and navigators because there was little geographical detail that helped them to differentiate one town from another. In fact, on 10 March, instead of hitting Essen, the bomber force bombed another town entirely, and did so again on 12 April. Hamborn was the unlucky victim of mistaken identity on the first occasion and Schwelm on the second.

The German defenders had also perfected the art of setting decoy fires that were brighter than the fires started by the incendiaries dropped by the first wave of attackers and so naturally presented a more attractive aiming point for the follow-on forces than the real fires. On two occasions the bombing force was diverted away from Essen by decoy fires, dropping its bombs on Rheinberg, 20 miles to the north-west of the target. Over the next years decoy fires, and the creation of large decoy targets that simulated whole towns, were to pose problems for Bomber Command.

Gee, then, was not the magic wand that would solve the problem of bomber crews' inability to see in the dark, but its success in aiding navigation and concentration over a target area was actually greater than the immediate results suggested. Harris, however, was alarmed at the failures of Gee. He had expected much more at a time when Bomber Command still had to prove itself, and in May 1942 he wrote to the commanding officers of the various groups predicting that continued lack of success would play into the hands of those who wanted to see the end of an independent bombing force and an independent Royal Air Force. If it appeared that the enormous support and resources that it had received in the past were being wasted, then Bomber Command would no longer be able to continue.

What Bomber Command needed, as well as an improvement in its performance, was some very obvious successes to reassert, in the mind of the public and therefore in the mind of the politicians and the War Cabinet, that it was the one organization that was taking the war to the enemy. If it was still not possible to hit significant industrial targets like the Krupps works, then other ways of inflicting damage on the enemy might be more successful.

The planning staff at Bomber Command headquarters in High Wycombe had been searching for an easily identifiable target in order to test another target-marking idea. If, it was thought, a large enough fire could be started in the centre of a town, then this might act as a reliable aiming point for the following wave of bombers. The town of Lübeck was examined and appeared to offer the best advantages for this test. It was near the coast and on the River Trave, so might easily be identified. According to intelligence reports, it was unlikely to be heavily defended and the town centre was a tightly packed group of buildings based on a medieval street pattern, with houses largely constructed of wood and plaster. It was, remarked Harris, built more like a firelighter than a human habitation.

The raid on Lübeck on 28 March was led by a group of Wellington bombers equipped with Gee. They marked the centre of the town with flares, then forty aircraft dropped their loads of incendiaries. Thirty minutes later, giving enough time for the fires to start and gain a hold, the next wave of bombers, armed with high explosives, flew over the burning town. A total of 234 aircraft took part, dropping 144 tons of incendiaries and 160 tons of high explosive. It was an extremely destructive operation, with the centre of the town – the former capital of the old Hanseatic League and an historic Baltic port – turned into an enormous, raging fire. Over 1,400 houses were completely destroyed and another 2,000 badly damaged, while 312 people were killed. Losses to Bomber Command totalled thirteen aircraft, most of them shot down over the route to the city.

The raids on the Renault works, Essen and Lübeck were hailed in the press as great successes – evidence that Britain, in the shape of Bomber Command, was starting to fight back against Germany. After Lübeck, another raid followed on a similar town, Rostock, once again an old Hanseatic port, built in the thirteenth century and with a similar ancient city centre. The operation, however, would not only be another fire-raising attempt, but would include an attack on the Heinkel aircraft works in the suburbs.

The attack, which started on 23 April, lasted for four days. The initial raids were disappointing, but on the third and fourth the target burned fiercely. Five Group attacked the Heinkel works and here too the bombing showed a high level of precision. Out of 521 aircraft sent over the targets, 12 were lost. The severe damage to the centre of the town alarmed the Nazi leadership. Thousands of people living there fled to the surrounding countryside, as of course many of the citizens of Coventry and Southampton had done when those towns were bombed in 1940. Many public buildings and commercial areas were flattened. The German Ministry of Economic Warfare wrote, 'It seems little exaggeration to say that Rostock has for the time being ceased to exist as a going concern'.

Despite the euphoric reaction to these raids in the British press, their strategic importance was limited. However, what they had demonstrated to Harris and his staff in High Wycombe was that, if raids were organized in a disciplined way, then the defences of a town could be overwhelmed and great destruction could be caused. The methods being adopted to make the best use of Gee – bombers dropping illuminating flares, followed by others dropping markers and incendiaries to act as a target indicator for a following wave – called for strict timing over the target and careful coordination amongst the various bomber groups on matters like routes, bomb loads and take-off times.

Up until this point, operational instructions had been passed to groups and stations ordering certain targets to be attacked within a specified time limit, but individual crews were allowed discretion to plan their own flights and, within limits, their own routes to and from the target. There was little coordination in detailed flight planning. Now, with Harris's determination to build up the effectiveness of Bomber Command, all this was changing and big operations had to be planned down to the last detail. He wanted to show how refinements in coordination and target-marking, and thus improved concentration of bomb loads on the target, could wreak enormous devastation. Such a raid would make the world take notice and underpin his ambition for Bomber Command to become a war-winning weapon.

Harris realized, however, that far larger numbers of aircraft were needed for an operation of this sort. The normal raids of 250 or 300 aircraft would never be able to produce the mass destruction around the aiming point that he wanted. His intention was to assemble a force of 1,000 bombers against a single target, and preparations were started in May 1942. There was an element of high risk in this. Bringing together that number of aircraft would require all the training squadrons and conversion units to make a contribution, raising the possibility of higher casualties amongst the inexperienced crews, as well as the disruption of the training programme. The OTUs put up a total of 302 aircraft, in addition to another 64 attached to 1 and 3 Groups. Diversionary raids on enemy fighter airfields were carried out by Blenheims of 2 Group, and Fighter Command provided 39 aircraft to attack airfields along the route to the target.

Harris wanted to bomb Hamburg, on the grounds that it presented an easily identifiable target. Like Lübeck, it was on the coast at the mouth of a river. The city was, however, outside effective Gee range and Bomber Command's scientific advisers argued that Cologne, being closer and within Gee range, was a better option. Harris later wrote suggesting that the final decision was made because of the weather, but others think that the decision to target

Cologne was a direct result of the 'boffins'' advice. Harris was determined that this operation would be a success. It was a key moment in his attempt to get the spotlight of publicity on Bomber Command and arrangements had been made to take forty members of the press on the raid.

On 30 May, with a forecast of a bright, moonlit night, 1,047 aircraft took off and set course for the German city. There was very dirty weather over the North Sea, but it lifted over the Dutch coast and then clear conditions prevailed over Holland and Germany, all the way to the target.

The bomber crews had heard the news that there would be 1,000 bombers taking part in the raid at their morning briefing and it produced a remarkable sense of awe, and of confidence. Group intelligence officers had already noted, in their reports to Bomber Command headquarters, that whenever crews were informed that they were going to try something new, or that the operation was going to test a new procedure, there was a lift in morale. The worst thing for the men, they had noted, was being asked to perform the same routine operations over and over again when the results and the casualties were already known.

There was some concern about the congestion that might be expected over the target, and the possibility of collision or of falling victim to the bombs from a plane at greater altitude, but the fact that a stream of bombers moving through a single sector of airspace made it harder for radar-controlled anti-aircraft guns or night fighters to select a target seemed to be a convincing argument.

Guided by their Gee receivers, 3 Group's Wellingtons arrived at the target first and proceeded to lay their flares for the next wave of Wellingtons and Stirlings with their incendiaries and high explosives. Finally, the Manchesters and Lancasters of 5 Group followed. Nine hundred aircraft made it to the target, dropping 1,455 tons of bombs on Cologne within the space of ninety minutes. The effect was dreadful and the bomber crews arriving after the attack was well under way could not believe their eyes. Nothing like this had been seen before. The fires of Lübeck and Rostock a few weeks earlier seemed minor affairs. The glow of the conflagration could be seen for 100 miles ahead, so vast that many people believed that some great forest was on fire. Some of the bombers flying at low altitude saw their wings and engine nacelles flickering with reflections from the red flames below. The flak and the searchlights seemed insignificant in this great blaze. The only identifiable indication that this had been Cologne was the River Rhine, which passed through the city, the surface of its water reflecting the sullen red of the fires on either bank.

So massive was the onslaught that many of the defending gun batteries were exhausted of ammunition, telephone lines were cut, searchlights lacked direction, and fire and ambulance services were trapped and ineffective, with roads destroyed and blocked and water mains ruptured.

Six hundred acres of the city, much of it in the centre, was damaged by the attack. This included 3,300 houses completely destroyed and another 7,000 damaged; 36 factories destroyed and another 270 damaged or put out of action; the central train station badly damaged; and the docks along the Rhine, the tram lines and railway lines all put out of use. In addition, 384 civilians were killed; 85 soldiers and members of the Civil Defence also lost their lives.

British losses overall were lower than average, with the highest casualties amongst the Wellingtons and the lowest amongst the four-engined heavies. Analysis later showed that the large number of planes did not prevent the defenders from tracking individual aircraft through the attack, but did stop them from firing on more than a small number.

The raid showed Harris that destruction of German industrial centres by bombing was a realizable aim if enough resources were devoted to achieving it.

The thousand-bomber raid made headlines around the world and was a great coup for the British propaganda effort. Churchill said that the raid was 'proof of the growing power of the British bomber force' and was a herald of what Germany would receive, city by city, from now on.

In a few months, Harris had reinvigorated Bomber Command and placed it firmly at the centre of Britain's war against Germany. The problems of destroying and weakening Germany's ability to wage war by striking at key industrial targets had been by-passed. He had proved that Bomber Command had the ability to destroy the very fabric of German society – factories, government, houses, civilian workers, towns and cities could literally be blown away. It was a remarkably successful few months for Harris and proof that he could go on to wreak greater and greater destruction.

However, Harris had not completely quelled the arguments for more precise and directed bombing, and with new improved aids ready to be introduced, his vision of Bomber Command would be constantly challenged. Portal, along with others in the air staff, had for some months wanted to introduce a special target-marking force of bombers into the command's structure. Harris had resisted this, for the good reason that he believed that creating an elite force would remove the most experienced crews from the other squadrons and so damage morale. He wanted the special crews to stay in the groups and the squadrons so that they could carry out a leadership role, rather than being hived off into a separate organization. The pressure for some reform was too great, however, and he gave in with the proviso that Don Bennett, a renowned airman and navigator with considerable experience in setting up civilian routes across the Atlantic, was offered the job as head of the Pathfinder Force, as the new target-locating aircraft were called.

It was duly created in August 1942, equipped with Lancaster, Halifax and Stirling bombers, and with another aircraft that had recently been brought into production, the de Havilland Mosquito. Powered by two of the ubiquitous Merlin engines, the Mosquito was largely constructed out of wood and was extremely light. With no defensive armament, it was fast enough to outrun most German fighters, but could still carry a 4,000lb bomb load. When acting as a Pathfinder, it carried a special target-indicator flare manufactured by Brocks, the fireworks company. These flares burned with a dull red light, then produced showers of green sparks as they descended, hopefully giving an unmistakeable signal to the bomb aimers overhead.

Their first operation was an attack on Flensburg, a submarine base north of Kiel. It was a failure. The Pathfinders had little training and none of the special electronic aids that were shortly going to be introduced into the main force. But they improved, raising the level of navigation and starting their own meteorological flights to improve weather forecasts. In a very short time the bulk of the bomber force relied on them to mark the targets. Harris, however, was never wholly convinced of their value and would later take the opportunity to create a separate target-marking force.

What Harris had achieved in such a short time was a demonstration of the potential impact a bombing campaign could have on the course of the war. One year on, this new determination and strategy were to shape the nature and frequency of missions that Geoff, George and the crew would be asked to undertake.

9

INTO BATTLE

In September 1943, Geoff, George and the rest of the crew, their training complete, waited to begin active service. It was common knowledge that 'freshman' crews, as the new arrivals were called, would not be thrown into the main bomber force on a raid straight away. It was customary for a first mission to be 'gardening' – a mine-laying operation in the Channel or the North Sea, where the only danger from anti-aircraft fire was a chance encounter with a German flak ship and where German night fighters would not normally venture.

They were posted to 57 Squadron, operating Lancasters from East Kirkby in Lincolnshire, arriving on 11 September to be picked up by one of the base buses from Stickney railway station. They were allocated to 'A' Flight. Geoff shared a billet in a damp Nissen hut with the Canadian crew of a pilot called Pat Paterson, whom he soon discovered were 'a mad bunch, but great fun'. They were a constant thorn in the authorities' side, but took flying very seriously indeed.

There were twenty-seven Lancasters in 57 Squadron, six more than in a normal squadron, although because of maintenance and crew training it was never possible to muster the full complement on a mission. Around one third of the flight crews were Canadian, a higher than normal percentage.

The squadron was part of 5 Group, commanded at the time by Air Vice Marshal Ralph Cochrane, and on arrival the aircrew were issued with a small, duplicated booklet called *No 5 Group Tactical Notes*, to which he had written the foreword. The opening paragraph, while saying that the weight of the bombing offensive was having an appreciable effect on Germany's ability to continue the war, proceeded with the warning that she was strengthening her air defences and that 'it is no longer possible to operate against German targets without a thorough understanding of the defence system and of the manner in which it can be breached'. The document went on to detail the workings of the German defensive radar system, how it was linked to the night-fighter forces, how they were directed and how the searchlights and anti-aircraft batteries were organized. It then described the various tactics that could be used to evade German night fighters and escape from the batteries of searchlights and anti-aircraft fire. Much of this had already been taught at the OTU, but the report stressed that the information it contained was compiled from the experience of those who had recently been engaged in

operations. In fact, for the first two weeks of their time at
East Kirkby the new boys, along with the remainder of the
squadron, did nothing but more training, both night and
day. There were no operations, there was a full moon
and clear skies, so they trained on the bombing and gun-
firing ranges, where Geoff, as a bomb aimer also
responsible for the forward turret, fired his machine guns
for the first time, loosing off 500 rounds at various targets
dotted around the mudflats on the northern edge of The
Wash. At the same time he was getting used to the countryside and its landmarks – the Boston Stump, the nearby
windmill, and the tall lighthouse at Grimsby, which the *Dock*
Luftwaffe had not attacked because they also found it a *Tower*
useful landmark on their journeys across the North Sea.
Evenings were spent in the mess, where they joined forces
with the members of the other five new crews that had
joined 57 Squadron in September. It seemed to Geoff and
the other crew members who were officers, the Skipper and
Curly, that the more established crews tended to be slightly
aloof, not making any effort to get to know the fresh faces.
It was only later that they understood why.

Normal routine was for Geoff to be woken in the morning by his batman, head off on the long walk to their toilet
and shower block, then make his way to the mess for breakfast. The flying instructions for that day would be pinned
up in the flight office, where the crews would see to which
aircraft they had been allocated if they were scheduled to
take part in an exercise.

On 22 September there was no exercise, but all the rest of
the squadron was flying on a raid to Hanover. All around

the perimeter Lancasters were having their engines run up, and the riggers and fitters were clambering over them.

All the aircraft taking part in the raid later that day had to take off to be given an air test before landing again to be bombed up and fuelled. All morning there was a constant roar of engines as the Lancasters slowly moved round the perimeter track into position at the end of the runway and gathered speed for take-off. There were twenty-two altogether, a maximum effort that engaged almost the whole of the squadron apart from Geoff's crew. He felt marginalized, and George felt positively discriminated against.

Later that day, at 18.30, the aircraft went through the same procedure, slightly more ponderously as they trundled round the perimeter fully loaded, sitting heavier on their huge tyres, taking longer to lift off. A group of senior officers, some WAAFs and ground staff in a cluster at the end of the runway saluted as each Lancaster rushed past them – a poignant farewell. The chances of all of them coming back were slim, although two operations earlier that month had seen all 57 Squadron's crews return safe. The Skipper and his crew watched from further away, from one of the hangars, as each bomber in turn slowly rose in the air, the undercarriage disappeared and it turned to the right into the departure route.

The bombers were back from Hanover and in the circuit waiting for permission to land by 23.00. Lying in his cot, Geoff could hear them flying over the threshold and the beat of propellers as they circled slowly back round to their hardstands. Next morning at breakfast he heard that one crew had been lost. Lancaster S Sugar, flown by Pilot

Spilsby

Officer Duff, had been hit by a German intruder over Spilsbury. The bomb aimer and the flight engineer had baled out, but the rest of the crew had failed to do so and died in the crashed aeroplane, which burned for some time afterwards.

It was sobering. 'Yup, stay on your toes or else,' said the Skipper as they walked to 'A' Flight. This time their names were on the flight list under operational flying and they had been allocated E Edward. They were flying tonight, not on a 'gardening' mission but as part of the main force on a target in Germany. It was remarkable, reflected Geoff, how the knowledge that at last they were going to face night fighters and flak in a few hours' time changed everything.

They went over E Edward at length, talking to the ground crew, Jock closely searching the engine nacelles for any oil or hydraulic leaks and inspecting all the systems for which he was responsible, which was in fact everything. A faulty oxygen system could kill them, as could a thousand and one other pieces of machinery that might suddenly develop a fault, but on the air test he closely monitored the temperatures, the variation in the revs of the engines and the oil pressures of each one. The engines kept the plane flying and powered the gun turrets, the electrical systems, the navigation aids, the radios – in short, they were the heart of the Lancaster and it was their sweet running, and the fuel system that fed them, on which he kept a close eye throughout any flight. Landing again, they signed it off and made their way to the briefing.

On a large board set on a low stage in front of 114 aircrew were the details of the mission, target, route, expected weather, latest intelligence about the defences and any diversions planned. All this information was covered by a white sheet, waiting for the intelligence officer to bound up the steps and dramatically reveal the 'mission for tonight, gentlemen'.

It was Mannheim. They were to be thrust into the thick of it, and it was going to be a big effort. Mannheim-Ludwigshafen was 450 miles inside Germany, much further than the Ruhr, and had already been pounded several times during the war, most recently on 5 September. The new raid was once again to be a major effort from Bomber Command, with 600 bombers scheduled to take part, of which 57 Squadron detailed twenty aircraft. The intention was to concentrate on the northern part of the town, which had not been hit on the earlier raid that month. There was also to be a diversionary raid on Darmstadt. The weather forecast was good and opposition was not expected to be fierce.

With a final 'Good luck', the intelligence officer left the stage, to be replaced by the met officer. There seemed to be no problems, no expected fog over East Kirkby or other alternates hindering the crews' return, and the winds antici-pated at the height at which the Lancasters would be flying, 18,000 feet, were not likely to be severe.

Each squadron had a section leader for each trade on the Lancaster – pilot, navigator, flight engineer, bomb aimer, wireless operator and gunners. These section leaders were usually aircrew who had completed one or more tours of operation. They would brief the various sections on the relevant aspects of the operation so that individual crews could be given more detail. Geoff was briefed on the type of bomb load to be carried, the height from which they would drop their bombs, the sequence that the armourers would set in the bomb-control panel so that the bomb load would be dropped in the right order, and the basic wind speed and direction over the target, which Geoff would feed into the bombsight. Their load on this their first mission was going to be standard for the main bomber force. There would be a 4,000lb high-explosive bomb – a 'cookie' – then seventy-six 30lb incendiary bombs and 1,080 4lb incendiaries in cases that would be dropped, scattering their load as they broke apart in the slipstream. Inside the bomb bay there were sixteen bomb stations, from which various sizes and types of bomb could be suspended. The load varied, depending on the type of target and the distance from the bombers' base. The further the target and the greater the fuel load, the smaller the bomb load. For heavy industrial targets the load would be one 4,000lb high-capacity bomb designed to create a massive blast, and this would be combined with ten 500lb general-purpose bombs. For a town, where fire would create more havoc than blast damage, incendiaries would be carried, as they were on this night.

Curly, the navigator, was given details of the route way points and the time that he had to ensure they were over the target. It was understood that an irregular spread of heights would help to confuse the fighters operating over the target area. Whatever pattern was adopted, the timing of each aircraft was vital. Stragglers were much more likely to fall victim to a fighter or to radar-controlled anti-aircraft fire. The navigator had a heavy responsibility. As a concession to their new-boy status, E Edward was scheduled to take part in the fifth wave, by which time it was hoped the flak would have been subdued and the German fighters would be low on fuel and ammunition.

The briefings finished, they went to collect their rations – sandwiches, some chocolate, a flask of tea or coffee – and to get their parachutes from the parachute store and their escape kit. Their personal possessions, anything that might help the enemy's intelligence services if they were shot down and captured, were put into a small, cage-like locker.

They got into the crew buses and were taken out to their aircraft. The bombs had already been loaded and the tanks topped off. Geoff inspected the bomb load, walking under the open bomb doors, checking for himself the loading sequence. The routine was distracting; he found that it helped to prevent too much speculation about what lay ahead. But as the minutes ticked away, the knot in the pit of the stomach, the fluttering thoughts that this might be the last as well as the first time any of them did this, could not be completely quashed.

Just before they started to climb aboard, the Squadron padre arrived. He knew that they were a fresh crew and wanted to know if they would like to speak to him or to say some prayers. The reaction from the Skipper was unexpected. He turned on the minister. 'If you want to talk to the Anglicans, talk to them in your chapel, not at my aeroplane. I'm not going to be a hypocrite and get down on my knees and pray that we come back tonight.' He gestured to the crew, who were all nonplussed. 'I want these guys to know in their hearts they're coming back, and they'll come back, but it will be through their own efforts, not because they're putting their hand out for help. So don't come back here again.'

George remembered that the minister was extremely annoyed; no doubt it was another black mark against him. He believed, though, that the crew appreciated his emphasizing that the outcome of the trip was their responsibility. He gestured to everybody to get going and they climbed aboard. There was nothing more to say. Whether the Skipper intended it or not, everybody's private fear had been brought out into the open. They might not come back tonight. He was worried, but he believed they had some say in it, and he trusted them. They started doing what they had to do.

The gunners, Flash and Tommy, satisfied themselves that the ammunition feed from the boxes in the fuselage was in order. Getting into the rear turret was a test of agility for Tommy. He had to climb in feet first, it was such a cramped position, then close and test the door. The standard drill was to check the gunsight fuses and spare bulbs, unlock the turret and test the guns for depression and elevation, and rotate the turret to make sure the hydraulics were working. Then he would test the oxygen outlet to his mask, plug the intercom in and test that, then put the 'fire and safe' switch to 'fire' and the master switch to 'safe', where it would stay until they were in the air. Then report OK to the Skipper.

The four engines were started, one after the other. The pilot and the flight engineer checked the rev counter, oil pressure and temperature on each one before the throttles were eased forward, the brakes released and the Lancaster slowly moved forward along the perimeter road to take up its position at the end of the runway. As each aircraft took off, the next one moved into position, the pilot did his final checks with the flight engineer and they waited for a green signal light to take off. Exhaust smoke and the smell of aviation fuel eddied across the airfield. The flaps were set at 15 degrees and the engines would be running at full throttle as the skipper pushed them all the way forward. The plane was vibrating with the revolutions of the four propellers and the Merlins running at almost 3,000 revs a minute, with the boost set at 9. The brakes were released, the Lancaster rolled forward, gathering speed, then at 100 m.p.h. the wheels lifted off the tarmac and the great plane rose slowly into the air. The take-off could be long, and it was tense. Fully loaded with high-octane petrol and a load of high explosive, any crash at this point was going to be both spectacular and fatal. But over the intercom came the words 'Wheels up', then 'Flaps up', and the aircraft gained height in the gathering darkness on their first op. The relief at taking off with a full bomb load for the first time was now replaced by the tension of their first flight over the North Sea and into heavily defended enemy territory.

After the take-off and slow climb out to rendezvous with the main force, Geoff went forward and lay flat in the nose, with a clear view through the bomb aimer's bubble of the landscape below. It was cramped and he was lying over the forward escape hatch. To his left, about 8 inches in front of his nose, was the bombsight computer, which was connected to the bombsight. On the right was the pre-selector box, which contained the switches setting the order in which the bombs were going to be released. Geoff's was the most exhilarating position, as it gave a true sense of speed as the bomber rushed past the tops of the clouds. As the coast approached, he started focusing on geographical features and landmarks to pinpoint the landfall and help Curly to get an accurate fix on their course.

Curly was stuck in his cubbyhole, screened by a curtain from the rest of the aircraft, getting regular fixes from the Gee transmissions and plotting the course on his sparsely covered map, devoid of most features. Conventional map-reading was superfluous; the navigator never saw the ground. Vince, the radio operator, was listening out to broadcasts from 5 Group headquarters every twenty minutes. This was usually the group number and a call sign, but occasionally there might be new orders.

As they got closer to the coast, searchlights started to flicker up into the clouds and the first bursts of enemy anti-aircraft fire appeared ahead of them. The Skipper had been flying the Lancaster in the recommended way to give the gunners a chance to cover the sky beneath them. The aircraft would bank slowly one way and then the other, and it required a lot of concentration to keep to the required speed and course that Curly demanded.

They approached the target, which they could see ahead outlined by a large number of searchlights and by fires burning on the ground. Many of the anti-aircraft positions had taken a pounding from the waves of bombers that had gone before them, and the flak was sporadic and not particularly focused. The adrenaline was flowing now. Geoff gave the Skipper a heading towards the markers that he had identified, and as the Skipper opened the bomb doors the Lancaster changed altitude and Jock increased the engine revs to maintain speed. The slipstream from the open bomb bay added to the noise, and all each crew member could do was focus on what they could see and strain to hear the words in their headphones. There were fires burning all over the area, making it hard to spot the target flares, but the Rhine, which split the towns of Mannheim and Ludwigshafen, helped Geoff. They flew straight and level, until Geoff, confident that his crosshairs were on the aiming point, pressed the button and the bombs dropped away. Suddenly free of the weight, the plane lifted in the air.

They had to wait a few more seconds while the photo flash dropped from the bomb bay and illuminated the fall of bombs, so it was three seconds before Geoff could utter the magic words, 'Bombs gone, Skip'. He felt a wave of relief at the success of their first mission. It was completely irrational, because they had to make the return trip back over Germany and often single night fighters would lie in wait over the coast, the pilot hoping that tiredness and the thought of another safely completed mission would make the bomber crew less vigilant. The Skipper was well aware of the dangers of loss of concentration and warned Geoff and the two gunners to stay on the alert. The Lancaster thundered on its course, every minute getting closer to home. Finally they sighted the coast of Britain and shortly before midnight they were given permission to land.

Geoff King (**above left**), here photographed at the start of his operations with 57 Squadron. A few months before, he was photographed on the old farm in Essex where he was born, helping his sister, father and grandfather with the harvest (**left**). George Laing (**above right**), the pilot and 'Skipper', had the dashing good looks which could sweep any girl off her feet. He learned to fly in Canada in the small Tiger Moth (**below**), and only graduated to the powerful twin-engined Wellington when he arrived in the UK. By this time, the Wellington was being superseded by new, even bigger four-engined 'heavies'.

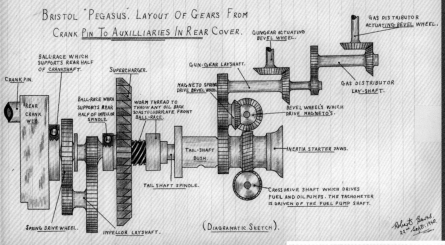

BRISTOL "PEGASUS". LAYOUT OF GEARS FROM
CRANK PIN TO AUXILLIARIES IN REAR COVER.

GAS DISTRIBUTOR
ACTUATING BEVEL WHEEL.

GUN GEAR ACTUATING
BEVEL WHEEL.

BALL RACE WHICH
SUPPORTS REAR HALF
OF CRANKSHAFT.

GUN-GEAR LAYSHAFT.

SUPERCHARGER.

GAS DISTRIBUTOR
LAY-SHAFT.

CRANK PIN.

MAGNETO SPRING
DRIVE BEVEL WHEEL

BALL-RACE WHICH
SUPPORTS REAR
HALF OF IMPELLOR
SPINDLE.

REAR
CRANK
WEB.

WORM THREAD TO
THROW ANY OIL BACK
SO AS TO LUBRICATE FRONT
BALL-RACE.

BEVEL WHEEL'S WHICH
DRIVE MAGNETO'S.

TAIL-SHAFT
BUSH.

INERTIA STARTER JAWS.

TAIL SHAFT SPINDLE.

CROSS DRIVE SHAFT WHICH DRIVES
FUEL AND OIL PUMPS. THE TACHOMETER
IS DRIVEN OF THE FUEL PUMP SHAFT.

SPRING DRIVE WHEEL.

IMPELLOR LAYSHAFT.

(DIAGRAMATIC SKETCH).

Roberts Burns
22 Sept. 1940.

Flight engineer Robbie Burns (**right**) left school
at fourteen, but the RAF gave him an education.
His drawing (**above**) of a gear train in a Bristol
Pegasus was in one of his first notebooks. By the
time he qualified, he was familiar with all the
engines then in service, and understood the
engineering behind them.

The Rolls Royce Merlin engines (**above**) that powered the
Lancasters were highly sophisticated machines and Robbie's
knowledge of their performance was often vital to the
crew's survival.

The crew's first posting was to 57 Squadron, here posing in front of one of their Lancaster aircraft on the base at East Kirkby. To George Laing's surprise, there was a high percentage of Canadians in the ranks.

Roy Davis (**left**), a grammar-school boy from Manchester, was the navigator. His skill kept them on course, and on target, and helped earn them a reputation as a highly proficient crew. His marriage, halfway through their tour of operations, worried George the Skipper. Vincent Day (**right**), the wireless operator, was a 'quiet cockney', always alert to last-minute signals and the stray clues that he could pick up about enemy activity.

The Lancaster Bomber was the most successful of the big four-engined aircraft in Bomber Command. It could carry more bombs higher and further than any other in service, and spearheaded the attacks on Germany.

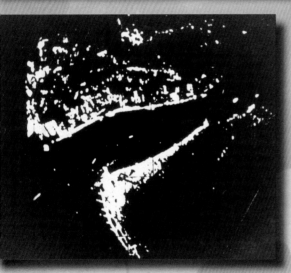

Developments in radar were vital to Bomber Command. In 1943 radar was being fitted to Lancasters, the transmitters and receivers mounted in a dome underneath the fuselage (**left**). It was hoped that it would provide a massive boost to the accuracy of the bombers. The first sets helped the navigator to easily identify geographical features such as coastlines and rivers (**below left**), but as the photo of the radar screen on one of the crew's raids over Stuttgart shows (**below right**), it took an experienced operator to use it over large built-up targets.

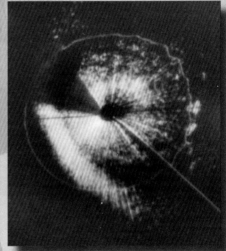

The cartoon figure of Jane in the *Daily Mirror* (**right**) was a forces' favourite. It was a shared liking for the newspaper that brought Geoff and Roy together, in a crew that fought over fifty missions.

JANE
FLAGS 'EM
DOWN

The Germans also had sophisticated radar. A chain of large ground-based radar stations (**below**) bordered the whole of occupied Europe. Their operators could be confused by clouds of aluminium strips called Window, seen here (**above right**) being run off before being cut up into shorter lengths. The Germans had an answer to this: they fitted radar sets to the Junkers 88 night fighters (**above left**), which could then independently hunt the bombers down.

This dramatically lit photo of a Lancaster (**above**) reveals the size and power of the machine, but in reality light was something that the crews hated. Once picked up and illuminated by powerful lights (**left**), the bomber pilots would throw their aircraft around the sky, diving and corkscrewing, but they had a slim chance of avoiding anti-aircraft fire or night fighters which could spot them, trapped by the beams.

Giant searchlights, which could throw an intense beam for thousands of feet into the air, ringed the cities of Germany, and they were coordinated and directed by local radar stations.

From the air the fires of a burning target looked like bright points of light (**background image**), but on the ground each one was a scene of burning devastation, like these smashed blocks in Berlin. On some raids Geoff felt that he was flying into hell.

A photo taken from Geoff's own Lancaster (**below**), when they were Pathfinders, shows another plane below them, searchlight beams reflected in the plexiglass of the bomb aimer's bubble and illuminating the clouds. This raid on the Phillips factory at Eindhoven was abandoned because the clouds made it difficult to mark the factory accurately, and they wanted to avoid allied civilian casualties.

The crew kept in touch after the war, helped by the fact that the Skipper, George Laing, became a captain for Air Canada. He and Geoff (**above left**) are now the only members of the crew still alive. George visited Frank Green, the mid-upper gunner, in Australia (**above right**). The visit, according to Frank's widow, helped Frank to talk about his experiences, and relive one of their most dangerous raids.

George also went up to Scotland to visit Robbie Burns (*in the cap*), where they reminisced about the numerous times they had dealt with engine failure, fires and low-level escapes over the Dutch coast.

The crew managed to get back to East Kirkby for a reunion, when a surviving Lancaster was put on display (**main image**). George (*left*) and Geoff (*right*) stand next to Frank Green, 'Curly'.

Geoff (*left*) and George (*right*) flank Vincent Day, wireless operator, with the wheat fields of Lincolnshire behind them.

Debriefed, they went, absolutely drained, for their bacon, eggs and strong tea.

To begin with the target-marking had worked well and concentrated bombing had fallen on the intended areas, although in the later stages of the raid the fall of bombs had crept back across the northern edge of Ludwigshafen and out into the countryside. A great deal of damage was done – an estimated 25,000 people were bombed out of their homes. Where there was creep away from the target, the bombs had tended to fall across the Rhine and into Ludwigshafen, where the IG Farben factory was badly hit. The smaller towns of Oppau and Frankenthal had also been damaged because of an error in marking. As a result, another 8,000 people were made homeless and the incendiaries started fires that completely gutted the centre of Frankenthal. Geoff was satisfied, however, that he had got fairly close to the aiming point.

They were not scheduled for a raid again for another four days, so there was ample time to absorb the feelings and experiences of their first mission over Germany. Everyone on the aircraft had felt fear and nervous anticipation, but they were all pleased that they had carried out their jobs without any major problems. The Skipper was upbeat, saying it had been a great show, but it was of course more taxing than any exercise they had ever done. The searchlights and the flak, however distant, had been real and threatening, creating a new, unparalleled level of danger. Out of 628 aircraft that had taken part in the raid, 32 planes and their 224 crewmen had crashed or been shot down. Estimates were that the vast majority of these were kills by night fighters.

Perhaps more seriously for Geoff and the rest of 57 Squadron, three Lancasters out of the twenty that had taken off from East Kirkby had failed to return. Pilot Officer Bourdon, Pilot Officer Hogan, Flight Sergeant Austen and their eighteen crew members were either dead or taken prisoner. Their possessions, in the cage lockers, were left to be gathered up and returned to their families.

The first mission naturally had a remarkable impact on Geoff and the crew. They had flown over Germany and returned to tell the tale. After that flight Geoff felt a far greater sense of security in the Lancaster than he had ever experienced on a training flight. Once inside the fuselage, with the engines roaring and the aircraft gaining speed along the runway, he felt not fear but a sense of safety and a belief that he would make it. It was irrational. Most crews died after only a few missions; statistics indicated that the first five were the most dangerous. The crew had another four to go. Whether they would make it would in part be due to the fundamental changes that Bomber Harris, their commander-in-chief, had wrought on Bomber Command.

10

THE WINNING WEAPON

Bomber Harris believed very firmly that Bomber Command could become large enough to cripple the German economy so badly that its leaders would sue for peace. In the nine months that preceded the raid on Mannheim by George Laing, Geoff King and the other members of the crew on 23 September 1943, he had gone some way towards demonstrating that this dream was perfectly achievable.

He had been disappointed by the Gee system, which had proved only a partial success in guiding the bombers to their targets. In practice it was not capable of providing a level of accuracy beyond 2 or 3 miles, even when used by the most experienced and adept navigators. Yet it had proved valuable in getting more of the bombers to the target, and at the start of 1943 a more precise system was tested. Known as Oboe, the new technology was similar to

Gee in that it transmitted signals from ground stations in the UK which were intercepted by a receiver on board an aircraft, but the additional feature was that the receiving aircraft was fitted with a transponder that sent a response back to the ground stations. This enabled them to measure accurately the distance of the plane from the transmitters and so signal the bomber when to release its bomb load. Accuracy was very high, within hundreds of metres, but Oboe could handle signals from only a few aircraft at a time.

Almost coincidentally with the introduction of Oboe, in January 1943 an alternative, wholly independent system of guidance that could be mounted on each bomber was being manufactured. Called H2S, this was ground-mapping radar mounted in a blister under the fuselage that enabled the navigator to see on a cathode-ray tube a representation of the geographical features over which the aircraft was flying. H2S required a considerable amount of skill and experience on the part of the operator, and it took some time before it became really effective.

Oboe, however, did have the possibility of delivering to Arthur Harris that holy grail of air forces, the blind-bombing instrument. The fact that only a handful of aircraft could use the system at one time was a severe restriction, but was solved by the expedient of fitting it only to the aircraft of the Pathfinder Force. The introduction of Mosquitoes fitted with Oboe and armed with target-indicator flares began a practice known as 'sky-marking', where the target indicators were dropped above the cloud cover over a target.

Used in conjunction with the H2S ground-mapping radar, it was found that a number of factors affected the results of this type of target-marking. The main one was the speed and direction of the winds and the frequency with which new flares could be dropped after the original ones burned out.

After several experiments on several different targets it was established that sky-marking would be used if the cloud cover was eight tenths or more – that is, if the ground was obscured by clouds that covered 80 per cent of the sky. Between five and eight tenths, the Pathfinders were told to drop flares to illuminate the target based on identification from their H2S sets, and then to identify the aiming point visually before dropping the target indicators.

The differing performance of the aircraft in Bomber Command affected their ability to use Oboe. The Mosquitoes of the Pathfinder Force could operate at great height above the clouds, while the number of main-force planes capable of bombing on the sky-markers was progressively reduced as the height of the clouds increased. The Stirlings and Wellingtons, which were being steadily withdrawn, could only really operate at heights of up to 12,000 feet and only the Lancaster could fly above cloud tops reaching 17,000 feet. In addition, like Gee, Oboe was limited by the range of the ground-based transmitters.

Despite these limitations, Harris wrote enthusiastically about the introduction of Oboe, which was first used on a mass raid in March 1943, that 'for the first time the Command found itself in a position to inflict severe material damage on almost any industrial centre in Germany'. It was a sweeping statement.

It was no coincidence, then, that that first attack using Oboe was directed at Essen and the huge Krupps foundry and steelworks. The target, as usual, was cloaked in smog and, but for the use of Oboe as a guide, the attack by 442 aircraft would have been as ineffective as the previous ones. On this night, however, the Pathfinder Mosquitoes dropped their red target indicators with great accuracy and the back-up marker bombers surrounded them with green markers. The attack was therefore much more concentrated than in the past, with 150 aircraft dropping their bombs within a 3-mile ring around the aiming point. The damage assessment was that 160 acres had been laid waste, with damage caused to another 450 acres. Harris could smell blood.

> It was not only that a hitherto invulnerable target had for the first time been seriously damaged but also that there was no reason why the success should not be indefinitely repeated in attacks on any other target within Oboe range. This had never been the case before; every previous success had been dependent on the caprice of the weather and usually had been won by seizing some opportunity that might never reoccur. But now the whole of the Ruhr was evidently at our mercy.

As a result of this attack, and two others that followed within the next month, about 600 acres of the built-up area of Essen was destroyed. In the course of these three raids, about half of the 300 separate buildings in the Krupps works were damaged. By the end of July 1943 three more attacks had seriously reduced the output of this industrial complex. The most effective of the operations, carried out on 25 July by 700 aircraft, caused as much damage as all the previous attacks on Essen combined. Among the list of damaged buildings was the giant Hindenburg Hall, where steam-locomotive production was halted and never restarted, despite the fact that locomotive construction was considered by the German government to be as important as that of tanks, aircraft and submarines. After Kassel, Essen was the largest locomotive factory in Europe. In addition, the bombers stopped production of large-calibre artillery shells for three months, and also artillery fuses, while the output of artillery pieces, gun-barrel tubes and liners was cut by half. Krupps also produced crankshafts for aero engines and the attacks reduced the output of these from 1,000 per month to 500. The British press was quick to publicize the raids on Essen. One of the reconnaissance photographs was splashed across a page of the *Daily Express* with the headline 'WHAT WE DID TO ESSEN'. The newspaper described the city as the most bombed in the world.

In between the attacks on Essen, other targets in the Ruhr were being hammered, again with an effectiveness never before achieved: Dortmund, one of the chief centres of heavy industry, Duisburg, an important inland port with its surrounding industrial satellite towns of steel-rolling mills and foundries, Bochum, Gelsenkirchen, Oberhausen and Mülheim. Other outlying towns such as Wuppertal, a centre for steel and stainless-steel fabrication, Krefeld, Münster, Aachen, Remscheid and München-Gladbach were all damaged, most of them very heavily, within this period. Over 14,000 individual bomber crews flew missions over the Ruhr, including Düsseldorf and Cologne.

Düsseldorf was a leading commercial centre of western Germany and the seat of the head offices of all the major heavy iron and steel engineering and armaments companies of the Ruhr and the Rhineland, as well as the location of important factories in its own right. It was the target for two attacks, each of about 700 aircraft. The first, on 25 May 1943, was not successful and showed that even Oboe could be rendered ineffective by very high cloud cover. With the tops at almost 20,000 feet, the sky-markers were completely obscured and the attack was widely scattered. The second, however, on 11 June, was carried out in good weather and the bombers attained a very high concentration around the target indicators. The air-raid services in Düsseldorf were completely overwhelmed, and once more a German city was engulfed in an uncontrollable, incendiary-fuelled fire. Some buildings were still smouldering a week after the attack, and engineering works and rail terminals were smashed in the devastation. Cologne was also attacked, by 600 aircraft, and again the concentration achieved by Oboe was such that more destruction was caused in this raid than by the famous thousand-bomber raid of the previous year. By the middle of July, conditions in the Rhineland and the Ruhr had reached a state of chaos, and the Germans were considering drafting in 100,000 men to clear the rubble and carry out repairs.

The campaign against the Ruhr took nineteen weeks

altogether from the first raid on Essen. Forty major raids were carried out and altogether 18,506 missions were flown in the period. The RAF's casualty rate was around 4.7 per cent, which meant that 872 aircraft were shot down and 6,104 young airmen were killed, wounded or taken prisoner over Europe. The losses were acceptable to Harris and the top brass of the RAF, and Bomber Command emerged from this major campaign against the heartland of Europe much, much stronger than it had started it. However, the losses meant that a crew starting a tour of operations on the first mission of the 'Battle of the Ruhr' had less than a one in three chance of living through to the end of the campaign.

Losses were not spread statistically across the whole of Bomber Command. Some squadrons were hit worse than others, and there was some evidence that crews flying in the Halifaxes were more likely to die than those in the Lancasters; the Stirlings, with their limited performance, were the most vulnerable of all. Lack of experience was a great killer; those crews taking part in their first few operations were far more likely to die than those whose successful missions reached double figures. Moreover, the losses from the Ruhr campaign had been steadily rising and obviously affected morale.

Bomber Command had set up an Operational Research Section to examine every aspect of its operations and it carried out considerable research into the reasons for the continued casualties. Figures suggested that the rise in losses was attributable to the German night-fighter force – responsible for as many as 70 per cent of losses, in fact

– and that half of these were radar-controlled intercepts. Of the losses due to flak, fully two thirds were caused by gunfire from radar-directed artillery.

But Harris was not prepared to call a halt. The Ruhr had been systematically attacked by the use of Oboe, and it was now time to test the effectiveness of the other new aid, the radar H2S.

Hamburg, Germany's largest port and, with a population of two million, the country's second largest city, had always been high on the list of Bomber Command's targets. It had of course been considered as the city to hit with the first thousand-bomber raid, but because at the time it was out of range of the Gee radio beams, Cologne had been chosen instead. Hamburg was similarly at the limits of Oboe, but the ground-mapping radar H2S had been tested on a smaller raid on Hamburg in January 1943 and the Mosquito observers operating the sets had reported that the image on their screens had been remarkably similar to what they had expected to see. The reason was that it was on the coast, on the estuary of a river, and the differences between land and water presented a very clearly delineated image on the radar. The town and its harbour were easily identified. Now, in July 1943, a major raid was planned using H2S as the main target-finding method.

One other innovation was also going to be used, and this represented a minor victory for Harris over the air marshals in the RAF and the members of the War Cabinet. Early in 1942 Joan Curran, a scientist at the Government Telecommunications Research Centre, had developed a simple method of interfering with German radar defences. The idea was that strips of aluminized paper, dropped in sufficient quantities, would reflect the radar beams back to the transmitters and make it impossible for the operators to separate these signals from those reflected by the bomber stream. Trials had proved that it would be effective, but the senior officers in Fighter Command had argued that, if it was used over Germany, the Germans would copy the idea and use it against Britain. The argument had gone up to the chiefs of staff, with a new potential vulnerability suggested at each discussion. By the time the operation against Hamburg was being prepared, however, Harris's constant complaints about the ban on something that he knew would staunch the haemorrhage of casualties in his command had started to bear fruit. The fears that had been put forward in June – that revealing a method of confusing radar to the Germans might endanger the tactical air forces in Sicily and the Mediterranean – was overruled by Churchill and Harris was given permission to deploy 'Window', as the strips were codenamed, against the defences of northern Germany.

Produced by a commercial printer who carried out a large contract for the government, the strips were about 6 inches long and 1 inch wide, fused on one side with aluminium foil and coated in a matt black ink on the other. They were bundled up in clumps of 2,000 or so, held together with thick rubber bands. For the first raid on Hamburg, on 24 July, twenty-six aircraft from 76 Squadron dropped the bundles of Window as they approached the target, at a point 3 degrees to the west of Hamburg, and they continued to do so until the same point on their homeward leg. Eventually the bombers were modified so that the bomb aimer could drop the bundles from his position in the nose, but on this first operational use they were dropped by the wireless operator from the flare chute in the fuselage.

The combined bomber force that took off on that summer evening from the airfields in Lincolnshire and Northamptonshire was made up of 791 aircraft – 347 Lancasters, 246 Halifaxes, 125 Stirlings and 73 Wellingtons. The Pathfinders easily identified the coast on their H2S sets and marked it with yellow target indicators, at the same time passing back accurate wind speeds for the main force, who were bombing without any navigation aids. Two more Pathfinder Mosquitoes were to illuminate the centre of the target area so that a follow-on force of Pathfinders could drop red target indicators at zero hour, the time that the first heavy bombers were due over the target. All the nearly 800 bombers were scheduled to pass over the city in just forty-eight minutes – a very high level of concentration, but one that the boffins believed would make the best use of Window. Despite the very short duration of the attack, back-up markers were to be dropped during the raid, with a two-second delay, so that the main-force bombers would have new target indicators to aim at. Operation Gomorrah, as the Battle of Hamburg was called, was going to incorporate all the lessons of the past raids on the Ruhr and would be a milestone in the development of Bomber Command's planning and research.

Window's effect on the defences was profound. There

was utter confusion in the night-fighter control rooms, and bomber pilots reported the searchlight beams over Hamburg swaying aimlessly through the night sky, as though they were operated by drunks. The night fighters, corralled in their boxes by the ground controllers, lacked any direction and some of them were extremely frustrated at their impotence in the face of a large attack. One German pilot, Peter Boden, could see the bombers silhouetted against the fires of the burning city but was not allowed to leave his box, even though the ground controller couldn't vector him to any targets or provide any other course of action.

The losses to Bomber Command reflected the disorganization of the anti-aircraft defences, because on this raid only twelve aircraft were lost. Three other raids on Hamburg followed, and only fifty-seven aircraft in total were shot down over the four raids – a rate of 2.4 per cent, compared to previous rates over the city of 6 per cent. The concentration on the target was also considered to be a marked improvement; on the first raid 306 aircraft dropped their bombs within 3 miles of the aiming point. On the further raids mounted on 27 and 29 July, and 2 August, the results were more mixed owing to problems with the weather and, on one night, a failure by the Pathfinder Force to account for the effect of low tide on the H2S image.

Hamburg, however, was doomed. The effect of concentrated raids over four days, including daylight raids by US bombers, was as though an army had invaded and sacked the city, then razed it to the ground.

The raid of 24 July started large fires that could not be

put out and continued to burn throughout the next day, sending enormous columns of smoke into the sky. Supplies of coal and coke stored in the cellars of large city apartment blocks caught fire and burned for weeks. Telephone lines were cut and efforts to fight the fires were hampered by lack of communication, with motorcyclists carrying damage reports and requests for help being forced to make large detours because rubble from collapsed buildings blocked streets and passages. The docks and factories were also damaged. The firefighters, stretched to the limit, could not prevent buildings and factories from flaring up again and again.

The first raid by Bomber Command was followed by two daylight raids by the US Eighth Air Force on 25 and 26 July, then the next large raid by the RAF on the 27th. The main weight of this attack was on the left bank of the River Alster, and the German authorities described it as one of unimaginable density; almost complete annihilation of those parts of Hamburg was achieved in a short space of time. Extensive areas were enveloped in a sea of fire within half an hour. The report went on to describe what was perhaps the most horrific effect of the raids on the city – the creation of a giant firestorm that engulfed the city.

> Tens of thousands of small fires united within a short period of time to conflagrations which developed into firestorms of typhoon-like intensity, in the course of which trees 3 feet in diameter were pulled out of the ground. As the fires spread and increased in temperature they created a

powerful convection current that sucked in air and helped to further fuel the conflagration. The German War Minister asked women and children in the city to take part in a voluntary evacuation. Hundreds of thousands left so that in the next attack [the Germans were convinced by now of British determination to destroy Hamburg systematically] only emergency services would be present in the town.

The firestorms created deadly conditions for emergency workers in the streets, who were knocked over and tumbled along the ground by the fierce winds, unable to breathe, and for civilians in their cellars and basement shelters, who were burned alive or asphyxiated in the fires.

The next raid, on 29 July, was even heavier, reducing the whole of Hamburg to one large fire. The port was severely hit and the remaining part of the crowded working-class area of Barmbreck was destroyed. Economically, the German authorities reported, Hamburg was knocked out, as even the undamaged parts had no water, gas or electricity.

The death toll was put at 45,000 and rescue work to recover the dead, and anyone still alive who might be trapped in the ruins, went on for days. Throughout the city corpses were lined up in the squares and streets, waiting for burial in mass graves. Over a million inhabitants left the city as refugees, fleeing to other towns in the area or to the surrounding countryside – a phenomenon that seriously troubled the German leadership. Albert Speer, the Reichsminister for armament and production, and one of the few Nazi leaders to escape the death penalty in October 1946, later said in his interrogation, 'The first heavy attack on Hamburg made an extraordinary impression. We were of the opinion that a rapid repetition of this type of attack upon another six German towns would inevitably cripple the will to sustain armament manufacture and war production.' Harris also believed this; he includes this quote from Speer in his account of Bomber Command written in 1945.

Yet what human beings can destroy, human beings can also rebuild, and while the shock and fear engendered by the Hamburg raids was very real amongst the German population, and indeed amongst the high command in its immediate aftermath, it didn't take long for the enormous resources of German-occupied Europe to be mobilized for the benefit of the German war machine. Speer found that Hitler was completely uninterested in the daily problems of production caused by bombing, so came up with his own solution. Formerly, many of the workers in the occupied countries had been transported to fill production gaps in the German armaments industry. In collaboration with the Vichy French minister of production, Jean Bichelonne, Speer worked out a plan in which, instead of French workers being conscripted as forced labour in Germany, German production would be shifted to France and the French workers would be protected and guaranteed security from deportation. The French factories would produce consumer and domestic goods for the German economy, freeing up all Germany's production facilities for armaments. The plan, known by Speer as a 'total war' measure, resulted in 10,000 new factories in France and was later extended to Holland and Belgium. Hamburg itself was also rapidly revived. Within two or three months services had been restored and the Blohm & Voss shipyards were functioning again, albeit with a reduced capability. In all, 10 per cent of their wartime submarine output was destroyed by the raids – a less than decisive blow.

Bomber Command, however, had carried out another devastating operation that resounded around the world and was greeted with jubilation in the press and by the bulk of the people in Britain. The details of H2S and Window were obviously still secret, but in the squadrons and bases of Bomber Command morale had been given an immense boost. The second largest city in Germany had been destroyed and the bomber losses were falling. Many thought that they were now Britain's major weapon of war, with the ability to bring Hitler and his regime to its knees. Harris certainly believed this and, after Hamburg and the Ruhr, was determined to go on to prove that Bomber Command could bring victory. What other target was left but the prize of Berlin?

11

THE NEXT FIVE MISSIONS

After Geoff and the crew's successful fulfilment of their first mission on 23 September 1943, two operations were cancelled because of bad weather over the targets, but they were called off very late on both days. It was unsettling to go through the preparations and the rising expectation of an imminent take-off and then have to stand down. It made everybody tense.

Four days after the raid on Mannheim, 27 September, a raid on Hanover was announced at the morning briefing. There was always a stirring of fear as soon as the target was announced, and Geoff, the Skipper and everyone in their crew had more or less accepted that that would happen. The Skipper believed that it was a healthy reaction. Their missions were dangerous. Flying itself could be dangerous for the lazy, incompetent or complacent, and the Skipper had resolved that that would never affect him or his crew.

Like everyone, he was determined to stay alive and he was going to drill into their heads that the best way to survive was to be vigilant and prepared for any emergency. The way to handle fear was to recognize it and understand that it existed for very good reasons, but not to become overwhelmed by it. Even after just one op, Geoff knew that they had only scraped the surface of what the future might hold for them. They had another thirty trips over enemy territory to carry out before their tour was over, and they all knew the statistics. They could look around the squadron and know, with an awful certainty, that some of these men would be dead, perhaps sooner rather than later. It might be them, but it was important not to dwell on it.

Years later, Geoff explained that there were a lot of other motives to take into consideration to understand why they did not succumb to fear. They had all volunteered and spent many months training and practising for this very job – flying a large, heavy bomber hundreds of miles over territory where enemy night fighters and anti-aircraft guns were determined to shoot them down. Their training had emphasized both the dangers they faced and the steps they could take to minimize them, whether it was breaking out of a cone of searchlights or going into a corkscrewing dive to evade a fighter. Combat was always a shock, because it was much more frightening and vivid than the training, but you came back from it knowing that it was possible to survive.

One thing they had discovered was that, being a new crew, they were assigned a different Lancaster for every op. The Skipper put a brave face on it, saying that he could fly anything, but it meant that there was little time to get to know the vagaries of the particular aircraft, or to establish a rapport with the mechanics and riggers. The spare aircraft that they were given also tended to be worn out, their engines in particular not quite as responsive and powerful as they could be.

This time they were flying H Harry, and would be one of 678 aircraft to attack the city. Hanover was an important industrial city, with large locomotive works, a tank factory and oil refineries that fuelled a vital source of synthetic rubber for German industry. It had already been struck in the raid that took place on 22 September, the day before Geoff and the others undertook their first operation, but that mission, a large one of 711 aircraft, had proved to be badly off target. The Pathfinder Force sent to mark the target had encountered unexpected winds, which caused their target-indicator flares to drift and the following aircraft, designed to back up the original markers, aimed for the wrong colour flares. The errors were compounded by the fact that the German anti-aircraft defences had covered a nearby lake with barges to camouflage it. This confused the H2S operators in the Pathfinder Force and they timed their run-in on the target from the wrong lake. The main force bombed what they believed to be the correct target indicators, but they were as much as 5 miles from the intended aiming point and the bombs gradually spread further away from the city on to suburbs and countryside. On this attack the defences had been guided by a strong concentration of searchlights, and intense anti-aircraft fire laid in a box barrage over the target.

The failures of the Pathfinder aircraft followed some previous ones over Berlin and Munich at the beginning of September and they prompted a critical letter from Harris to Don Bennett, head of the Pathfinder Force. Air Vice Marshal Cochrane, CO of 5 Group, had also put his oar in, writing to Harris that he believed he could pick twelve good crews from 5 Group to do just as good a job as the Pathfinders. Cochrane was speaking from a position of some strength, of course, because of 5 Group's experience and its success with precision raids such as those made on the Dortmund–Ems Canal, the Renault factory and the Dams by 617 Squadron earlier that year.

While the dispute between Bennett and Cochrane simmered, the second raid took off for Hanover. H Harry was scheduled for the fourth wave, once more arriving over the city towards the end of the offensive. The bombs had been dropped on time, but again the Pathfinders had been surprised by strong winds over the target and the raid spared the centre of Hanover this time, focusing instead on the north of the city. The strong defences of searchlights and anti-aircraft fire were still in place and so too were the night fighters. A post-raid report by Bomber Command's Operational Research Section said that so many bombers were observed falling out of the sky in such a short space of time that it was hard to assess whether the casualties were due to flak or fighters. All the victims, however, seemed to have been caught in the searchlights before being shot down. The sky over the target was, according to flight engineer Jock Burns, 'very hot' – a verdict echoed by Geoff.

The Skipper manoeuvred well enough that they were

never caught by the searchlights, but with searchlights there were bound to be night fighters and as Geoff lay prone, looking through the bomb aimer's sight, he knew that everyone was keeping an urgent lookout. Their run-in was meant to be steady and straight, despite the puffs of smoke from exploding flak. Geoff found that he could focus on the bombsight and push everything else out of his mind, but he had no idea how the Skipper, Jock and the gunners ignored the malevolent chaos outside the cockpit. Hanover was well alight and there were fierce fires burning on the ground. As H Harry flew over the burning city towards the turning point where they could start their course for home, Geoff could see many of the main-force fleet silhouetted against the flames on the ground. If he could see them so could the pilots in the Junkers 88s hunting them. Hearing the bomb-bay doors thump closed and the noise of the slipstream change was like standing on top of a mountain – there was a sense of achievement, even though there was an equally arduous return journey to be made. On this return leg, Vincent, the wireless operator, picked up a message from Group headquarters that there was severe fog at East Kirkby, so they should divert to Waterbeach in Cambridgeshire. Sixteen of the Lancasters put down there and spent the night.

The photographic reconnaissance afterwards showed a good concentration of bombs falling on open countryside or small villages to the north of Hanover. There was not much the main force of bombers could do about this. Their instructions were to bomb on the target indicators, so little could be changed once the Pathfinders had marked the target, even if it was possible for any of the main-force bomb aimers to ascertain the errors. Whatever the success of the targeting, the risks to the crews were still the same.

Before leaving Waterbeach, which is just a few miles to the north of Cambridge, Geoff persuaded the Skipper to make a detour and fly south on their way back to Lincolnshire. He wanted to fly over his old home at Manuden, to show his parents and his grandfather what their son had achieved. George, irrepressible as ever, thought it was a grand idea, so they took off and diverted, without giving any notice, to the south.

Geoff read the map from the bomb aimer's position and when they got to Manuden they circled briefly, then did a low pass over the tiny hamlet. Geoff's grandfather was standing outside the cottage, his face turned up, with a small group of neighbouring children clustered round, waving their hands and leaping into the air. Geoff discovered later they had guessed that he was in the great Lancaster thundering above them.

Now they had two missions under their belts and were as proud as punch. They wanted to show off to the world what they were and what they had done. Geoff in particular wanted to impress his parents and show the neighbours just how much he had achieved since he was a little boy in a stone-flagged, thatched cottage in the heart of rural Essex.

The flight over the village finished, they set course again, flying over Bishop's Stortford then on towards East Kirkby. As they headed north, two Boulton Paul Defiants arrived as if from nowhere and positioned themselves on the wing tips of the Lancaster. Long since pulled out of any role in the fighter force, these aircraft, which were armed with a rear-firing gun turret, were occasionally used for gunnery trials and air-sea rescue operations. The crew were at first alarmed about their intentions and Geoff frantically waved at them from the bomb aimer's dome, showing them the map he had been using to indicate that they knew where they were, but the two fighters accompanied them back to Cambridge before peeling off. Arriving at East Kirkby, they expected to be hauled up and questioned about their little jaunt, but nothing was ever said.

Wing Commander Fisher, the CO of 57 Squadron, had other things on his mind. One of the Lancasters returning from Waterbeach, flown by Pilot Officer Hargrave, had gone into the circuit at East Kirkby with a serious problem. Both port engines had failed and, as the aircraft circled to make its approach, it lost height and crashed into a low hill to the north of the aerodrome. It caught fire and the aircraft was destroyed. Remarkably, the bomb aimer, the two gunners and the wireless operator escaped, but the pilot, the navigator and the flight engineer were killed – three more casualties to add to the list since Geoff had joined the squadron.

There was little time to dwell on this, however, and Geoff found that it was much better not to. The next day, 29 September, the crews assembled in the briefing room again and were told that their target was Bochum. An audible groan went up amongst the older hands. Bochum, of course, was in the centre of the Ruhr and had already been hit in the course of the bombing campaign against the heartland of German manufacturing power back in the spring and summer of that year. During that onslaught – the so-called Battle of the Ruhr – almost 9 per cent of the bombers taking part had been lost. That was more than twice what was considered acceptable. The stories about the heavy defences had been readily absorbed by Geoff and his crew, so they were more than nervous about what lay in store for them on this, their third raid into enemy airspace.

As their aircraft, F Freddie this time, approached the target, Geoff realized that their previous two raids had been relatively easy. Looking forward out of the bomb aimer's position, he saw a mass of searchlights projecting into the sky, moving with a weird mechanical precision like something out of *War of the Worlds*, with bursts of anti-aircraft fire stretching before him. The Skipper could also see what he had to fly the Lancaster through, but nobody spoke about it; they kept the conversation over the inter-com to the job in hand. Geoff read off the height, the heading to the aiming point and then the final corrections to their course as they lined up on the target indicators. For the first time, the weather over the target was clear and Geoff could see some of the detail of the target, the railway lines leading to the central station. Also for the first time, he saw his 4,000lb 'cookie' explode on what appeared to be a ramp leading to a very large factory. It shook him. For the first time he realized the effect of what he was doing. It was akin to being a god sending thunderbolts of destruction on to the earth beneath. However, thunderbolts were also rising to meet him, and he was happy to hear

Curly give the return heading to the Skipper and to feel the Lancaster bank into the turn. It was almost a ritual now for the Skipper to say, 'Keep a good lookout now, guys – you too, Kingy,' as they left the target. The good visibility and lack of smoke and cloud allowed Geoff to see that the targeting, unlike in their raid on Hanover, had been good. The Pathfinders had been using Oboe and relying less on H2S, and the target indicators appeared to be spot on. Bochum's Altstadt, the old centre of the city, was particularly severely damaged, with over 1,300 buildings destroyed by fire.

The flak had seemed impenetrable as they approached the target, but casualties were much lower than had been experienced in previous raids on the town, with just 9 aircraft lost out of the force of 352 that had taken part in the raid. The group's casualty figures and a selection of the bombing photographs were available in the squadron office the next day but, as George remarked later, there was always a reason not to be affected by the deaths announced on the green sheets of paper pinned up on the notice board: 'You had only met him briefly, or he came from a different town, or they must just have had bad luck. It was a way of keeping those black thoughts at bay.'

The confidence of the crew was growing, and in particular the calm voice of the Skipper, issuing instructions or checking in with the rest of them throughout the flight, acted as a reassuring focus. No one chatted or said anything distracting and Geoff, lying at the front of the aircraft, felt that everybody behind was alert and getting on with their job – a feeling that did not diminish after the bombs had been dropped and they had turned on their course for home. He felt sure that the rear and mid-upper gunners were on the ball and as vigilant as they had been when heading towards the target, and that their route was being accurately plotted by Curly.

The next day, 1 October, brought another attack on the Ruhr, this time on the town of Hagen. Again they had a different Lancaster, which the Skipper said was beginning to be a little wearing, and it was unfortunately named D Dog. George was smart enough, whatever his private feelings about the name, to tell the rest of the boys that it handled fine.

Mosquito aircraft fitted with Oboe dropped their sky-markers with precision over the town and its industrial areas. One of the key targets in Hagen was a factory that made the large batteries used to power U-boats. Again the concentration of searchlights and anti-aircraft defences was intense. D Dog was part of the main force, which was a small one for the time, amounting to only 243 aircraft, but the raid was a total success, achieved on a small, completely cloud-covered target and with the remarkably low loss of just two aircraft. The bombing caused severe damage to Hagen. Two of the town's four industrial areas were badly hit, a third suffered some minor damage and the factory producing the U-boat power cells was put out of action, hitting the submarine programme. It was a 'decent prang', recorded Jock in his unofficial diary.

There was no let-up in pace at this time. On 2 October they were again detailed to fly on an operation, their fifth, and this time the target was Munich – a long stooge to the south of Germany, eight hours in all from base to base. Again they had a different Lancaster, this time I Ink.

The chief of 5 Group, Air Vice Marshal Cochrane, had been lobbying Harris to allow him to employ some different methods of marking targets that the group had started to use where accurate and precise bombing was called for. After the Pathfinder Force's problems with H2S on the Hanover raids, Harris had given way. The raid on Munich was to be carried out with Lancasters from 5 Group and 1 Group, with target-marking by Lancasters from the Pathfinder Force. The 5 Group method to be tried out was known as 'offset marking', and was indeed just that. Pathfinder aircraft would drop target indicators a set distance from the centre of the target and the main bomber force would be expected to locate these flares in their bombsights, then the bomb aimers would direct the pilots on to a predetermined course for a timed run to the real target. This, it was hoped, would prevent the target flares being obscured by smoke from the fires started by the raid. However, it required the bombers to fly straight and level over the target, and for this reason it was unpopular with some of the crews, who thought it increased their chances of being hit.

At Munich the target point to start their run was to be the Wurmsee, a lake about 17 miles to the south-west of the city. On the night, none of the Pathfinder aircraft could locate it. Despite fairly good visibility, the target-marking was scattered and the weight of the bombs fell on the southern and south-eastern districts of the city. But as the raid continued, bombs started to be dropped 15 miles back along the approach route, because bomb aimers were confusing flares intended to guide them to the target with the actual target indicators themselves. The results were not impressive and conflict between Cochrane and Bennett was exacerbated. Cochrane, of course, was not prepared to abandon his campaign, while Bennett found the criticism of his Pathfinder Force extremely irksome.

Munich was very well defended, with heavy anti-aircraft fire and thick bands of searchlights. As they flew over, with the city spread below them, Geoff saw another Lancaster fixed by a searchlight. As soon as a bomber became caught by the focused glare, other searchlights quickly created a cone of beams that followed the bomber whatever manoeuvres he made. The crew on I Ink saw the plane passed from cone to cone as it twisted and dived, until anti-aircraft fire started to cluster in bursts around it and it staggered as it was hit. Part of the wing seemed to disappear and it slowly tipped, then began to dive steeply to the ground.

There was silence on I Ink, as Geoff tried to focus on the bombsights and read off the seconds before he could say 'Bombs gone' over the intercom. George turned the Lancaster on to its departure heading, and still nobody remarked on the sight they had just witnessed of a bomber plunging to its death.

This was the first aircraft that Geoff had seen hit and plummet to the earth. Even on raids where there had been heavy casualties, it was possible for many bombers in the middle of the stream not to be anywhere near the un-fortunate aircraft that fell victim to either German night fighters or anti-aircraft fire. Now they had had a taste of what could easily befall them, and it was a sombre and slightly subdued crew that assembled later that morning for the debriefing. Was it a coincidence that their fifth raid had brought them this close to death?

They had a day to ponder it, because after three operations in three days they were tired and needed a rest, but on 4 October they were again slated for a mission against Frankfurt, another very heavily defended target. Their aircraft was to be the same one that they had flown over Munich, I Ink.

After their section briefings they went out to look over the plane before the air test and George had a discussion with the engineer. Returning to his billet, something prompted Geoff to look for the old leather belt that he had worn on his previous missions. The crew had talked amongst themselves about the extent to which every member of the squadron seemed to have their lucky charm, or some other way of keeping luck on their side. Some crews insisted that they leave the briefing last, or be carried to their vehicle in a particular truck, and at first it had seemed slightly alarming to Geoff. Now, however, he had been affected by a sense of anxiety about the future. He noticed that others in the crew had quietly been becoming a bit more obsessive about arranging their pencils, pads and maps in the aircraft, or wearing the same scarf on every mission; now he was looking for his old belt. The only person who didn't seem to have a lucky charm or mascot was George, the Skipper, who was matter-of-fact, confident and still insisted on strict discipline in the air. In fact, Geoff would have commented on the Lancaster they had seen shot down if he hadn't felt that the Skipper would have issued a curt demand for less chatter and an instruction to everyone to keep a good lookout and get on with it.

Later they took off for Frankfurt, heading out to sea. They were approaching the coast over Clacton-on-Sea and Geoff was trying to get an accurate time over the coast for Curly when he felt the aircraft dip. To his alarm, his sandwiches and briefing notes started to fall past his head. Through his earphones he could hear gasps and a muffled 'Christ almighty!' and then Flash, the mid-upper gunner, said loudly, 'Skipper, why am I looking at the sea?' Sure enough, Geoff was looking at the stars, the plane was upside down and he felt a surge of alarm electrify his body. The Merlin engines were roaring and the Skipper and Jock were yelling numbers and trim-settings at each other. Geoff's heart was in his mouth and, after what seemed like an eternity, he heard rather than saw maps and his Thermos flask crash down next to him. The Skipper had apparently got the Lancaster back out of its inverted flight and he throttled back. The artificial horizon – the instrument that a pilot uses to keep the plane flying straight and level in darkness – had failed and the Skipper and the flight engineer couldn't fix it. The loss of the night-flying instruments was serious, so the flight controllers at base ordered the Skipper to return, but even the trip back to base was hazardous. There was also the question of what to do about their bomb load – the 4,000lb of high explosive and the incendiaries they carried in the long bomb bay beneath them.

The jettison area was to their north over part of the North Sea. Jock anxiously asked the Skipper, 'Can you make it?'

There was a pause, and the implications of several course changes and manoeuvres sank in to the rest of the crew. The bomber roared on, every creak, every tremor and change in attitude threatening to become a deadly plunge into the ocean, or so they all imagined.

'I'll give it a go,' said the Skipper. There was another pause.

Then, without more discussion, Curly said quietly, 'OK, Skip, please steer fifteen degrees. We'll be there in seven minutes.'

There was a gentle bank and everyone held their breath. The plane levelled out and, after seven minutes, the Skipper announced that he was opening the bomb doors. The bomb jettison switches were on the instrument panel in front of Jock and he, not Geoff, said, 'Bombs gone.' Again a change of course, then Curly called the heading and time to base.

Everyone on board waited tensely until the flare path came into view. It was, thankfully, a fairly clear night, but a night landing without instruments was running a huge risk. George held the Lancaster, still heavily laden with fuel, rock steady and, as the tyres hit the tarmac with a thump, Geoff for his part suddenly became almost limp as he relaxed. He realized for the first time how tense his body had become as he waited for another, perhaps more catastrophic, loss of control. The Skipper had got them home.

The attack on Frankfurt should have been their sixth mission, but the necessity to abort it over the North Sea meant that it could not be counted as part of their official tour of thirty ops. Geoff felt that this was unfair, as at the time it had seemed to him as dangerous as anything else they had experienced, but there was no point in arguing the case. Nobody would have paid the slightest attention.

The Skipper's coolness during the emergency had given everyone pause for thought. He was a good pilot. He was not just some Canadian shooting a line. Geoff was occasionally asked to leave the Skipper's crew and move to that of his other Canadian friend, George Kain. After the inverted flight on 4 October, though, Geoff made it clear that he was not moving. He had been relieved at the way that the Skipper, Jock and Curly had reacted without any fuss.

On 8 October they were in the air again as part of a 343-plane raid on Stuttgart. At the briefing they were told to be especially careful of Pforzheim, a small town to the north-west of the target, which apparently had the most deadly anti-aircraft defences. Curly had no difficulty setting a course to do just that, but there were still plenty of searchlights and exploding anti-aircraft shells over Stuttgart itself. On this raid, Bomber Command had set up a diversionary raid by sending Mosquito aircraft to Munich. Dropping Window as they went, they could appear to be a much bigger force than they were and the German night-fighter controllers were misled. It wasn't until the end of the raid on Stuttgart that night fighters arrived to attack the last of the bomber force.

The Skipper and his crew returned safely to base and were now, after six missions and one aborted, beginning to be considered part of the squadron. No longer new boys, with a good chance of disappearing before anybody noticed their arrival, they had proved to the squadron commander and to themselves that they could get to the target, make as accurate a bomb drop as possible and get safely home. All these things were important – for their confidence and for their nerves over the target. It was impossible not to feel apprehensive approaching a target and seeing the searchlights and flak reaching up to hit them, but they now knew that death was not inevitable. Most importantly, over the seven missions and the problem with the night-flying controls in I Ink, they had discovered that they could work well in an emergency. They trusted each other. Strangely, the I Ink incident had created a strong bond because the Skipper had asked them to trust him to get the plane back to base and they had, quietly, given him a vote of confidence. Nobody realized it at the time, but they had crossed a watershed, and it would prove to be extremely important in the future.

They also now understood why few people in the squadron had befriended them when they first arrived. It was, as George described it in later life, 'a sick society. You ignored the new guys in case they would not be around for long. We did the same thing. We didn't want to know them until they had done a decent amount of missions. You were friendly with the guys in your hut, but it was your crew that was important. After all, you all went together.'

Geoff echoed the sentiment. 'You could see who had a

better chance of making it quite quickly. The ones who were not very good, or were beginning to show the strain, were more likely to get the chop. You avoided them.'

For the next few days East Kirkby was beset by dense fog. During the following weeks training programmes were continued and Geoff was able to try out H2S for the first time. He thought it was remarkable. He couldn't wait to get a Lancaster that was fitted with it.

He would get his chance soon; meanwhile, Bomber Command was preparing itself for another onslaught on the most important target in the whole of Germany. It had been bombed before, but always with disappointing results. Now, however, in the almost eighteen months since the thousand-bomber raid on Cologne, the bomber force had been transformed. It was composed of nothing but four-engined heavies, mainly Lancasters and Halifaxes. The two-engined Wellingtons had been withdrawn, as had the poorly performing Stirlings. New technology was promising to improve the accuracy of bombing and cause further disruption to the German defences. Once more, the great city loomed in Bomber Harris's sights. Berlin was going to be tested again.

12

LUCKY C CHARLIE

On 3 November the Skipper and his crew were once more gathered in the briefing room along with the crews from another twenty Lancasters. There was to be a major effort for 57 Squadron, on Düsseldorf this time – another target in the Ruhr, or 'the Happy Valley', as Jock Burns had christened it in his diary. It would be a substantial raid for Bomber Command as a whole. In all, 589 aircraft were slated to take part, plus there was to be a diversionary operation on Cologne mounted by fifty-eight Lancasters and ten Mosquitoes. Düsseldorf had not been targeted since the Battle of the Ruhr in June, five months ago, and the aiming point for this raid was to be the Mannesmann-Röhrenwerke steelworks, a major manufacturer of high-pressure seamless steel tubes and large gas cylinders for the chemical and synthetic oil industries. The command was also going to use the mission for the first real operational try-out of a new blind-bombing system known as GH, which had been fitted to some Lancasters from 3 Group and 6 Group. The system relied on Gee to guide the planes to the target, then transmitters on the aircraft would send signals to ground bases which would triangulate their position and send a signal back to the navigator, who could then give very precise guidance to the aiming point.

George hadn't hidden his feelings about being allocated spare aircraft for missions, and with the experience of I Ink as ammunition he had been promised a permanent aircraft when new ones were delivered. They hadn't arrived yet, so they were assigned another orphan plane for this trip, G George. Their outbound journey to the target was uneventful. Düsseldorf, like every target in the Ruhr, was heavily defended, but the diversionary raid on Cologne did succeed in confusing the German night-fighter controllers and they sent many of their squadrons to the wrong destination. However, around eighty Luftwaffe fighters still succeeded in assembling over the target and others also managed to intercept the bomber stream over Holland.

The new GH guidance system appeared to work well, although there was some teething trouble. Five of the aircraft fitted with it had to return early, another two were shot down on the raid and the equipment in sixteen of the others didn't work well enough to provide the accuracy that had been hoped for. But some target indicators were dropped accurately and the main force unloaded the majority of its bombs on the south and centre of the city. The steelworks was badly damaged and there were reports of a carpet of fire stretching 7 miles long and a mile wide across the town. Casualties to the bomber force were relatively low, with the loss of only eighteen aircraft. One of these was a Lancaster of 57 Squadron flown by Lieutenant West, with Flying Officer Clements as a second pilot in the flight engineer's seat. The squadron diary reported that fighter activity had been slight, but the Skipper saw two bombers getting hit by fighters, neither of which escaped. Even with losses of just eighteen aircraft out of the 589, that still meant a potential death toll of 126 or so airmen, and there were other casualties in planes that returned.

While in their OTU, the crew had met a pilot instructor, Flight Lieutenant Bill Reid, with whom they got on very well. He had already completed one tour of operations, but had rejoined 61 Squadron in 5 Group. He too was on the Düsseldorf mission and shortly after his Lancaster crossed the Dutch coast he was pounced on by a German night fighter. His rear gunner's intercom had been affected by ice, so he received no warning of an approaching attack. An exploding 20mm cannon shell hit his windscreen and pieces of shrapnel injured Bill in the head and tore through his hand and his shoulder. The rush of air whistling into the shattered cockpit was so cold that it froze the blood pouring down his face into his eyes. The crew urgently asked him if he was OK, but he said nothing about his injuries and kept on flying. As they got closer to the target, another fighter came up on them and once again the fuselage of the Lancaster echoed with the sound of shells piercing the aluminium skin. This attack killed Bill's navigator, Flight

Lieutenant Jefferies, and fatally wounded his radio operator, Jim Mann. He still plugged on to the target, using the Pole Star as a navigation aid, because he could easily see it through the broken canopy. He saw Cologne, where the diversionary raid was taking place, and knew from the briefing that he had to make a turn towards Düsseldorf. His bomb aimer, Sergeant L. G. Roulton, got a fix on the target and they dropped their bomb load. Remarkably, the target photo developed later showed that they had released right over the aiming point.

With a dead or wounded crew, Bill tried to make it home, but the oxygen system started to fail and he became unconscious. The flight engineer then took over the controls and reduced their height, allowing Bill to recover for the last leg of the flight. Low on fuel, they were diverted to an American base at Shipham in Norfolk. As they touched down on the runway, one of the main wheels collapsed and the Lancaster crumpled on to its wing.

Bill was carried off and taken to the base hospital, where he eventually recovered. It had been a remarkable effort on the part of the whole crew and Bill awoke in hospital one morning to find Air Vice Marshal Cochrane sitting by his side to tell him he had been awarded the VC. He then asked Bill what he would like to do next. He volunteered for 617 Squadron, the Dambusters.

On their return from Düsseldorf the crew of G George were once again diverted because of poor visibility and ended up at Dunholme in Lincolnshire. On their return to East Kirkby the next day they were told that a brand new Lancaster Mk1 that had just been delivered to the squadron was theirs. It was call sign C Charlie. To Geoff and the others it would become lucky C Charlie, although it required a rather odd definition of luck. But it was their plane and nobody else's, with riggers and maintenance bods who would, over time, almost become part of the crew, energized and motivated by the Skipper.

For his part, George thought that flying the new Lanc was a fantastic treat. The engines had no problem delivering their rated power, and everything was tight and responsive compared to the old warhorses he had been flying until then. The ground crew were anxious that they look it over thoroughly to rectify any faults or missing components, which they were sure the civilians at the factory would have let slip through.

C Charlie, unlike the planes they had been flying previously, was fitted with an H2S set, with the bubble under the fuselage for the radar aerial and the controls, and the circular screen mounted next to the navigator's table. Geoff and the Skipper decided that Geoff would now occupy the seat next to Curly for most of the flight so that he could use the H2S as another plotting device. He found the cramped little cubbyhole far more uncomfortable than his prone position in the nose. It also meant that he would no longer have that god's-eye view of the coast slipping away beneath him, nor experience the clouds rushing past as they crested them into the clear sky above. Often the fears about the coming raid would be counterbalanced by the beautiful tints of clouds and sky painted by the last red rays of the sun setting in the west.

H2S had originally been hailed as the breakthrough that

would provide Bomber Command with accurate bomb aiming whatever the cloud cover or visibility over the target. It had proved a disappointment in this respect, but Curly and Geoff had a different view of it. Arriving at the target on time was vital, because a high concentration of bombers over the target did overwhelm the defences. For the same reason, Curly plotted their course assiduously to ensure that they would stay in the bomber stream for maximum protection. H2S might not be able to give detailed images of a city centre, but it was an exceptionally good aid in plotting the position of the bomber when they were out of range of Gee.

For the next few days they took C Charlie into the air whenever they could to get the feel of their new aircraft and for Geoff and Curly to get some idea of what the H2S set could achieve. They knew from the course that they had done at the Operational Training Unit that when it was working well – and each set needed to be tuned by a technician who knew what he was doing – then it should be able to show as much detail of rivers, towns, villages and coastal outlines as they would get from looking at a map of the ground beneath them. It could provide a more constant and far more accurate test of wind speed and drift than traditional navigation. A more advanced H2S system was being introduced using a smaller wavelength, but this was going as a matter of priority to the Pathfinder Force. One of the technicians on the squadron responsible for the H2S sets was a Canadian and a good buddy of George's. After a brief conversation with him, a few components on C Charlie's set were replaced and after this Geoff thought that it provided quite remarkable definition even though it was just a standard set.

The Skipper first took C Charlie on a war mission on 10 November. The target was different from the mass area attacks on cities that they had been carrying out up till now. This time they were directed to hit marshalling yards and a junction at Modane, a town in the French Alps close to the Italian border. Intelligence believed that this junction was a crucial link in the movement of German troops and supplies between France and Italy, where the Allies, as they advanced up the Italian peninsula, were encountering very fierce opposition from the German army.

The flight was a long one. Overall the mission was expected to last more than nine hours, with take-off scheduled for around 21.00 and a return due at 05.00 next day. The squadron put up fourteen Lancasters and the outbound trip was made in brilliant moonlight, with the crystal-clear air providing perfect visibility for mile after mile. Jock was intrigued by the French countryside unrolling beneath them as they roared south, then the Alps, with their gleaming white peaks, appearing on the horizon. The target in the floor of the valley, however, was obscured by deep shadows and the only aiming point was the Pathfinders' flares. Geoff lay in the nose, in his bomb aimer's position, listening to the echoes from the enclosed valley reflecting the blasts of the exploding bombs upwards. As they rose they created a wave of hammer-like blows on the aircraft, so that the explosions felt as if the Lancaster was rolling over a very widely spaced cattle grid.

As they returned, Geoff caught a last sight of Mont Blanc gleaming in the moonlight, white-capped and still, with fir trees clinging to its lower slopes. It brought back memories of childhood Christmases in safer, more peaceful times.

The Pathfinders' flares had again been slightly off target, but the photo intelligence suggested that enough bombs had been dropped within a mile of the marshalling yards to hinder the large expected troop movement south to the Italian front.

Eight days later, 57 Squadron was once more assembled at a briefing. The CO, Group Captain Taft, announced, 'Well, gentlemen, your target for tonight is Berlin.' For a few moments there was utter silence. It was possible to hear a pin drop. Then the main briefing continued against a shuffling backdrop of mutterings and whispered discussions. However, when the section briefings began, the noise rose considerably. Urgent questions were asked about the targets, the route and the intelligence on the current state of the defences they would have to face. It was clear that everybody was nervous, and with good reason. Very few of the crews had taken part in earlier operations against Berlin, but the stories about the fierceness of its defences were now part of the mythology of Bomber Command.

Sir Arthur Harris was determined to mount a successful bombing campaign against the Nazi capital and in fact raids on the city had been an important part of Bomber Command's overall strategy ever since the first German attacks on London in September 1940. The difficulty was that the command had had neither the aircraft nor the technical capability to make sure that the raids were seriously damaging. By the middle of 1943, however, with H2S radar and larger numbers of Lancaster aircraft at his disposal, Harris felt that he was in a position to prove that Bomber Command, if used correctly, could win the war without the need to invade Europe, and Berlin was the cornerstone of this belief. In fact, a few weeks earlier Harris had written to Churchill that if the American Eighth Air Force, now fully established in Britain, could be persuaded to join in the campaign, Berlin could be wrecked from end to end. It would cost 400–500 bombers, he said, but it would cost Germany the war.

This was an exceptionally bold statement, although the evidence of the destruction wreaked on Hamburg and Cologne over the course of a few days of heavy bombing raids could partly be used to support his view.

The difficulty was that there was no agreement between Lieutenant General Ira Eaker, commander of the US air force, and Harris about how best to use strategic bombers. The American policy was to carry out daylight raids on specific industrial targets to cripple Germany's war industry. At the start of the war the British had had a similar policy, but it had proved disastrously costly in men and machines. The adoption by Bomber Command of night-time area bombing had not been done on a whim. It was the best that could be achieved without throwing away the lives of trained airmen. The Eighth Air Force believed that they would not suffer the same fate. Their aircraft – B-24 Liberators and B-17 Flying Fortresses – could fly higher than the planes of Bomber Command, possessed an extremely accurate bombsight and were sufficiently well armed to be able to defend their formations against fighters, even in daylight.

On 8 October, the US air force had mounted a raid on a ball-bearing factory at Schweinfurt, part of a campaign to hit the German aircraft industry that included planned raids on the Messerschmitt plant at Regensburg. The attacks were successful in part, for they did reduce the output of the factories, but the American losses were unsustainable. Sixty bombers were shot down and another 120 damaged out of a total of 291 taking part. This level of casualties was crushing, and the Eighth Air Force carried out no more missions until long-range fighter escorts could accompany them.

There was pressure on Harris from within the RAF to follow the policy of specifically targeting strategic industries, especially now that technical developments such as H2S were available to assist the bomber force achieve higher levels of accuracy. Harris knew that these policies came at a high price. His critics within the Air Ministry could – and often did – point to the success of missions carried out by 5 Group, hitting precision targets like the Renault works, the Dams and the Peenemünde V1 flying-bomb plant. Harris could retort that, six months after the Dams raid, 617 Squadron had still not sufficiently recovered from its 50 per cent losses and that there was no future in training men for six months for one suicide mission. In any case, he could argue that in fact he *was* targeting the critical industries that supported the Luftwaffe. His raids in the Ruhr had been directed against industrial targets. There was the Bosch sparkplug factory in Stuttgart, as well as the BMW engine plant, the ball-bearing manufacturer VKF, and the Daimler-Benz aero engine factory, all of which had been hit. The big Focke-Wulf 190 factory at Bettenhausen, Kassel, had been heavily damaged. If anyone still wanted to doubt his commitment to smashing German industry, he could point out that Berlin was the biggest manufacturing city in Germany. It was the administrative and transport hub of the nation, and it also contained large numbers of armaments industries, including the aircraft firms Heinkel, Dornier, BMW and Argus, as well as many important electrical and wireless equipment manufacturers, not to speak of the giant Siemens plants in Siemensstadt in the industrial suburbs.

The target of Berlin was decreed by Harris on the morning of 18 November and so Bomber Command's huge planning machinery moved into action, working out bomb loads, routes, fuel capacities, diversions, liaison with Coastal Command and aircraft availability from the various group headquarters. It was going to be a well-planned and significant operation that befitted the start of a major aerial assault on Berlin, the 'Big City'. That night, 835 heavy bombers would be flying over Germany, including 395 Stirlings and Halifaxes which would be conducting a diversionary raid on Mannheim-Ludwigshafen. A third 'spoof' raid by twenty Mosquitoes on Frankfurt was intended as a diversion from the Mannheim operation. So great was the size of Bomber Command now that a mere diversionary raid mustered more heavy bombers than had existed in the whole of the command eighteen months ago.

These two bomber streams would enter German airspace 250 miles apart. Over Berlin, the command hoped to get a much higher rate of concentration than before, with as many as twenty-eight bombers passing over the target in a minute, to swamp the freelance night fighters. At that rate, the raid itself should last only around fifteen minutes.

Having by now survived two months of operations and eight completed missions, the crew of C Charlie were moved up from the rear echelon of the main force and on this operation were in the second wave. They were going to be one of sixteen aircraft put up by 57 Squadron and their take-off was scheduled for 17.20. Breaking up from the briefings, they went back to their billets to gather the final pieces of gear before collecting their flying rations and parachutes. The prospect of flying against Berlin weighed heavily on everyone. This was bound to be tougher than anything that they had done up till now, and was sure to be far worse than the Ruhr. They took off, and as they flew over Manuden Geoff thought of his parents in bed beneath him. They would hear the bombers flying over, as most people in the eastern part of England did every night, and they would be wondering if their son was up there and praying that he would make it back home safely.

Geoff knew that thoughts like that were no help to him, so he was glad that he had the new piece of kit, the H2S set, to occupy his mind. He found that it was an invaluable tool for navigating on long trips. It provided constant fixes against the landscape below, which Geoff could pass on to

Curly, but it could also be used to map-read their way along the route, enabling them to remain on track and avoid the more heavily defended areas. Their route that night was to head east over the North Sea, crossing the coast above the easily identifable Frisian Islands, then to take a leg to the north close to the target and approach the city over the north-west.

Their return trip was routed on a south-west heading, passing south of the Ruhr, crossing Belgium and turning north for home around Dieppe. It meant a long route over enemy territory, but again it was designed to avoid enemy fighters.

There was little to make their pulses race on the trip over Germany, but on their approach to the target it suddenly seemed to Geoff that they were suspended in mid-flight hardly moving. The forecast fair weather had in fact turned into heavy cloud, with the tops at around 15,000 feet. The diversionary raid had confused the night-fighter controllers and they had failed to ascertain in time that Berlin was the target, but the absence of fighters meant that the flak barrage was given its head. As C Charlie approached, they seemed to be flying into an impenetrable wall of explosions. The batteries below were laying an extremely well-coordinated box barrage that tested George's nerve. The current doctrine was that it was a waste of effort manoeuvring to avoid flak. Evasive efforts by the pilot increased the time the bomber spent over the target and so increased its vulnerability. It was better to gain maximum speed, then head straight and level through the barrage. It demanded iron self-control to do this. Geoff could only ask himself, 'My God! How on earth can we get through this lot?' It was the most frightening experience of any raid he had been on so far.

As C Charlie flew over the clouds, lit up from below by searchlights, the flash of bursting shells blossoming into black puffs, Geoff saw two Lancasters lower than him and just to his starboard side. Both were hit, flames running along their wings and licking the fuselage. Then one fell apart, suddenly, as though hit by a giant axe, and the other toppled over and dived into cloud. It was a sight that chilled his blood, sent fear running through him like an electric shock, and it has stayed with him all his life.

Nearing the aiming point, he tried hard to concentrate and search for the Pathfinders' flares. They too, however, had been surprised by the weather and had relied on ground markers. There was just one yellow signal flare and Geoff attempted to guide the Skipper on to it, all the while tensing inwardly for a sudden explosion and for the shrapnel to come ripping through the Plexiglas dome in front of him. It was impossible to avoid the flak; they just had to pass through it. Geoff and the Skipper went through the formula: 'Bomb doors open. Left, left, steady, steady', the rest of the crew listening and praying for the words 'bombs gone'. The illuminated cross on the bombsight crossed the yellow flare and Geoff pressed the bomb release. Feeling the bombs tumbling out and the aircraft immediately trying to rise, he heard the Skipper say, 'Bomb doors closed.'

Then, thankfully, they headed for home, still navigating the barrage of anti-aircraft fire, climbing now, throttles full forward to get away, with the glow of the fires flickering like embers in a grate, even from 100 miles away.

Because of the cloud cover, the attack on Berlin was widely scattered over the city and its suburbs. Four industrial premises were destroyed and twenty-eight damaged, among them eleven explosives factories and four chemical plants. There were 169 houses destroyed and 476 seriously damaged. Several fighters were seen, but there were no intelligence reports that they had shot down any aircraft. In all, 9 went missing, including one from 57 Squadron, flown by Flight Lieutenant Gobbie. However, 100 aircraft came back with some degree of damage caused by the anti-aircraft fire.

The increased concentration over the target did not produce the rash of collisions that some crews had feared. There was just one, resulting in one Lancaster crashing and the deaths of two men. Even this collision occurred during the run-in, not over the target area. An aircraft from 207 Squadron hit the tail of another from 9 Squadron, possibly killing the rear gunner and taking off the tops of the tail fins. The 9 Squadron aircraft started to lose height rapidly and the skipper, Pilot Officer Lees, ordered his crew to bale out. The other Lancaster had a shattered nose with the loss of the bomb aimer's bubble and escape hatch, and damage to both starboard propellers and radiators. Its pilot, Pilot Officer Baker, regained control, but the bomb aimer was missing. Eventually his body was found 100 miles away, near Hamburg; it had probably fallen into the River Havel and been carried along on the current. Baker did not want to lose any height, because he believed he would be vulnerable to the flak, and could not drop his bomb load because of the damage, so he elected to make a run for home. The icy wind roared through the smashed nose, but he flew a direct route across Germany, evading night fighters and searchlights, and as a lone bomber was extremely lucky not to be picked up by German radar and hunted down. He eventually jettisoned his 4,000lb bomb over the North Sea and made a safe landing at Spilsby. Baker's hands were so severely frostbitten that all his fingers and thumbs had to be amputated. Other members of the crew were also affected by frostbite, but fortunately not as severely as their skipper.

Three more raids on Berlin followed that of 18 November. They were more successful, in that they were carried out with a more sophisticated target-marking strategy and there was much clearer weather. This, however, meant that the bomber force was more vulnerable to the night fighters, so their losses were higher. Geoff, the Skipper and the rest of the crew of C Charlie missed these raids. As George said later, you have to know when to go on leave.

13

LIVING DANGEROUSLY

Anybody with any sense wanted to have a life outside the base if they could. Geoff King believes that the fact that he and some of the other crew members found a social life in the small towns and cities around East Kirkby helped keep them from becoming obsessed with the dangers that they faced over Germany. If you couldn't forget it, even for a brief interlude, he says, it would overcome you.

George, the Skipper, would often disappear to London on a weekend leave, sometimes travelling down with Geoff, but more often with other Canadians from the squadron, and they had no trouble meeting girls and generally having a good time. George would frequently return from these trips the worse for wear, and hard up; more than once Geoff lent him 10 shillings to see him through the week. Both Geoff and Curly had regular girlfriends, and Geoff would often make the trip to Aberystwyth to meet up with Eleanor, although the distance and her parents' strong Welsh nationalist views sometimes made the journey more of an effort than he would have liked.

Curly's fiancée Laura would make weekend trips from Hyde in Cheshire to Boston, where she would take a room in the Red Cow in Wide Bargate. She remembers that often the hotel would become a second home for the crew, with Geoff also taking a room there for a weekend. There was dancing to a live band at the Glyder Drome, a former ice-skating rink, which was heaving on Saturday nights with local girls and aircrew from all the neighbouring bomber stations. George, she recalls, was extremely handsome and funny, and could sweep any girl off her feet, while the quietest members of the crew, Tommy Thomas and Jock Burns, both used to sit out the dances, sipping their beer and chatting. Even now, Laura remembers that whenever she spent time with the crew all together, she felt that there was a bond between them that nobody else, not even she, could penetrate. They were like a very close-knit family. Life in the Red Cow over a long weekend's leave was far removed from life on the base. After closing time the owner's wife, Ruth, would make supper for the guests; some of the locals, including the police sergeant, would call in, a few pints would be pulled and games of darts and cards would go on into the small hours.

Curly rode a 500cc Ivory Calthorpe motorbike, and he and Geoff would often make a quick dash into Boston for a surreptitious night out in the Red Cow, or another, quieter pub called the Black Horse. The Calthorpe never

GLIDER !

NOT a Black Horse IN BOSTON AS FAR AS I CAN Remember.

had a reputation as a racing bike, but it was a powerful beast and could be lethal after Curly and Geoff had had a few drinks. Early one winter's morning, after an overnight in Boston, they were speeding back to base when Curly lost control. The heavy Calthorpe slid down the lane, emitting a shower of sparks, while Geoff and Curly were hurled off into the hedge. Geoff lay there, winded and battered, not daring to move, believing that he must have broken every bone in his body. Slowly he pulled himself to his feet and saw Curly on his hands and knees, his overcoat ripped, one leg of his trousers scraped through, looking down the lane at his bike. They didn't dare be late, so they hobbled to the Calthorpe, picked it up and painfully kick-started it. The foot rests had been bent and there were dents in the exhaust, but it sputtered into life and they rode it through the gates and managed to report to the flight office. Geoff was stiff and bruised for days afterwards. Years later, looking back, he thought how peculiar it was that, with so many people in Germany trying hard to kill him and Curly, they so nearly succeeded in doing the job themselves. One of the mechanics fixed the foot rests and the Calthorpe was as fast as ever.

Returning from their week's leave in November 1943, the crew found that a combination of a full moon, fog and dense cloud was limiting operations for the squadron, so it was not until 2 December that another raid was announced.

Once more it was Berlin. Nobody could hide their lack of enthusiasm. The first Berlin raid that Geoff, Curly and the rest of them had been on had been frightening enough, so the idea of going back was enough to make the blood freeze. While they had been on leave, the squadron had carried out three more in quick succession on 22, 23 and 26 November, and they had been just as hot as the one on the 18th. The flak over Berlin and its approaches was unprecedented, making it a target that called for the utmost determination on the part of the aircrews. They coped with it as best they could, some, like Geoff, busying themselves with preparation and details of the forthcoming operation, others by whiling away the time playing cards or in conversation. All of them believed that they were pushing their luck by flying over Berlin again.

The raid was meant to be another stage in the attempt to destroy Berlin and was a maximum effort, but the threat of fog forming over the Yorkshire airfields meant that 210 Halifaxes were withdrawn from the operation. That afternoon, 458 Lancasters and just 15 Halifaxes formed the main force. The route was direct on outward and return trips, hitting the Dutch coast, then crossing north Holland over Alkmaar, and passing north of Hanover and Brunswick before approaching the north-west of Berlin.

C Charlie took off at 16.30, with an expected arrival over the target at 20.04. The bombers were again going to attempt a high rate of concentration, with the 473 aircraft streaming over the target in twenty minutes. After take-off they flew on a south-easterly heading to make the rendezvous point before starting their climb to 20,000 feet. They were carrying a standard main-force bomb load of one 4,000lb 'cookie' and 6,700lb of incendiaries – not the maximum payload for a Lancaster, but a substantial weight to carry on the long trip to Berlin.

Climbing out over the North Sea, they encountered a towering weather front of very high cumulonimbus clouds. It was a tense time onboard C Charlie as the bomber struggled for height. The clouds seemed to go on for ever, and Geoff wondered if they would ever reach the tops and break out above them. Ice started forming, with bits breaking off and smashing against the fuselage. Tommy Thomas, the rear gunner, was in a very exposed position in this weather. The Skipper would occasionally break his rule of silence to offer him some encouragement. The heating system in the Lancaster was a hit-and-miss affair. The warmest places in the aircraft were the navigator's and wireless operator's positions, where Geoff now sat monitoring the H2S set. The heating ducts poured out a stream of hot air and he can hardly remember a time when he ever needed his thick flying jacket. The rear gunner's position, however, received scarcely any heat; moreover, the central panel of the turret was left open to improve visibility. Tommy was encased in an electrically heated suit, but it was barely enough in the conditions through which they were flying. Condensation would collect in his oxygen mask and freeze, and often at the end of a trip a sheet of ice covered his chest. He was always checking his guns to make sure that the heaters for them were still working. The icing was so bad that night that 10 per cent of the force heading for Berlin turned back because of it. The Skipper plugged on, however, with Jock encouraging the engines, keeping warm air flowing to the carburettors so that they didn't ice up. Finally, after what seemed an eternity, they broke out of the tops and saw stars above them.

The high cloud cover continued over Holland and then Germany, with some variable and strong winds affecting various bomber waves, so that the bomber stream started to become split up. This was bad news because it helped the German fighters. The spread of the bombers reduced the effectiveness of the Window strips which were scattered over the approaches to the target and there was a strong force of German fighters up that night. The attacks on some of the stragglers started over Holland. Vincent reported that the German controllers were very active, rapidly changing their frequencies and clearly on top of events; they were already predicting to their fighter pilots that the target was Berlin over a quarter of an hour before the attack was due to start.

Their route took them into the north-western part of the city, where the new industrial estates of Siemensstadt, and others in Tegel, Wittenau and Spandau, had been built. So extensive were the German capital's defences that it took around twenty-five minutes to fly through them. The last twenty minutes to the target were like their previous raid, although this time there were many airborne illuminating flares dropped by the night fighters. The flak once more looked like an impenetrable wall, a massive barrage from the giant flak towers that the Germans had constructed around the city and from the large batteries of 88mm guns that ringed the city. They had come through it unscathed before, however, and C Charlie headed in from Magdeburg. There were flashes of red light in the clouds, reflecting in the cockpit and gun turrets as Geoff looked at the H2S screen for a final check of their position.

The Skipper had put the nose down for a gentle dive to gain as much speed as possible over the target when Geoff heard a massive explosion, loud enough to overpower the noise of the engines. The plane jolted in mid flight. Flash, in the mid-upper gunner's position, and Tommy, in the rear turret, felt rather than heard the almighty bang, and the smell of cordite filled the fuselage. The Skipper felt the yoke of the control column jolt in his hands, but he held the plane steady as he called for any damage reports. Jock looked at the oil pressure and temperature gauges; they seemed to be steady and the revs had not dropped. It was the oil pressure that was most important. He remembered the words in the manual, 'a Merlin will not survive long without adequate oil pressure'.

Geoff felt a pain in his leg, but responded to the Skipper, saying he was fine. He turned to see Curly slumped over his chart table, his oxygen mask off. Geoff put the mask back on him, then looked him over but couldn't see any injuries. The rest of the crew were fine. After a few minutes Curly started to recover from what was probably a slight concussion. Geoff could see no traces of blood on his leg and could find no reason for the sudden pain, except perhaps an attack of cramp caused by the shock and a surge of fear.

There were no more explosions and they had not been trapped by searchlights. The gunners, now extremely alert, could see no fighters moving in. George kept C Charlie flying straight and level; pulling out of the bomber stream now just didn't make sense. It would increase the risk of collision and draw attention to them on the ground directors' radar. They pressed on, heading into what looked like the jaws of hell. Geoff went into his bomb aimer's position and on the final run-in saw several bombers hit by fighters, one or two burning as they went down. His emotions were in complete turmoil and the sight of the bombers tumbling in flames out of the sky almost made him physically sick. He dragged his shattered concentration together and focused on the illuminated crosshairs of his bombsight. C Charlie continued to run in, responding to the slight touches of George's hands on the yoke, and Geoff lined up on what he assumed were the target indicators and pressed the tit. They turned for their route out, climbing now to get as high above the flak as they could, with everyone again keeping a vigilant lookout for enemy fighters.

Their journey back was uneventful, except that the fuselage seemed much colder. They returned to East Kirkby, but when the undercarriage was extended Jock warned the Skipper that there was no pressure on the brake hydraulics. They landed normally and Jock immediately throttled back, George fishtailing the rudders to slow down. They stopped at the extreme end of the runway. The crew sat in their seats for some minutes afterwards, too drained to move, until the Skipper said, 'OK, guys, let's go. Well done.'

Next morning they went out to their beloved C Charlie to see what had happened to their new aircraft. Geoff was aghast at the damage. Shrapnel from a bursting shell had hit the airscrew casing on the port inner engine and smashed it. The hydraulic pipes from the starboard inner engine had been cut by another metal fragment, and there were rips and punctures in the metal of the wings and fuselage. The largest hole was the size of a football, caused by a huge chunk of shrapnel that had hit just forward of the rear turret, missing the rudder and elevator controls by a matter of inches. Geoff, who had of course been trained as a fitter, looked at the damaged engine and was amazed that it had continued to run for three and a half hours from the time it was hit to the time they landed. They had been unbelievably lucky. This was just their second trip to Berlin, and the tenth in their tour. They had another twenty ops to go. Nobody needed to say anything. How long could they last at this rate? From then on, each member of the crew was even more determined not to take their luck for granted. Geoff knew that he would never fly without his lucky leather belt.

The raid from which they had been so lucky to escape had not been successful and the casualty rate had proved that it had been extremely unlucky for some. The poor wind forecast had again caused problems for the Pathfinder Force, who had not been able to establish their positions correctly. Harris was becoming increasingly dissatisfied with the Pathfinders' performance. Their aircraft had been fitted with some of the latest high-definition radar sets, but it had not improved their ability to mark the targets on Berlin. Photographs of the target area showed that bombing had been scattered over a wide area of countryside to the south of the city, although some damage had been caused to industrial areas to the east and west.

The crews on the target-marking aircraft, however, were trying to overcome enormous difficulties. The radar-controlled flak was extremely well coordinated and dense over Berlin, causing a lot of casualties in the small groups of Pathfinders that led the raids. Squadron Leader John Searby described how on one mission he saw the flak shoot down the two Mosquito aircraft in front of him and the one behind, leaving his as the sole marker aircraft. As well as German flak, they also had to battle strong winds, which the weather forecasters never seemed able to predict, and dense cloud cover over the target. Berlin was a significantly bigger target than any other in Germany. It extended for 30 square miles, and even the advanced H2S sets that the Pathfinders were using could show only what lay beneath them – mile after mile of built-up areas. It was a difficult target in which to pick out specific aiming points.

The losses on this raid were severe, with a total of forty aircraft, nearly 10 per cent of the numbers taking part, being shot down. One squadron, 460, of the Royal Australian Air Force lost 20 per cent of its aircrew. Harris was always jealous of the publicity generated by the army and navy and was assiduous in courting the media. Just as Bomber Command had arranged for journalists and broadcasters to be taken on the thousand-bomber raid over Cologne, similar encouragement was given for coverage of the Battle of Berlin, as it was beginning to be known. It wasn't difficult to arrange, because the onslaught on the heart of the Nazi regime was a popular story in the press. However, two war correspondents were killed on this raid, and another was shot down and taken prisoner. The famous American broadcaster Ed Murrow was also on the raid, a passenger in a Lancaster, but it and he returned safely.

*

The extraordinary level of defences surrounding Berlin was not the only reason for the high number of losses on this mission. Since the use of Window on the Hamburg raids in July had unhinged the German radar and night-fighter defences, they had gone through a radical reorganization and were once more in a condition to mount effective attacks on the bomber stream. The growing size of operations by British bombers, first on Hamburg then subsequently on other cities in the Ruhr, had forced the Germans to increase the night-fighter force and by the time the raids on Berlin were being carried out in November and December 1943, around 1,650 fighters had been allocated to the defence of the homeland.

Prior to the use of Window, German night fighters had been controlled from the ground and directed to intercept bombers in their own specific part of the airspace. Demarcation between each patrolling aircraft was strictly adhered to. Bomber Command had sought to counter this by narrowing the stream of bombers so that they over-whelmed a fighter in its patrol space and so limited the number of defenders the bombers could come into contact with. With a concentrated bomber stream, the narrow night-fighter zone in the west was quickly penetrated and the number of fighters that came into actual contact with the bombers was reduced. The narrower the width of the bomber stream passing diagonally through the ground-control area, the fewer the number of controllers that could have bomber aircraft within their range; and the shorter the journey through the zone, the fewer the number of possible interceptions.

The German response was to deepen the night-fighter zones by adding a second, more easterly, belt of ground stations and developing it so that two or more night fighters could be brought into action. This tactic was enhanced by the use of Lichtenstein, radar carried in the aircraft itself. The second tactic was the use of what were called Wild Sow aircraft. These were single-engined fighters, usually Focke-Wulf 190s, which were deployed close to the targets. In place of ground control, a system of flares and visual signals was used to guide the fighters to the bombers. At the same time, Tame Sow flights were also used. These were stronger twin-engined night-fighter formations employed against the bomber streams during the outward and homeward flight.

Night fighting had started to become a coordinated operation over a large area. This was the state of the system when Window was deployed on the Hamburg raid of 24 and 25 July 1943. The old night-fighter system, with its rigid boxes, collapsed completely, but the Germans quickly responded with a development of the Wild Sow technique. A new airborne interception radar, with a wavelength immune to interference from Window, was fitted to the twin-engined Me 110s and the bomber stream was illuminated by high-flying Ju 88s dropping flares to guide the single-engined fighters.

Individual control of the night-fighter force was abandoned and both single- and twin-engined fighters were sent to the target areas in large numbers, directed by a special radio running a commentary on the air situation. The fighters were assembled at radio beacons where they were directed to circle until the controllers had worked out Bomber Command's target, at which point they were despatched at speed to intercept the bomber stream. The flak batteries were usually given a ceiling above which the fighters were free to operate. The system was flexible because in some instances it allowed fighters based in northern Denmark to intercept bombers over Stuttgart.

The response of Bomber Command was to concentrate raids even more and ensure that an attack could occur in a short space of fifteen to twenty minutes. They not only used feint or decoy raids, but also set up a system code-named Mandrel, in which aircraft transmitted jamming signals on the radio frequencies used by the German ground controllers. They also had German-speaking operators sending false signals to the fighters.

Such diversionary methods were countered by the Germans with improvements to their ground-based spotting system and with new radar systems called Wassermann and Mammoth. These were very long-range systems which were able to detect the bombers when they were still over the North Sea. German ground stations also started to monitor the radio transmissions of the Pathfinders and the bomber streams to provide inform-ation that was fed to the night-fighter force. Perhaps the most secret and most dangerous development in the German armoury, however, was a system known as Naxos. This was a receiver fitted to German night fighters that could pick up the beams from the bombers' H2S radar sets and allow the fighter pilots to home in on them. The device was sufficiently accurate to guide the fighters close enough that the operators in the night fighters could use their own radar to pick up the bombers. These airborne radars, called SN2, used a smaller wavelength and were not jammed by the use of Window like the earlier Lichtenstein radar sets. With all these measures introduced, the German night-fighter force had bounced back from the effect of Window in July.

The Wild Sow fighters were now slowly being withdrawn because they suffered from too many accidents, and there was a general re-equipping of the night-fighter squadrons. The older Me 110 and Dornier 217 aircraft were being withdrawn and replaced with the ubiquitous Ju 88, the twin-engined workhorse of the Luftwaffe, which, like the British Mosquito, proved to be remarkably versatile. Originally designed as a bomber, it became a very effective night fighter. Its numbers were gradually expanding and it was planned that they would reach a formidable 775 at the beginning of 1944. As well as being fitted with the new radar sets, the aircraft were given heavier armament, with the bomb aimer's position being replaced by the radar aerials and blister that contained four forward-firing cannon. Some of them were fitted with upward-firing cannon – known as 'Schräge Musik' – mounted behind the cockpit, similar to those fitted earlier in the Me 110.

The crew of C Charlie was going to see the results of these deadly changes sooner than they would have liked.

14

OTHERWISE A QUIET TRIP

The crew of C Charlie, along with the rest of 57 Squadron, had another period of intensive exercises and training because of poor weather, then on 20 December everyone was put on standby for another mission. It was Jock Burns's twenty-fourth birthday but, unless the weather got very bad, there would be no drinks in the bar tonight. As they walked from the flight office to the briefing room, Geoff observed that it was their eleventh op. Only nineteen to go. It seemed like an eternity, but he knew that it was fatal to think like that. You just had to take each day as it came.

There had been a big raid on Berlin just four days earlier, during which the Luftwaffe had shot down over 5 per cent of the attacking force. Another thirty-four Lancasters had been damaged trying to land back at their bases in fog. The fact that a major campaign was being mounted on Berlin was obvious to the German government and the night-fighter command was not being fooled by diversionary raids. As part of a continuing strategy of deception, the raid on which George, Geoff, Curly and the others waited to be briefed was going to be not on Berlin but on Frankfurt. It was another major effort, with 650 aircraft taking part. It put a considerable strain on the various bomber groups' headquarters. The fog on the previous raid had not only resulted in a lot of crashes, but bombers had diverted all over the country and they all had to be retrieved and often repaired. Relieved that the target was not once again 'the Big City', the atmosphere was slightly less tense in the hours before take-off.

For this operation 57 Squadron detailed sixteen of its crews and C Charlie was fourth in line as they taxied round the perimeter track. At 17.06 they rolled down the runway, Geoff still, after all this time, anxiously waiting for the undercarriage to thump home and the flaps to wind in before he relaxed.

The German night-fighter control and the new long-range radar picked up the bomber stream almost as they crossed the English coast, with the result that night fighters were directed to the bomber stream on the approach to Frankfurt. In addition, a diversionary raid to Mannheim didn't succeed in misleading them.

Over Frankfurt there was the usual combination of flak and fighters, although Curly consistently managed to keep C Charlie on course and in the middle of the bomber stream. The raid overall did not go according to plan. The Pathfinders had prepared a ground-marking plan but found that the target was obscured by eight tenths cloud. The Germans had also lit a large decoy fire 5 miles to the south-east of the city and set off dummy target flares. This misled many bomb aimers in the main force, with the result that a train halted 6 miles south of Frankfurt was hit and, inexplicably, so was the town of Mainz along the Rhine.

The Germans, however, had not accounted for the tendency for bombs from the main force to creep back from the main aiming point – something that was continually worrying Bomber Command at its High Wycombe headquarters – and so parts of Frankfurt did suffer, despite the decoys, as did the towns of Sachsenhausen and Offenbach.

Another forty-one British aircraft were lost on this raid, although all sixteen aircraft from 57 Squadron returned safely. The losses the night fighters were causing were beginning to hurt Bomber Command, and more and bigger course changes to confuse the night-fighter controllers were needed. This meant longer routes, more fuel and smaller bomb loads, while for the crews it meant more time over enemy territory and greater fatigue, both of which could prove deadly.

While preparations were being made for the raid on Frankfurt, photo reconnaissance missions had been flown by several Mosquitoes over Berlin, in the first period of really clear weather since the main raids had begun in November. The results were impressive. A large area of the city appeared to be burned out – almost 8 square miles, from the centre of Berlin to the districts of Charlottenburg in the north-west and Wilmersdorf in the south-west. There were also signs of heavy damage to the industrial areas of Spandau and Reinickendorf, and there were burnt-out blocks in Tiergarten in the centre, home to many diplomatic missions, and considerable damage to the Mitte, where many government offices were located. Satisfying as this was to the planners at Bomber Command head-quarters, Berlin had hardly been wrecked from end to end. There were intelligence reports of large-scale evacuations from the city, particularly of children, and more and more people were living almost permanently in the cellars of the large apartment blocks, yet there was no sign of any weakening of resistance. For the bomber crews, the missions were actually becoming tougher.

The next Berlin raid, on 23 December, was longer than usual in another attempt to fox the German radar chain and ground controllers. Bomber Command had become aware of the German tactic of assembling fighters around radio beacons, so care was taken to avoid routing the bomber stream anywhere near these.

Tactics were in fact becoming increasingly complex. The raid was originally set for a five o'clock take-off, but was delayed for seven hours because of the fear of bad weather over the UK. George finally lifted C Charlie off the runway at fifteen minutes past midnight. There would be daylight for their return. The planned route was for a long southerly approach, which would appear to threaten Frankfurt again, and then Leipzig, before the true target, Berlin, was hit. There was even going to be an actual diversionary raid on Leipzig by a force of twin-engined Mosquitoes as the main bomber force passed close by. The Germans used the same tactics that they had in recent raids, sending out fighters to engage the bombers on their run-in, but bad weather over the German airfields meant that they did not find it so easy to locate the main force. Over Berlin there were, thankfully, almost no fighters, and only a few search-light batteries seemed to be in action. However, the Pathfinders again found it difficult to mark the correct aiming point. Five aircraft in the force were fitted with H2S Mk3 and each was loaded with eleven green target indicators, but only one of them was able to drop its markers, the rest finding that their radar was not working properly. These markers were released 6 miles south of the actual aiming point, so were not a lot of use. The Pathfinder back-up force tried to shift the aiming point by dropping new markers, but it was too late – most of the bombs fell on the south-eastern suburbs of Köpenick and Treptow.

Sixteen aircraft were lost altogether, but only six of these were shot down over the target. One of Geoff King's fellow bomb aimers in 57 Squadron, Harold Chadwick, saw one go down. He was on his bombing run when a Lancaster just above him and to the left appeared in his vision, both its port engines on fire. As he watched, he saw three crew members bale out of the rear door in the fuselage, while it was obvious that the pilot was still struggling to keep the Lancaster flying level, but no one else escaped.

It was a very quiet night for C Charlie. Geoff dropped the bomb load, the usual assortment of a 'cookie' plus incendiaries, and they turned for home, continuing north before making a turn to port and heading 260 degrees west. Their course was taking them north of Hanover and across Holland, then over the North Sea. They were flying at 22,000 feet, at their best economical air speed of around 155 m.p.h. Geoff had just identified Hanover on the port side on the H2S screen to give Curly a fix, when 'Fire!' was heard on the intercom. Geoff's immediate thought was that they were under attack, but in that case the correct call should have been 'Corkscrew' to the Skipper. Then it became clear to him that Jock had pressed the fire extinguisher – a bottle of compressed gas that filled the engine nacelle with ethyl bromide – and with the Skipper was going through the drill of shutting down the engine, isolating a fuel tank and feathering the propeller. The starboard inner engine was on fire.

Flames whipped back from under the cowling, licking over the wing, smoke trailing behind, curling in the air as they left it behind. Had it been caused by a fighter attack? Would there be another? There was no call from either of the two gunners. Geoff's next thought was that if the fire didn't go out soon – it was taking a long while, it seemed to him – either a fighter would spot it and then they would be under attack, or the fire would spread and they would be in real trouble. There was still a lot of fuel in the wing tanks. Thankfully, the flames finally disappeared.

The Skipper called for a few more revs on the remaining three engines to keep up the speed. A few minutes later there was a muffled oath from Jock and the port inner engine stopped. Pressing the boost pump did nothing and after a few minutes he feathered the propeller, shut the fuel down and switched off that engine too.

It seemed to Geoff very quiet in the cabin with both inner engines out of action, their propellers rigid and useless in the slipstream, the cowling and wing behind the inner starboard engine blackened and blistered from the flames. C Charlie started to lose height and the Skipper told everyone to keep a good lookout for fighters. Geoff went back into the nose to keep an eye open to the front. They were getting lower and lower.

'I don't know what height we can maintain, guys,' said the Skipper. 'It might be better to bale out than ditch in the North Sea.' There was a long silence.

'Guys, what do you want to do?' There was another long silence. The Lancaster was still sinking despite the revs on the two remaining engines increasing.

'Ten minutes to the coast, Skip,' said Curly.

It was strange to hear the Skipper talk of baling out. He was always most critical of the escape hatches in the Lancaster, often saying that the one in the nose, on which Geoff was lying, was ridiculously small for someone like him wearing a flying jacket, Mae West life jacket and parachute. This was true. If they baled out there was a good chance that the Skipper would not make it. He would stay at the controls until they had all gone, then struggle to get out himself, hoping that the aircraft would maintain enough speed to keep the autopilot on. But time was running out. They had descended through the cloud layer and were down to around 6,000 feet. There would be flak at the Dutch coast, the sun was coming up and they would be an easy target, and then it would be the slog over the black, cold North Sea.

Geoff lay in the bomb aimer's position and looked out. C Charlie was like a cocoon around him, and the thought of plunging out through the escape hatch into the cold, whipping slipstream revolted him.

'I think we should go on, Skip,' he said. One after the other each crew member muttered assent.

So they flew on, and sure enough searchlights flicked on and tracer from low-level anti-aircraft guns shot up into the sky as they crossed the Dutch coast. Shells exploded – unusually, above them – with a crump and a flash of red. Jock recorded in his diary a laconic 'hot time over the Dutch coast'. Then they flew on over the North Sea, still at 6,000 feet, Geoff and probably everyone else on the crew reflecting that they had no idea why the second engine had failed and losing a third would be the end. Vincent asked the Skipper if he wanted to radio for an alternative air base to put down, but the Skipper said no, he thought they would make it.

Approaching their base, it seemed strange to see it in the morning light. They were very tired – they had been awake for twenty-four hours and only adrenaline was keeping them on their feet. The Skipper and Jock had been nursing the two remaining engines for almost two hours, the Skipper not daring to switch on the autopilot. With both inner engines gone, they had to use the auxiliary pneumatic systems for the undercarriage and flaps, but there were no more warning lights on the panels. They touched down on the runway at East Kirkby at 08.25. They had been in the air for eight hours and ten minutes. Never had bacon, eggs and chips tasted so good.

'Literally came back on "a wing and a prayer",' wrote Jock Burns in his diary. Then, in the final sentence on the page for 23 December, 'Quiet trip apart from that.'

15

Maximum Effort

There was some respite from flying after C Charlie landed on Christmas Eve with two engines out. There was a spot of leave and, unbeknown to the Skipper, the squadron CO had put his name forward for a Distinguished Flying Cross (DFC) for bravely getting the Lancaster back and for his overall determined approach. It was noticeable that the crew of C Charlie were getting through to the target and were attempting to bomb on the aiming point.

On New Year's Day 1944 they assembled for another briefing for a raid on Berlin. It seemed to be an obsession with the high command in High Wycombe, as indeed it was, and Geoff wondered if it would prove to be their death. The planned route was meant to outfox the German night controllers, with the bomber stream passing over the North Sea, crossing northern Germany parallel to the

Danish border and heading east, before turning and heading south-east to Berlin. A spoof raid on Hamburg was also scheduled to take place.

The weather was very bad over the North Sea and take-off was delayed until midnight. This meant that the return journey south and west across Belgium would be carried out in daylight, so a more direct route to the target was substituted at the very last minute. The raid on Hamburg did not outwit the German radar and the night-fighter controllers. Fighters were directed on to the bomber stream at an early stage and were most active between two of their ground beacons on the way to the target. The Lancasters kept up a fast approach, but they could not evade the fighters. Sixteen bombers were shot down as they flew south of Hamburg.

The new equipment that the Germans were throwing into the fight was really formidable in the hands of an experienced pilot. A twin-engined Ju 88 with long-range tanks giving exceptional endurance, and fitted with the latest SN2 airborne radar and an upward-firing cannon, was flown by Major Heinrich Sayn-Wittgenstein. Up until late 1941 he had been a bomber pilot, but then turned night fighter. He was successful at both and had just been given command of a night-fighter wing, NJG 2. He infiltrated his way into the bomber stream as the RAF planes made their way to Berlin that night and shot down six Lancasters.

In all, 28 aircraft were shot down out of a total strength on the raid of 421. Again the Pathfinder markers were poorly targeted. Eight of the Pathfinder Force had been lost before reaching the target and another exploded when it was hit during its marker run. The clouds extended up to 18,000 feet over the target and there were strong winds, so a modified marker plan was used: those aircraft equipped with the latest version of the H2S carried extra-large loads of sky-markers, which were dropped throughout the fourteen minutes of the raid. They immediately disappeared in the clouds and were scattered across the target by the wind.

As George flew C Charlie towards the giant city, the box barrage of flak over Berlin was as intense as ever. It seemed impossible to penetrate it without suffering a hit that would kill them all in a welter of exploding bombs and petrol, but by now they knew that they had penetrated it before and survived, and that they had a good chance of doing so again. They had become less fearful with experience, though Geoff couldn't help wondering whether there was a danger in this. Would it lead to a complacency that in the end might prove just as deadly?

George was unlikely to allow that to happen. His exhortations to keep an unremitting lookout for enemy fighters never ceased. His preparations for each trip were meticulous, closely observing Curly's route plan, the approach to the aiming point and the marking methods. He was on top of the routes, turning points and everything that could affect the safety of the crew. Some things were out of his control, however, and one of them was the pressure that would be put on them by their top brass.

When C Charlie approached East Kirkby at 07.00 on 2 January, a Sunday, the weather was absolutely foul. It had started to snow and they let down through very low cloud, with poor visibility and icing conditions almost all the way down to the ground. They stumbled out of their aircraft, tired and exhausted, sat through the debriefing barely able to speak, ate breakfast and went to sleep, to be woken after a few hours with the news that they were scheduled once more to fly to Berlin that evening. There was a mixture of horror and amazement amongst the crews of the thirteen aircraft detailed to carry out the raid.

At the briefing they saw that their route was almost straight in and out, abandoning the previous attempts to avoid the air defences. There was just one small dogleg close to the target, which would enable the bombers to take advantage of a strong tailwind from the north-west. The weather forecast was extremely bad, with an expectation of thick clouds threatening heavy icing and electrical storms. Facing the utter disbelief of the crews, the met officer said that they would find lanes through this lot of dense weather, but he must have known that the chances of this happening were slim. His cynical announcement was met with hollow, sarcastic laughter. The atmosphere was poisonous.

There was a lot of bitching and moaning as they left the briefing room, but George would have none of it. He was as unhappy as the rest but didn't want any negativity creeping in. It was going to be tough, but they would come back. Nevertheless, for the rest of the day Curly and George, along with the other navigators and pilots, were in and out of the met office for news of any improvement in the weather. There was none.

They took off at 23.13 with a reduced bomb load

because of the headwinds they would face. Over the North Sea they entered thick cloud and were unable to climb out above the tops even at 22,000 feet. Sixty aircraft out of the 340 taking part turned back with heavy icing, communications problems or just out of sheer disbelief in the mission. C Charlie plugged on, but it was hell, as they encountered belts of severe turbulence and freezing conditions. The Lancaster bounced heavily through the clouds, the airframe creaking and banging, George and Jock fighting to keep it on an even keel. These atrocious conditions continued until they were just thirty minutes from Berlin. The weather also affected the airfields of the night fighters, but those that were relatively clear managed to mount a major effort and, with their radar following the RAF bombers, the Germans assessed their destination forty minutes before the first wave was due over the target. The Luftwaffe put up 200 fighters, one of the largest forces for some time, many of them assembled around a radio beacon near Bremen. The German controllers, however, got their timing wrong and the British bombers flew past without the enemy planes being released.

With the 80 m.p.h. tailwind, the bombers had a fast run in to the target, and the sky-markers were plentiful and fairly well concentrated. Geoff took an H2S fix and it seemed that the main group of flares was over the centre of the city, but thick cloud cover at 10,000 feet prevented any observation of damage. They flew back through the same poor weather. To add to the strain on the crew of C Charlie, a device called Boozer had been fitted to the tail to give a visual signal when the Lancaster was being scanned by a fighter's radar. It could not provide any more information, however, and Tommy Thomas, from the rear gunner's turret, cursed the thick clouds that prevented him from seeing any approaching aircraft, knowing that if the fighter was fitted with radar it would have an easy job to home in on them. It was an acute version of the dilemma that the air gunners had to deal with every day. The cannons on a Ju 88 had a much longer effective range than the machine guns on a Lancaster, and often all that a gunner would achieve by firing at an enemy was to alert him to their presence. It was 5 Group's policy to instruct their gunners to shoot at anything, but Bomber Command insisted that gunners get positive identification that they were shooting at a fighter and not another bomber. Often the first identification was the cannon shells blasting into the rear fuselage or fuel tanks, and then of course it was far too late. Tommy and Flash both knew that the effective range of their guns was 400 yards at best, while a Ju 88 was happy to fire at 600 yards and would be accurate. They sat extremely tensely in anticipation of cannon shells ripping through them, the indicator light from Boozer flashing on and off, George throwing the Lancaster into a deep diving corkscrew, before hauling back on the yoke for a climbing turn. There were no bullets, however, and the fighter, if there was one, lost them. It left them feeling drained and utterly exhausted, but despite their fatigue they were almost elated at being able to walk on the tarmac at East Kirkby.

It was Geoff's twenty-second birthday on 20 January and he and the rest of the crew of C Charlie were detailed to take part in another raid on Berlin. With 769 aircraft participating, it was one of the biggest yet – a maximum effort. The course to the target was similar to the one that had been abandoned because of the weather on 1 January, flying over northern Germany before turning to head for Berlin. The weather this time was reasonably good, and take-off was scheduled for 16.30. The crew of C Charlie were now veterans, sufficiently experienced and trustworthy to take up newer pilots to get them accustomed to combat. The Skipper was playing host to Pilot Officer Castagnola and it was going to be an impressive first trip.

The weather helped not only the British crews but also the German night fighters, who started to infiltrate the bomber stream long before it reached Berlin. They picked off thirty-five bombers, ceasing their attacks only when the force was well on its way home. A smooth sheet of cloud at 12,000 feet covered the target and was heavily illuminated by the massed batteries of searchlights on the ground below, so that the bombers flying above were silhouetted against it, greatly aiding the German night fighters. The flak was extremely heavy, so the twin-engined fighters avoided the target area, waiting instead for the bombers to turn on to their return route before they once more started attacking them. However many times Geoff had flown into the intense barrage over Berlin, he still found it hard to imagine that he could come through it unscathed. He pitied Pilot Officer Castagnola, in the dickie seat experiencing a raid for the first time.

The fires that were being started were also much more visible through the thin cloud layer; they were spreading over an area almost 8 miles long, over the eastern part of the city. It was an inferno. The glow of the flames could be seen for almost 100 miles after leaving the target. When they landed back at base Castagnola seemed stunned. It was hard to tell whether it was the intensity of the flak or the widespread destruction beneath him. Geoff remembered that the first time he had seen an enormous city burning for miles beneath him he had felt profoundly frightened. The sight of such destruction was terrible. Jock's feeling was that they wouldn't stop until Berlin had become another Hamburg.

C Charlie had landed at 23.05 on the night of the 20th, and on the morning of the 21st they were told that once more they were flying to Berlin that night. They were going to be one of only two from 57 Squadron, flying a spoof raid on the capital while a larger attack was directed against Magdeburg. It occurred to them that this time there would be no safety in numbers as there was in a concentrated bomber stream.

This was the second time in three weeks that they had to carry out back-to-back raids on Berlin, and the whole crew found this type of operation extremely exhausting. It was, Geoff remembers, like being in a deep wood with no way out. It was as though you flew to Berlin in your dreams, with no escaping the nightly flight through tracer and shell-burst. It seemed that your whole life was spent in the noise and vibration of a Lancaster bomber.

C Charlie was in a small group of twenty-two bombers flying at the head of the main force. Geoff lay in the nose, dropping bundles of Window out of the chute in the side of the fuselage, hoping to convince the German radar operators that a large force was making for Berlin. Heading across the northern outskirts of the city, they then dropped a 'cookie', three 1,000lb bombs and two red target indicator flares, to simulate an attack. Immediately a flak battery fired illuminating flares to indicate their presence for night fighters, but the ground controllers had not been fooled by the ruse. All the night fighters were concentrated on the attack on Magdeburg and they shot down fifty-eight aircraft.

C Charlie returned safely. Others didn't. The overall losses suffered by Bomber Command were starting to rise as the campaign against Berlin continued. In the six raids in which C Charlie had taken part since 22 December, more than 200 bombers had been shot down, with the loss of over 1,400 aircrew, killed or taken prisoner. These casualties were serious and it was becoming apparent to everyone in Bomber Command, from those at High Wycombe headquarters down to the men in the squadrons, that the numbers were not sustainable.

Yet there was to be no let-up. The bombing of Berlin was the keystone of Harris's strategy and it was too early to admit defeat. Five days later, on 27 January, another raid on the city was scheduled, this time with 515 aircraft taking part. Having taken off at 17.35, the Skipper was flying C Charlie across the border between Holland and Germany, with the gunners keeping a very watchful eye for night fighters, when Jock noticed that the starboard outer engine was running hot. He reported it to George, then in a somewhat more alarmed voice said, 'Oil pressure's gone –

cut ignition. Feathering now,' and in several rapid moves he switched off the fuel cock, pressed the button to feather the propeller and then pressed the fire extinguisher. Flames were spreading out from the cowling, blown back in the slipstream, and next to this conflagration sat two main petrol tanks containing high-octane fuel. If they caught fire, there was no hope.

It was difficult to assess what was more dangerous in their situation because any bright flame was likely to catch the attention of the pilot or observer of one of the many fighters hunting for them. George was already calling for a position from Curly – how far to target and so on – but it was obvious that they were losing height and speed. No one wanted to be a tail-end Charlie, bringing up the rear of the main force on this sort of night, too slow and too low, while fighters swarmed all over the skies. George announced that they were going back. He put C Charlie into a wide, sweeping turn to starboard to avoid the main force behind them, then looked for a place to drop their bomb load. They were now heading back over Holland, so Geoff waited for them to be safely over the Zuider Zee, the shallow inland water that would be free of civilians, before jettisoning their high explosives and incendiaries.

They were first back to base, the eggs and bacon tasted exceptional, and they got a very good night's sleep. They needed it. The next day they were heading for Berlin again.

These relentless operations were extremely stressful for the crews. Geoff remembers that the indications of severe strain were sometimes very obvious. People would chain smoke, or start to appear dishevelled. Their level of attention in the section briefings before an operation was sometimes very poor, and the rest of the squadron would avoid men who were so clearly stressed out. Yet nobody was immune and Geoff believes that people became unbalanced in quite subtly different ways. There was, of course, the obsessive superstition about small good-luck charms and items of clothing, while the Skipper had revealed to Geoff that he believed the spirit of a good friend who had died earlier in the war was looking after him.

At times they were all close to collapse. Geoff remembers once it was Flash's birthday, so he and George took him back to Geoff's village, Manuden. They cycled to a local pub, the Raven, which like many isolated rural pubs never paid attention to the licensing laws. They were stood drink after drink by friends and relatives, and one of Geoff's uncles told them not to leave until he had returned. He cycled off and came back with one of his chickens, which he had killed, and told them to take it home for their dinner. When they were leaving, Flash said that both Geoff and George were too drunk to manage their bikes and the chicken as well, so he would carry it. After a few miles of cycling down the lanes at breakneck speed, Flash went hurtling off his bike and slid along the ground. When the other two picked him up he had a bad graze to his lip, but they couldn't find any other injury. There was a lot of blood over the front of his battledress, however. Then George noticed that the neck of the chicken had been caught in the front wheel of Flash's bike and the head had been torn off. All three of them laughed hysterically while they gathered up the head and the rest of the chicken. Eventually they made it to Geoff's home, where the chicken was put in the oven. It was incidents like these, away from the base and the rest of the squadron, that helped them deal with the strain of operation after operation and the prospect of yet another night spent flying through a barrage of flak.

Their take-off on 28 January was delayed twice because of bad weather, so once more it was a few minutes past midnight on the 29th when they lined up at the end of the runway and the Skipper and Jock pushed the throttle levers forward. There was a higher level of anxiety about this operation than normal and the delayed take-off didn't help. The crew was due for some leave starting the next day, and Curly and Laura had arranged to be married on the 31st. Geoff was to be best man, then they were all going to Aberystwyth, Curly and Laura for their honeymoon and Geoff to stay with Eleanor. It had been planned for some time, but the Skipper was unhappy. He didn't think that Curly should get married. What Curly did in his private life was no concern of his, but when it affected his performance in the crew it was. Getting married was an unnecessary distraction, and having a wife was bound to affect his concentration. In George's book that was dangerous. This was the gist of his argument. Curly vainly protested that he had known Laura since he was eighteen and that marriage would make no difference to how they felt about each other. But George was opposed to the wedding and was not going to be at the ceremony. It was a delicate issue.

The weather forced at least one in ten of the bombers to turn back early. The route took them over Denmark, then on a south-east leg to reach Berlin. The operation was another complex one, as diversionary raids by Mosquitoes were being mounted on night-fighter airfields in Holland, mine-laying operations carried out in Kiel harbour and a spoof raid made on Hanover. But the Berlin raid itself was successful. Flying towards the target, Geoff saw large fires glowing through the clouds, some more concentrated and vigorous than normal, with a white intensity at their centre, as though some extra-large explosion had occurred there.

The searchlights, however, were also very active, and several bombers were coned by them. The German night fighters were concentrated over the approaches to the target, single- and twin-engined planes circling as they waited for the bomber stream. Twenty-seven bombers were shot down over Berlin that night and, with the casualties exacted over the route, the losses to Bomber Command were 46 aircraft in all, with their 322 crew, out of a total of 611 aircraft that attempted to reach the target.

Geoff had seen aircraft fall victim to flak and night fighters on other raids. They sometimes seemed to stagger in the air before slowly diving, with an eruption of flames from a wing. Others would start to break up in the air. The most dreadful were those aircraft hit in their bomb load; they would erupt in a giant fireball of high explosive, with a fountain of burning incendiaries and wreckage falling to earth. On this night C Charlie had just completed its bombing run and taken up course to leave the target when Geoff saw a huge explosion just ahead on the starboard side. A massive ball of flame, with spikes of fire and smoke shooting out from it like a huge airborne fireworks display, erupted upwards. Before Geoff or George could even utter a warning, C Charlie was flying through fire and whirling debris, and the aircraft filled with the sickening smell of burning petrol and explosives. The Lancaster started to fall from the sky like a lift whose cable had suddenly snapped – they fell hundreds, perhaps several thousands of feet. They had flown into the vacuum caused by the expanding fireball and lost any lift from the wings. As they re-entered calm air, they felt as if their stomachs had floated up to their mouths. For a moment they had been in free fall, and they jolted hard against their seats, but the Lancaster immediately regained lift and continued straight and level. Then George's voice came over the intercom, 'Jesus Christ what was that?' They all knew what it was, of course. They had just flown through the pyre of seven aircrew and a bomber. Curly read out the return course, a long trip over Denmark, and they landed safely at 08.30. It had been another twenty-four hours without sleep, but Curly and Geoff made it to the wedding in Cheshire on the 31st.

The next operation for the crew of C Charlie was on 15 February. In another major effort on Berlin, a raid of almost 900 aircraft was mounted – fewer than the thousand-bomber raid on Cologne but, in terms of the weight of bombs carried by the Lancasters and Halifaxes, much more destructive.

The Germans detected the aircraft while they were only

a quarter of the way across the North Sea. There was then a running commentary by the controllers describing the course of the bomber stream accurately and in detail. Every fighter that sighted a bomber was instructed to fire a green flare to help their comrades find the bomber stream. First contacts were made near the east coast of Denmark and from then on fights took place all the way to the edges of the Berlin flak defences.

Berlin itself was once again covered by cloud for most of the raid, but there was a better than normal concentration of bombs on the target. Heavy damage was caused in the central and south-western parts of the city, and some of the most important industrial areas were hit, including Siemensstadt. There were many civilian deaths, and huge fires were started. Again, to Geoff, the impact of hundreds of searchlights probing into the sky, barrage after barrage of exploding flak and star shells spreading out before them, while the fires and flashes of exploding bombs lit the ground beneath, made it seem truly like flying into Dante's inferno. But it was to be even worse on the way out. The low cloud base was lit up by the searchlights, helping to outline the shape of the bombers flying above them, but Geoff saw for the first time the German fighters use their own illuminating flares. They flew above the route of the returning bomber stream and dropped enormous numbers of parachute flares which lit up the bombers as much as 100 miles from the city. The crew of C Charlie suddenly felt ten times more vulnerable than they had as they bored through the flak barrages. Geoff's heart sank. If they had to face this after every raid on a German city, then their luck was never going to last. The only consolation was that the bright illuminating flares allowed the approaching fighters to be identified and gave the crew some warning of the need to take evasive action. However, once more they avoided trouble. Lucky C Charlie got them home again.

This was their last raid on Berlin, although at the time they didn't know it. Their last raid of the Battle of Berlin, however, took place on 19 February, though it was not on Berlin but on Leipzig, and it was this raid that marked the beginning of the end for Harris's attempt to wreck Berlin from end to end.

Leipzig was a bitter disaster. The operational log for 57 Squadron recorded that the opposition was the fiercest ever encountered. There were, however, other reasons for things going wrong. The met officer at the briefing gave the crews a completely inaccurate wind forecast, which, if they had followed it, would have brought them over the target much earlier than the planned zero hour. Fortunately Curly had not lost any of his concentration as a result of his wedding and, quickly realizing that the wind was much weaker than predicted, he figured out some dogleg interruptions to take up time. It was a pretty good piece of ad hoc navigation; moreover, they found that they had to contend with more severe icing problems than had been forecast as well. Other crews had not been so competent and did arrive over the target before the target-indicator flares had been dropped. Some of them circled, while others dropped their bomb loads anyway and headed out.

The target was covered by thick cloud up to C Charlie's operational height. As they took up their approach, working to the prepared schedule, Geoff thought that they might indeed have arrived too early, but Curly was adamant that he had been spot on. He was right. It was the Pathfinder Force that had been delayed. The sky-markers practically lit up in front of them as C Charlie made its run, and Geoff barely had time to make a couple of adjustments before pressing the release button. Up until that point the searchlights and flak had been non-existent. No sooner had the target indicators ignited, however, than everything came to life and anti-aircraft fire blasted into the sky. Geoff was aghast as the shells exploded all around them. The Skipper rapidly closed the bomb-bay doors and called for maximum revs and boost from Jock, desperate to get out of this death trap.

Around twenty aircraft were shot down over the target. In the confusion caused by poor wind forecasts there were more collisions over the target than normal, and many bombers on the return trip found themselves drifting off course, flying over the Ruhr where they were hit severely by more flak and night fighters. In all, 823 aircraft had been detailed for the raid, but a high percentage of crews had aborted so only 730 actually attacked Leipzig. Of these, 78 were shot down. A loss of almost 10 per cent of the whole mission was an extreme shock to Harris and the air staff.

There were two more raids on Berlin after this. Both were maximum efforts, and were very concentrated, but both had losses almost as bad as those at Leipzig.

Harris's attempt to bomb Berlin and win the war had been far too costly and had failed to achieve the collapse of the German government for which he had hoped. The

German defences had been getting stronger rather than weaker, and not only the raid on Leipzig but also one on Nuremberg on 30 March, when 97 bombers were shot down, drove this fact home in the most brutal manner. In the three months from 1 January to 31 March 1944, Bomber Command had lost 771 heavy bombers and 5,397 airmen were dead or taken prisoner, almost all of the command's front-line strength. With the days lengthening as spring arrived, the bombers would lose the safety of darkness on their long round trips. Moreover, Harris was now having to bend to very strong pressure to look for more militarily significant targets as the great invasion of Europe approached. He protested at this interference, but he had little real option. The Battle of Berlin had been lost.

16

THE END OF C CHARLIE

The citation for George Laing's DFC, awarded for the
trip to Berlin when they returned on two engines, read:
'Flight Lieutenant Laing has participated in many sorties
and has always displayed praiseworthy skill, courage and
determination.' In truth, all the members of George's crew
had shown similar skill and determination, and now at the
beginning of March 1944 they were considered to be
reliable veterans in the ranks of 57 Squadron. They could
be trusted to carry out a mission and cope with any
emergency. It was no guarantee of safety, however. The
Operational Research Section of Bomber Command had
noted that there was an increase in fatalities amongst crews
as they approached the end of their tour. Whether this was
a result of complacency or because these crews were
detailed for the more difficult missions it was hard to say.

On 10 March C Charlie was to be one of thirty-three

Lancasters that were going to attack the airfield at Clermont-Ferrand, in Occupied France, in preparation for another attack planned for a few days later on the town's Michelin plant. The target was to be bombed from a much lower height than normal in order to avoid damage to the French town and French civilian casualties. The run-in over France was peaceful, with little opposition. It was a clear, moonlit night, but there was thick haze over the target. The target indicators were dropped about 100 yards south and 400 yards south-west of the aiming point. The Pathfinder leader tried to give corrections to the aircraft over the VHF radio, but most crews bombed the markers. Geoff pressed the button as they came in on an attempted correction, and at 10,000 feet instead of their normal 21,000 feet the concussion of the bombs was felt through the aircraft, much the same as the rumbling effect he had noticed over Modane. That seemed like a lifetime ago, so much had been crammed into their tour. Geoff knew that he was now a respected veteran in the squadron, and remote from the new arrivals as the veterans had been from him when he first joined. He realized that he expected some of them would not be around for very long, and he kept his distance.

They then took part in another raid on Stuttgart, once more with many casualties falling to the night fighters. Again, problems with the Pathfinder Force caused the start of the attack to be delayed, then winds took the flares and moved the aiming point back well short of the target. A great many bombs fell on open countryside to the south-west.

There were two more raids on Frankfurt in quick succession. The first, on 18 March, passed off without incident for the crew of C Charlie, although there were again some losses to night fighters. The second, on 22 March, was another large effort with 816 aircraft taking part. The route to the target was indirect and at the same time a diversionary raid was carried out so that the German air defences would mistakenly think that the primary target was Hanover.

Geoff had lined up the Lancaster on its bombing run and had just called 'Bombs gone' when, to his dismay another Lancaster loomed out of the cloud directly beneath them. It was remarkable that it had not been hit by the bombs that Geoff had just released. The plane was climbing into C Charlie's course and Geoff yelled to the Skipper to 'Pull up, pull up!'. The Skipper immediately did so, with Geoff continuing to shout until he was sure they were clear of the other bomber. No sooner had they levelled off than they were, to Geoff's complete horror, caught in the beam of a master searchlight. It filled the front turret and bomb aimer's dome with a brilliant white light and George had to look down at the instrument panel to avoid being blinded. As it was, his night vision had gone. The flak was exploding close around them, tossing the aircraft, and with the threat of a collision far less of a worry than that of being coned by the searchlights, the Skipper threw the plane into a diving turn and sought the safety of the cloud. The searchlight must have been radar-controlled, for it lit up the cloud around them. The flak bursts also seemed to follow them, but at full throttle, free of the bomb load, the Lancaster bored through the cloud on the course home and the searchlight faded. Now there was a danger that a night fighter had picked them up while they were fixed in the searchlight's glare and might even now be homing in on them. There was little they could do but try to keep as vigilant a lookout as possible. Eventually George allowed the Lancaster to climb out of the cloud, telling Geoff to stay in the nose and search the sky forward and below.

Their return journey was over south-eastern France and they had been flying for around twenty minutes when, without any warning, a terrific explosion on the starboard side suddenly lifted the aircraft into a steep bank and C Charlie plunged into a dive. The Skipper shouted over the intercom, 'What was that? Kingy, have you seen anything?' and struggled to right the plane. There was nothing; it was as black as pitch outside and neither the rear nor the mid-upper gunner reported anything either. The explosion wasn't repeated and the Lancaster flew on, but there seemed to be a loss of lift from the starboard wing, a reduction in their speed, so George needed to compensate with some left rudder to keep on course.

There was no other sign of any damage and so they continued. As they crossed the French coast, Geoff unstrapped the Aldis lamp and climbed back into the nose to shine a beam over the starboard wing and the engine nacelles. There, in the yellow light, was the starboard landing gear hanging down. East Kirkby advised the Skipper to land at an alternative airfield, Syerston, which was not operational at the time so an accident on its runway would not prevent other returning bombers from landing. It was an intelligent, if callous, call, and they proceeded on the changed course and started their approach. George and Jock could not tell whether the starboard undercarriage leg was locked down. The Skipper ordered the crew to take up their emergency landing positions, which meant sitting down in the fuselage and bracing themselves against the wings' main spar running across it.

George slowly brought the aircraft in to land, keeping the starboard wing slightly high. The left wheel touched, and then as they lost speed the starboard wing was lowered. As the tyre made contact with the tarmac it ripped open with a bang, the rubber wrapping around the wheel and jamming it. Still travelling at 70 or 80 m.p.h., the Lancaster spun round horizontally, throwing the crew members around in the fuselage like a fairground ride, and in a shower of sparks from the landing leg and the starboard propellers it eventually came to a halt. The crew stumbled to the rear exit, where they were met by the station's fire crew and ambulance. They were badly bruised and shaken, but nobody was seriously hurt. Vincent had hit his head and had slight concussion. Frightened of a fire starting, Curly had hauled him out by whatever he could hang on to and had pulled out a tuft of his hair in the process.

Their lucky C Charlie, however, had been badly damaged in the crash. Closer inspection also showed that the inner starboard engine's oil tank had been buckled and some of the hydraulic lines had been cut. Whether there had been a single burst of flak or whether the tyre had exploded in the air was unclear. There was no sign of damage to the skin of the aircraft, nor any sign of shrapnel, and it was hard to work out why the tyre had burst in the wheel housing. But C Charlie needed extensive repairs and all the crew could do was once again thank their lucky stars that George had brought off a very tricky landing.

Back at East Kirkby, there was a new aircraft waiting for them – another C Charlie – and on 26 March, four days later, they went back in her to bomb the Ruhr. The town of Essen was covered by cloud, but it was within range of Oboe and the Mosquitoes of the Pathfinder Force were able to mark accurately. There was little fighter activity and very little flak; Jock remarked almost nostalgically that it wasn't like last time.

Weather was poor for the next week, but then on 9 April there was a full moon and the weather forecast was good. Geoff was woken by his batman and told that he was on ops. Later that day, after the air test on the new C Charlie had been carried out, they were taken aside and told that there would be a special briefing for them and two other crews after the main brief. Nothing more was said but, intrigued and naturally slightly apprehensive, they were first into the briefing room that afternoon.

This was not going to be a bombing mission over Germany, but 103 Lancasters were going to drop mines in the Bay of Danzig and Pillau. George and his crew, however, were then given another briefing, this time by a senior officer – a captain, no less – from naval intelligence. They had been selected, they were told, because of their excellent bombing record, for a target that called for skilful flying and accuracy.

While the main force was going to drop mines in the Bay of Danzig and at the entrance to other Baltic ports, the crew of C Charlie would liaise with two other Lancasters and meet up at the mouth of the River Pregel. Then at low altitude, to ensure pinpoint accuracy, they would drop mines along the ship canal at the mouths of the docks in Königsberg harbour, which was a major landing point for supplies and reinforcements for German troops fighting the Russians as they advanced into Poland.

This was a mission that called for accuracy and really cool heads. Flying low over a German port in bright moonlight was going to be dangerous, but the moonlight was necessary for the three Lancasters to meet up, and it was also essential so that the aiming points could be properly identified. If the mines were not dropped precisely in the dredged channel at the entrance to the docks, then it was unlikely they would be closed. The mission would have its required effect only if it could guarantee to close the docks for at least a week.

Their planned route was over Denmark, then over the southern tip of neutral Sweden, then across the Baltic to the Bay of Danzig. The only opposition they encountered was a token burst of tracer anti-aircraft fire from the Swedish air-defence forces when they were over Sweden, but nothing else.

The moonlight lit up the scene and the ships in the bay below were perfectly visible, their wakes gleaming against the dark of the sea. The two other aircraft scheduled to make the attack with C Charlie were easy to spot, and they formed up in line astern and headed up the river channel to the mouths of the docks, flying at well below 1,000 feet. As they snaked along the course of the river, Flash said, 'Skip, fighter behind at five o'clock!' They all knew this was serious. There was no height for any evasive action, and if Flash had seen him, then he had definitely seen them. Geoff was in the front waiting for the target zone to appear.

Flash stayed calm and said, 'He's got to come lower, Skip, to get a shot. Wait.'

George, in the cockpit, was focused on the height and speed of the heavy Lancaster. At 200 m.p.h. a slight misjudgement of height would be catastrophic. 'What the fuck are you on about, Flash?'

'Wait, Skip, wait!'

The rest of the crew couldn't believe what was happening. The noise of the engines was echoing back from the water, they were so low. Geoff was chanting out the range as it shortened and they bored on.

Then, 'He's crashed!' shouted Flash. 'The bastard's gone in!'

Flash had guessed that the fighter would be so intent on getting a long burst in that he would misjudge his height. He had proved correct. The fighter, a Focke-Wulf 190, had come to grief in a fireball on the bank of the river.

There was a whoop of joy from George – a Canadian 'yee-haw' – then 'Steady, Skip, steady!' from Geoff, and a 'Bombs gone.' Despite the immediate instinctive desire to pull out, George knew that to do so might silhouette him against the sky – an easy target for anti-aircraft gunners. Instead he kept low, turning to port away from the docks and their cranes, before climbing and taking a course from Curly for the run home. They had done it!

The raid was very successful and secured the crew of C Charlie's reputation. The docks were closed to traffic not for a week but for almost a fortnight, as the mouths of the docks and the river channel were laboriously trawled to recover all the mines that had been dropped. An eyewitness to the attack was a German woman who was on leave in Königsberg that night. She looked out of the window and to her it seemed that the big four-engined Lancasters were flying lower than her bedroom window as they roared in to the target. George met her many years later in Germany. At that point, she told him, she suddenly understood that Germany would lose the war.

Two days later they were once more briefed, this time for a raid on Aachen, as part of a 341-bomber mission. They turned on to the runway, got a green light and George pushed the four throttle levers forward, then they started their long roll along the runway, laden with fuel, a 4,000lb bomb and several thousand pounds of incendiaries. As they gathered speed and the tail came up, there was a sudden cry from Jock, 'Shit – starboard inner has gone!' There was a burst of flame from under the cowling, and burning fuel and oil with thick smoke poured back over the wing. They had passed the point of no return, so George eased back on the stick, pulling the heavy plane into the air, while Jock called, 'Fire extinguisher on, fuel cut, feather prop,' and George juggled the throttles to compensate for the loss of power. The fire persisted all the while.

This was the most frightening moment that Geoff had ever experienced, and he believes that was true for everybody else on the aircraft. It was more frightening than flying through flak over Berlin. They were a flying bomb, just a few hundred feet in the air, unable to climb, while flames licked just a few feet from hundreds of gallons of fuel. They couldn't jettison the bombs because they themselves would be caught in the resulting explosion, and anyway there were farms and cottages in the countryside below them; and they were too low to bale out. Eventually, starved of fuel, the fire died out. The Skipper and Jock raised the undercarriage and flaps as the Skipper struggled to keep the aircraft straight and the Lancaster flew at rooftop height over Skegness towards the North Sea. At last gathering some speed, they managed to gain some extra height, then safely dumped the bombs into the ocean. Relieved of the weight, they returned and George brought the plane into a steady landing. They were all completely drained, elated to be back on the ground, enormously thankful to be alive and light-headed from having once more escaped the jaws of death.

Next day they were called into the squadron office and there the adjutant told them that they had completed their first tour of thirty operations. The squadron had been prepared to count the last aborted mission as part of their tour as they had all exceeded 200 hours on operations anyway. No one was going to question that, and Geoff felt a surge of relief flow through him. They went outside into a blustery spring day and congratulated each other. They had beaten the odds; they had survived. They had faced the worst that the enemy could throw at them and come through. There was no briefing to go to, no target for tonight, no air test to carry out before lunch and no flak to be flown through. They stood, a motley group of seven young men from distant corners of the UK and the empire, far older than their years, exhausted to the bone, and they looked from one to the other. What now?

They already knew the answer to this question, at least in part. They were united by two things. They had the utmost belief in their own abilities and they had a determination to stay alive. They also knew that those two things were inextricably linked. There was almost no formal discussion, but they were a united group of seven comrades and they had an overwhelming desire to stay that way. Whatever Bomber Command told them to do, they would do their utmost to stay together. Deep down, they all knew that this was a matter of life or death.

17

LEADING THE WAY

The crew returned from fourteen days' leave and walked through the gates of East Kirkby on 27 April. In the adjutant's office they were told that they could be posted to various training units for a few months before being drafted back to another operational squadron. On the face of it, this was the most attractive option, the one that most crews took after completion of their first thirty ops. But the seven men of Geoff's crew were in one mind about their future, and they had made this decision before they went on leave. Even though the opportunity to leave front-line operations – to abandon the sometimes daily fear of what that night's target might be – was a dream that they had often talked about in the past, they knew that they would eventually be recalled for a second tour of operations and that all seven of them would be working with different crews, perhaps in different squadrons. One thing they were adamant about was that they would not split up. They had worked together over thirty operations, braved the hell of Berlin, survived accidents and become a highly proficient bomber crew because they trusted each other implicitly. They had all come to the conclusion that their best chance of surviving the war was to stay together, even if this meant that they would start another tour of operations immediately.

In the face of this show of commitment and solidarity, Bomber Command offered them two options. They could either stay in 5 Group to join the famous 617 Squadron, the Dambusters, under Group Captain Leonard Cheshire, or volunteer to go for an intensive training period as Pathfinders in the Pathfinder Force under Don Bennett in 8 Group.

Geoff remembers that there was a general consensus amongst them that the casualty rate in 617 Squadron was far too high, but the raids on Berlin had also proved to be dangerous for the Pathfinders whose losses were higher than average for the main bomber force. However, two operations by 617 Squadron were firmly in the minds of the Skipper and the rest of the crew. The first was the Dams raid itself on 17 May 1943, and the other was a raid on the Dortmund–Ems Canal in September 1943, in both of which almost half of the crews had been killed. The problem was that 617 was committed under Air Vice Marshal Cochrane's aegis to low-level precision bombing. So it was the Pathfinders for them, and a slight increase in pay.

A few days later they were flown to the Pathfinder Force night-training unit at Warboys in Cambridgeshire for an intensive two-week conversion course, which for Geoff meant that he got further instruction in using the advanced H2S Mk3 sets and got to grips with the target-marking and aiming techniques of 8 Group.

Sadly, this move did mean one change to the crew. They all had to undergo further medicals, in one of which Tommy Thomas discovered that his night vision had deteriorated and he would have to be taken off operations. There was some sadness amongst them at this, and a long, drink-fuelled farewell, as well as some unsettling thoughts in most of their minds about how long Tommy's night vision hadn't been up to scratch. When the course was over they were posted, still missing a rear gunner, to 97 Squadron.

Unbeknown to them and to the other members of the squadron, and indeed to Don Bennett and 8 Group, Air Vice Marshal Cochrane's long campaign to establish his own target-marking unit in 5 Group had paid off. Together with 83 Squadron and 627 Mosquito Squadron, 97 Squadron was being removed from 8 Group and transferred to Cochrane's command, where along with 617 Squadron and 106 Squadron they were to become a special target-marking section in 5 Group at 54 Base in Coningsby and Woodhall Spa.

The crew in 97 Squadron soon began training on a new set of techniques in which they would perform the function of a flare force, with a role to illuminate the target so that a master bomber could more easily select the correct aiming point and mark it. Other target-marking methods were also being made more systematic. These required, for example, precise identification by H2S of a landmark from which a course could be set to the aiming point – a technique that would, it was hoped, overcome the problems caused when a target became heavily obscured by dust or smoke. They could also be required to act as back-up markers, dropping coloured spot flares during an attack to mark a specified distance from a primary marker, or dropping cascading slow-burning markers set to burst at 3,000–6,000 feet above a target that was obscured by smoke.

The increased reliance on radar for target-finding dictated that Geoff spent all his time at the radar screen next to Curly, while in future Jock would physically press the bomb-release button in the bomb aimer's position. This required some split-second coordination between them. They picked up a new rear gunner at this time as well. 'Dickie' Polson was a veteran of over 100 operations, wearing the ribbon of a DFC. He was small and dapper, smoking constantly with a long, elegant cigarette-holder which he used no matter where he was in the squadron. Geoff believes that he probably thought of his new crew as a bunch of tyros, and they never really got to know him; he remained an enigma throughout their stay in 97 Squadron. He was considered rather mad, and would spend the whole time on operations in the rear turret, muttering, 'Come on, you bastards, come up and fight!'

Life in 97 Squadron was focused on two things: training to perfect bombing accuracy and operations. Their first mission was on 23 May and the target was Brunswick, a raid in which 225 aircraft took part. Their bomb load was twelve flares and one 2,000lb bomb. The weather forecast was for clear skies, but on their arrival they found between seven tenths and ten tenths cloud cover. The master bomber decided to use a sky-marking technique, but the flare-force leader had some problems with his radar set and the master bomber and his deputies experienced a breakdown in their radio communications. When the Skipper arrived over the target in their Lancaster – call sign S Sugar – he observed flares 2 miles to the east of the target. He circled the target three times but saw no more indicators, so he told Geoff and Jock to bomb on the best radar target they could find.

It was not a successful raid. There was a high level of flak and fighter activity, and circling the target was really asking for trouble. They returned safely, but another aircraft flown by Flight Lieutenant Chatten was hit by a Ju 88, whose cannon shell blasted open the Perspex nose and wrecked the bombing compartment. Chatten and his crew pressed on despite the freezing cold. Over Brunswick they were hit by flak and lost all their instruments. On their return they were attacked by another fighter, but the mid-upper gunner fired at it and drove it away. As they flew over the coast of England, the coastal batteries opened up on the plane, hitting it with their first two shots. Chatten made it to Coningsby and landed, as the squadron summary of events records, 'safely'! Another Lancaster crashed in a mid-air collision over another airfield and all the crew were killed.

A day later, problems with the weather and concern about Dutch civilian casualties led to a completely aborted mission. Their target was the Philips electrical factory in Eindhoven, but the cloud cover completely obscured the target and the master bomber ordered the fifty-nine aircraft that were taking part to return to base and jettison their bombs over the North Sea.

The crew's first real success in bombing a pinpoint target was on 27 May 1944, when the weather had cleared and they were sent to destroy a gun emplacement at St-Valéry-en-Caux, near Cherbourg on the French coast. The target-marking and bombing proved to be very accurate, and Jock left his position next to the Skipper to lie in the bomb aimer's bubble, dropping their flares and bombs right on the button.

Just after this, Geoff learned that he had been awarded the DFC and had been given seven days' leave. He returned to Manuden, where the village had put out bunting and flags to welcome him home, and to celebrate his award he was given an engraved cigarette case.

While he and the rest of the crew were on leave, the squadron was given a mission to attack a battery of coastal artillery at St-Pierre-du-Mont on the south-eastern base of the Cherbourg peninsula. As instructions were telexed to them before the raid was due to take place, it became obvious that the invasion of France was under way. The squadron commander, Wing Commander Carter, said, 'Thank God I'm still on ops and not at an OTU.'

The attack started at 04.50 on 6 June, thirty minutes before dawn. Both target-marking and bombing were extremely accurate, and on the return journey over the

Channel the crews saw thousands of landing craft heading towards the French coast. The squadron suffered severe casualties on this mission, however. Wing Commander Carter and his crew, including Squadron Leader Bryan Smith, the gunnery section leader, and Flight Lieutenant Chambers, the signals leader, all of whom had been determined to take part in an operation that was paving the way for the most momentous event of the war, were shot down by a Ju 88, as was a Norwegian crew in a Lancaster flown by Lieutenant Jespersen.

Early in the morning of 6 June, Geoff, still on leave, was woken by a spectacular display of signal flares, Very lights, star shells and anything else that would light up the night sky as the airmen at the US base at Stansted celebrated the landings in France. The Skipper, meanwhile, was woken by a maid in the Regent Palace Hotel in London and was told, 'They've gone to war!' His response, so he says, was 'What else is new?' However, he phoned the base and heard about the loss of the squadron commander. He was told to stay on leave, but he and his crew all made their way back to the base quite spontaneously.

They didn't fly on an operation until 8 June, when they were sent on a mission to bomb a railway bridge just outside Rennes. It was part of the overall Bomber Command task to isolate the areas in Normandy where the Allied landings had taken place and so prevent reinforcements reaching the German forces. Curly navigated using Oboe, as it was well within range, and the illumination and target-marking were very precise. The bridge and railway line were destroyed.

Four days later, two operations were mounted by the squadron. The first, on a railway junction at Poitiers, was successful. The second, on which the Skipper and his crew were detailed, was on a series of bridges at Caen which the British artillery had not been able to attack. There was a stalemate and the mission, it was hoped, would cut off fresh German troops from reinforcing their positions. Armed with clusters of flares and five 1,000lb bombs, Curly located the target by a Gee fix, but a marker from an Oboe-equipped Mosquito had already been dropped. This aircraft had to retire because of flak damage to his port engine, but his deputy in a Lancaster took over. The Skipper reported that the bombing seemed very concentrated, and it seems that the bridges were destroyed. The commanding officer of the British Field Forces, who had observed the strike, sent a congratulatory message of thanks.

Three days later another raid was launched in support of the Allied ground forces when a large munitions depot at Chateau Rault was targeted. Nine Lancasters from 97 Squadron took part, and again an accurate marking and bombing mission was carried out. Jock observed that the munitions were undoubtedly hit and the target was left burning vigorously, with some dramatic explosions occurring. No opposition was encountered, but again one of the returning Lancasters was fired on by the London anti-aircraft defences, who got several good hits.

In June, a few weeks after D-Day, the squadrons at 54 Base, Coningsby, were directed by 5 Group to start training for daylight operations. Whatever Bomber Harris's views about diverting Bomber Command away from its role of strategic attacks on German cities, he was losing the argument and there were demands on him both to commit more forces to precision raids in France and to attack specific industrial targets in Germany. The US view that destroying the German synthetic oil industry would be a severe blow to the German war effort had won the day and Bomber Command would have to make some effort to go along with it.

Any daylight raids would need a strong escort of fighters if the bombers were not going to be decimated, but Cochrane toyed with the idea that a tight formation of Lancasters might be able to provide some collective self-defence. This concept, which had been the keystone to the USAAF daylight raids, had proved a deadly mistake for the Flying Fortress and Liberator crews in 1943, but 5 Group none the less went ahead and called for training exercises in close-formation flying.

The Lancaster was not an ideal aircraft for this sort of flying. It was a big plane, and maintaining a precise speed and position in relation to other aircraft took great concentration on the part of the pilot and flight engineer, as well as good coordination. Jock Burns professed to hating it. George the Skipper, unlike home-grown RAF pilots, had learned to fly formation in Canada, but even he found it tiring. The problem for him was flying with people who didn't know what they were doing. An exercise was carried out on 20 June in preparation for a daylight raid, which was later cancelled. There were more exercises over the next few days, but on the 23rd the crew were involved in one which went horribly wrong.

George was flying with three other aircraft, one piloted by another Canadian, Flight Lieutenant Bill Gee from Montreal; one by an Australian, Flight Lieutenant Van Raalte; and one by Flight Lieutenant Perkins. The Skipper told them all to stay separate to give themselves some air. As they were turning, he saw the two forward Lancasters getting closer and closer, and shouted to his wing man, Flight Lieutenant Gee, 'They're going to hit – break right!' As both the Skipper's plane and Gee's broke away, Van Raalte's aircraft side-slipped and dropped on to Perkins's, shearing away its tail and damaging the nose of Van Raalte's. Both aircraft crashed into the fields north of Sleaford.

The squadron was ordered back to base and the exercises were cancelled. George, Jock, Geoff and the rest of the crew were badly shaken by this experience, seeing so many of their friends killed. Van Raalte had been a veteran of many tough raids and was seen as a natural survivor. Not all the aircrew died in this crash. A wireless operator, Flight Sergeant Coman, managed to bale out when his aircraft broke in two at 1,000 feet. He told Vincent later that he had no idea how he had managed to get out. The accident disturbed him so much that he found it impossible to fly again and he was taken off missions.

The death of their wing commander over Cherbourg on D-Day had meant a change of personnel in the squadron. They had a new commanding officer, Wing Commander

Heward, and George and several of the other empire pilots found him insufferable. Even this late in the conflict there were some officers who had not understood what had happened to the RAF. Heward had graduated out of Cranwell, the RAF Officer Training College, and was very much of the old school. He insisted on a strict uniform code; everybody had to wear their hats and salute the flag that fluttered from the flagpole when they crossed the parade ground, even if they were cycling. Soon many of the senior pilots were on a charge.

A Canadian in the squadron, Flight Lieutenant Duncan, had been a lumberjack in Saskatchewan, and one night in the mess Squadron Leader Locke, an Australian, offered him 10 shillings if he would go out to the parade ground and chop down the flagpole. At this offer several other pilots also produced 10-shilling notes, which were folded up and put under a pint glass. The former lumberjack needed no more prompting. He ripped the fire axe from the wall of the mess and went out. After ten minutes he came back with the axe and scooped up the 10 shilling notes. George estimated it must by then have been at least £20 – a very profitable ten minutes' work.

The next day the group captain, Evan Evans, arrived and addressed the officers' mess. He pointed out that the flagpole had been donated to the base by the Royal Canadian Air Force Officers Corps in British Columbia in 1935. 'It is unlikely,' he said, 'that it will be replaced, so there will be no saluting on the base from now on.' He then left. Discipline was relaxed after that. The problem, Geoff thinks, was that in the period following D-Day there was a considerable amount of training and very few operations, with many cancelled at the last minute because of bad weather. Boredom easily set in, although no one wanted to return to the awful grinding regime of mission after mission over Berlin.

The weather continued to be so bad that the crew's next mission was not until 12 July. During this long period they had not been idle, however; there had been daily bombing exercises over Wainfleet ranges, and the squadron's accuracy had gradually become very good. Geoff and the Skipper were nominated as deputy controllers on this raid, which was on a railway junction in France at Culmont-Chalindrey.

The target was identified by Mosquitoes after it had been illuminated and they dropped red spot flares. The controller had experienced some problems with his radio, so George took over, ordered the flares to be backed up with target indicators and passed an accurate wind speed to the main force for them to enter in their bombsights. The raid was a quiet affair, according to Geoff, with only a few searchlights, no flak and very little fighter opposition. It was a very accurate raid, destroying the junction.

The deaths on the formation flying exercise earlier in June had diminished 5 Group senior staff's enthusiasm for formation flying. If daylight raids were going to take place, then there would inevitably be a fighter escort and the bombers would form up in a 'gaggle' rather than in any precise close-knit formation. This was safer, but Jock still didn't like it.

Their first daylight raid was on a marshalling yard 70

miles south-west of Paris at Joigny-Laroche, with seven
Lancasters from 97 Squadron taking part. On this trip, for
some reason which nobody explained and with which the
Skipper went along, Flash and Dickie changed positions,
with Flash taking over the rear turret. The operation was a
totally new experience, flying over open countryside in broad
daylight in a gaggle. They felt very exposed, particularly to
anti-aircraft fire. They were flying at a much lower altitude
and when the Lancasters were in range of radar-controlled
anti-aircraft guns the flak could be deadly accurate. The raids
were accompanied by British and American fighter sweeps,
so they were protected against German fighter attacks. The
target was well marked, but the main bombing, which started
at 20.26, focused on the markers rather than on the yards
themselves, ignoring the briefed marking plan. Even so, the
yards were badly damaged and the raid was considered a
success. The weather was superb and, flying across the
Channel, they saw scores of ships waiting to unload their
cargoes at the artificial ports that had been built on the
French coast in the days after the Allied invasion.

This was the last of their missions in support of the
Allied ground offensive in Normandy. Harris had been
agitating for his bombers to return to their main task – in
his view – the strategic destruction of Germany. These
raids started in July, barely six weeks after D-Day, but there
were still some very important targets that demanded precision bombing and that kept them flying in daylight.

The first time 5 Group had tried out some of its target-
marking methods, particularly offset marking to avoid the

effects of smoke and dust, had been on 18 August 1943 on a raid on Peenemünde on the Baltic coast. This was the experimental station that was developing the V1 flying bombs – pilotless aircraft powered by a pulsejet that could carry a heavy warhead over about 150 miles. The operation had caused considerable damage and set back the V1 programme by a year. The success of this mission had been an important factor in Harris's decision to allow 5 Group to develop its own target-marking unit. It had, however, proved to be an expensive mission for 5 Group, with 17 Lancasters out of 120 from the group being shot down. The V1 'buzz' bombs, as they were called, were eventually produced and the Germans began launching them against London in June 1944. They caused a lot of damage, and because they were launched throughout the day and night they were extremely disruptive and affected civilian morale. There were a number of launch sites along the French coast and in Holland, and Bomber Command was tasked with eliminating them as well as the depots where the bombs were being assembled.

The launch sites were small, as were their storage depots, so the attacks had to be made in daylight. The first one in which the Skipper and Geoff took part was on 3 August 1944, against a site at Trossy-St-Maximin. This was just one of the V1 sites bombed that day; altogether there were over 1,000 aircraft from Bomber Command in the air. There was, however, very heavy flak in defence of the sites, and the Skipper's crew bombed the most heavily guarded of all, Trossy, where the gunfire was frighteningly intense. Bombing at 14.30 meant that the target was easy to identify, but very quickly after the start of the raid the whole area was obscured by smoke and dust. Five aircraft were shot down. Geoff's Lancaster was hit and when they returned they found twenty holes caused by small arms and shrapnel, although they had not noticed being hit when they were over the target. The next day there were more raids, and they flew in over St-Leu-d'Esserent. Again the target was quickly obscured by dust reaching up to 12,000 feet. The Lancaster was hit again by cannon shells and the fuselage was ripped into, but the shells missed the crew and they returned safely.

The next day they took another Lancaster over another flying-bomb store, at L'Isle-Adam, and Geoff thought that they were beginning to push their luck. As they approached the target there was once more the chilling sound of metal smashing against the aircraft and the pungent smell of explosives filled the fuselage. The bomb bay was packed with marker flares and bombs, and they all experienced an involuntary tightening of the gut. Just one hot piece of shrapnel hitting their load would cause an instant fireball. At least death would be practically instantaneous. The heavy impact of the flak hitting the plane convinced Flash that they had been badly hit, and he rotated his turret and locked it in the 'abandon' position, thinking that the instruction to bale out was imminent. The Skipper, however, didn't feel anything wrong and decided to keep going, with everyone finally reporting in OK. They unloaded their markers and turned to escape, but as they did so they saw a stick of bombs fall from a Lancaster and strike another aircraft directly underneath it. The stricken plane was cut in half and plunged uncontrollably to the ground. No one escaped. When the Skipper finally landed, they counted fifty holes in the rear of the fuselage and the tail plane. Another lucky escape.

18

THE END GAME

There were to be no more daylight raids on the V1 sites. In fact, there was only one more raid for the Skipper and his crew on France – a target that they had already hit, Chateau Rault, a large ammunition and fuel-supply base. This attack, on 9 August, was again successful, resulting in very large fires, with several explosions seen by the attacking bombers.

In the previous month, on 25 July, they had been selected as Pathfinders for a raid on Stuttgart, their first German target since joining 97 Squadron as target-markers. They had flown to Wyton, Cambridgeshire, where they were briefed by the CO of the Pathfinder Force, Don Bennett, and they had bombed up with a load of illumination flares and target indicators. They flew almost at ground level over France; there was still enough light to see the farmworkers in their fields, who waved as they sped over.

Approaching the border with Germany, they started to gain height before making their approach to the target. Stuttgart had remained almost untouched throughout the war, because it was set in a series of natural valleys and had never been successfully targeted by Bomber Command. This raid, however, was successful and the central district of the city was devastated, with many of the public buildings destroyed.

The Stuttgart operation had come as something of a relief to Geoff, not because he relished a return to the German targets of his former tour, but because he was in a turmoil of guilt and despair. His romance with Eleanor in Aberystwyth had foundered on the rocks of her parents' intransigent opposition to the English. His visits there had become difficult, and one weekend at the start of his time in 97 Squadron when he was in Nottingham with George they visited the Victoria Ballroom, where Geoff met a beautiful woman, Irene, a nurse with striking raven hair and a translucent white complexion. They fell for each other immediately and from then on they were in each other's company during whatever leave Geoff could get. One weekend Irene came to Manuden to meet his parents. The visit went well and she was a popular figure in the local pub. Geoff was serious about her and decided that weekend to ask her if she would marry him.

Her reaction shook him to the core. She broke down in tears and said that she was already married. Her husband was in the army, serving somewhere in Italy. Geoff was heartbroken. He was also extremely ashamed, because he felt that he had betrayed her husband who, like him, was in uniform, perhaps facing as much danger as Geoff did over France and Germany. They agreed not to see each other for a month, but Geoff knew that he could not go back to the relationship, however much he desired her. George was not particularly sympathetic and worried how it would affect Geoff. 'Jesus,' he would say, 'you guys and women. Just don't get too involved with them, like me! Do me a favour, Kingy, just don't tell me you've got nothing left to live for!' Stuttgart followed quickly after and Geoff was keen to prove to George that he was still on top of his game, and also to have an operation to immerse himself in.

At the end of August the invasion and advance of Allied troops into occupied Europe had done much to shift the advantage towards the attacking bomber force. Many of the German early-warning radar stations had been destroyed and the night-fighter force had had to abandon some of its forward air bases. Not only were the night-fighter defences weakened, but the RAF bombers' target-marking capability had been improved. Mobile transmitters were able to be positioned in liberated France and the range of Gee and some of the associated radio-navigation devices had consequently been extended to more distant parts of Germany. The overall effect was that casualties in the bomber force did start to go down from the very high levels experienced at the end of the Battle of Berlin. Yet it was never going to be a picnic. On 29 August, Geoff and the crew were sent on another mission to Germany, this time to Königsberg, where they had once before carried out a precision raid to mine the docks.

They flew out on the same route that they had taken on their previous raid in 57 Squadron, and again the reception over Sweden was a token firing of anti-aircraft tracer into the sky, with apparently no attempt at accuracy. The Skipper's load this time was not mines, but a mixture of red, green and yellow target indicators, a parachute flare and one 1,000lb bomb. Identifying the target – the marshalling yards and the dock area of the town – they came in on their bombing run. They intended to drop target indicators to mark the target for the main force, but the controller, Wing Commander Woodruffe, lost all his VHF communications and Geoff was unwilling to drop without permission. George flew round again on a wide circuit to see if Vincent could establish some contact with the controller or his deputy. As they doglegged round the target the searchlights coned them. The Skipper managed to wriggle out of them, but they were then forced to make a number of runs over the target before they could get a clear aiming point.

As they came in for a fourth run, they were bounced by a single-engined Focke-Wulf 190. There was no question this time of waiting for him to misjudge his height and dive into the ground. Both Dickie and Flash started firing, shouting urgent instructions for the Skipper to corkscrew. The Skipper shouted to Geoff to get into the front turret and for Flash to keep a sharp lookout. The Focke-Wulf had begun firing, then turned away to make another pass, the shells from its cannon ripping through their wing. Fortunately, it didn't seem to have hit a fuel tank.

The initial surge of fear had been replaced with high

levels of adrenaline. They had practised on fighter-affiliation exercises so many times, but this was the first time in forty-one missions that Geoff had got behind the two .303 machine guns in the front turret.

Dickie, in the mid-upper, shouted, 'There's a second at two o'clock, Skip.' Then Flash said, 'Number one starboard beam.' There were two!

Geoff's heart was in his mouth when he heard George shout, 'Kingy, get ready to take a shot,' and the Lancaster, which had been flying at full speed, slowed dramatically, inertia pushing Geoff forward in his straps. As the Focke-Wulf shot past, it appeared in Geoff's vision from the top of his turret and he pressed the button, the machine guns filling the turret with fumes and smoke and a deafening report, the guns leaping in his hands, cartridges pouring on to the floor. It was impossible for him to see whether he had hit the enemy plane, which had disappeared ahead of them at a relative speed of about 150 m.p.h. The two other turrets were also firing and he heard Dickie shout, 'Got him, Skip.'

The Skipper had put the Lancaster in a dive, and the Merlins were going at full power again, the plane turning into the direction that the second fighter had taken after it passed under them. Dickie was convinced that he had put forty rounds into him – 'He won't be back.' Curly gave them a course for home. Their original target in Königsberg was some way away and nothing had been heard from the controller. George was going to call it a day. The excitement slowly subsided, but Geoff stayed in the front turret until they were in sight of base. They had an absolutely amazing feeling of euphoria at having beaten off two attacks. Geoff was elated, but couldn't help feeling that his luck was beginning to be pushed to the limit.

They were lucky, although George's coolness under pressure certainly had something to do with it. The fighter presence over Königsberg that night was so heavy that 15 aircraft were lost out of just 189 taking part.

Their trip to the east German port had lasted for ten hours there and back, but their delays over the target and their encounter with the fighters had stretched their resources even further. As they approached for a landing, Jock told the Skipper that they were low on fuel. They landed steady as a rock and, as they taxied towards their dispersal point, Jock announced, 'Fuel zero, Skip.' They had barely a thimbleful left. The Skipper was awarded a bar to his DFC for that effort, evading so successfully the attentions of the night fighters, which had shown on that raid that they could still be extremely deadly.

The raid was one of the most successful 5 Group attacks of the war. Severe damage was caused around the four separate aiming points selected, and it was estimated that 41 per cent of all the housing and 20 per cent of all the industrial buildings in Königsberg were destroyed.

After Königsberg there were three missions in very quick succession that showed the extent to which Bomber Command had finally solved the problem of target-marking and was, moreover, capable of massive area raids with impunity. Casualties might still be taken, but towns could now be almost effortlessly obliterated.

Geoff saw this on 11 September 1944, just three months after D-Day, when the small town of Darmstadt was the target. There was an obvious change in the ability of the German defences to defend their airspace. Bomber Command was now starting to dominate in a way that had been unheard of prior to the Allied invasion. The Skipper flew their Lancaster over Allied-occupied territory safe from any attack, passing over the Franco-Belgian border, then made a sharp course change to port at Karlsruhe and flew on to the target.

Another new method of marking and bombing was being tried out by 5 Group. Instead of bomb aimers being briefed to look for different markers for different aiming points in a town, each section of the force was told to aim for just a single marker, but was directed to run in on the target on different headings so that the bombs were distributed more evenly over the area. The illumination and marking on Darmstadt were devastatingly accurate, and Geoff and Jock between them put their markers within 30 yards of the aiming point.

Darmstadt had survived a poorly organized raid by 5 Group in August, so was relatively intact. This time the bombing was intense and concentrated. A fierce fire was started in the centre and in the district immediately to its south and east. Estimates of the dead varied considerably, but many suggest that more than 12,000 were killed that night. The town was virtually wiped out as the fires spread from the centre. There was some fighter presence on the return trip, but Jock recollected that there was not much opposition and the raid was a 'wizard Prang'.

The next night, the 12th, they were on another raid, over Stuttgart again, following the same marking and bombing technique they had applied to Darmstadt. They were the primary blind-marker on the raid, and again between them Geoff and Jock got their flares on the button. This time 97 Squadron sent thirteen aircraft and the squadron summary of events says, 'This would seem to be the most successful raid ever on this target, or perhaps the only really successful one in some thirty attempts.'

The marking went like clockwork and the main force bombed exactly at the prescribed time, 23.10. A firestorm was started, and the northern and western parts of the city were totally erased. There were 972 deaths. Despite defences consisting of eleven heavy anti-aircraft batteries, thirty-eight light flak batteries and a fighter station a few miles to the south at Echterdingden, only 2 aircraft were lost out of a total of 217 taking part.

Bremerhaven was the next town to be hit by 5 Group, on 18 September, and, as Jock wrote in his diary, the town was wiped out. Again they were spot on in dropping their flares on the aiming point. It was a perfectly executed raid. Almost every building in the centre of the town was destroyed, as were about half those in the industrial areas and the port.

The next night their target was München-Gladbach. Before the briefing that afternoon, the target-marking force had lunch with the master bomber for the raid, Wing Commander Guy Gibson VC, who had led the Dambusters in the Dams raid, and whose idea of talking his fellow pilots on to the target during the raid had initiated the concept of the controller, which had been taken up by Cochrane.

It was a potentially difficult mission because there were two aiming points, the more northerly of which was to be marked by green target indicators and bombed by a bomber force known as Green Force; the southern one was to be marked by red indicators and bombed by Red Force. The first flares were scheduled to be dropped at 21.33, but in the event there was some confusion about the target-marking. The southerly aiming point had not been marked because of a problem with the bombsight on the Mosquito and as a result of the unexpected delay all the main-force bombers dropped their bombs on the northern aiming point.

It was not a good raid for the Skipper and Geoff. Curly had been given the wrong wind speed at his briefing, which had become apparent as they approached the target. He quickly worked out some doglegs in the route to take up time and passed the course changes on to George. As the Lancaster approached the target, Geoff's radar set started to play up and wouldn't show enough detail of the target to get an accurate flare drop. Despite their precise time of arrival, they had to continue circling the target, waiting for orders from Squadron Leader Gibson to back up any target-marker. They followed his instructions, then returned to base. It was a very quiet trip for them, with almost no flak or fighters in evidence.

When they returned to Coningsby, the CO of 5 Group, Air Vice Marshal Cochrane, met them as they got out of their bus for debriefing. 'When did you last hear from Gibson?'

George was taken aback by the abruptness of the question and merely replied, 'He was yacking away and then we all packed it in, but he was there all right.' Cochrane rushed away to another crew without another word.

It was not until the next day that they were told that Guy Gibson VC had not returned from the raid and was missing. In fact, he had been shot down over Holland.

This news was overshadowed by what the adjutant told them at the same time – that their second tour had expired. They felt an enormous relief. It was just twelve months since they had taken off from East Kirkby on their first mission to Mannheim. That night they went into Boston with their ground crew and had an extremely raucous and drunken celebration. They were then given fourteen days' leave.

That was the last time they were all together. As they returned from leave to Coningsby they were all individually posted on to other units. They never flew together again and never heard from each other for the rest of the war.

'It was a very sad time for us all,' recalls Geoff. 'For the rest of the time I was in uniform I felt that there was something missing. It was the crew, the men I had shared a Lancaster with for fifty missions. We all felt like that.'

The bond, however, was not broken. It resurfaced many years later, when all that was left was memories.

Conclusion

REUNION

After his last mission for 97 Squadron in September 1944, George Laing returned to Canada. He travelled back across the Atlantic on another once luxurious ocean liner, the 43,000-ton *Ile de France*. Sadly, the Admiralty had stripped the interior of its famous art nouveau decorations and converted her to carry 9,300 passengers as a wartime troop ship. At least George was now a Flight Lieutenant, so was entitled to slightly more cabin space than he had been given on his journey on *Queen Elizabeth*.

In Canada George found himself once more at school, learning the principles of gunnery and bombing, then it was on to study navigation, then to the Central Flying School. Finally he ended up flying Lancasters in an OTU in British Columbia, passing on to the slightly younger, far less experienced bomber pilots the tricks to staying alive that he had learned over Berlin. George then went on another posting to Comox, an air base on Vancouver Island, where he was taught long-range night flying and navigation. He completed this course by making a non-stop flight across Canada from Comox in the west to Greenwood, Nova Scotia, in the east. Finally, with the war over for more than a year, he was discharged from the RCAAF in 1946 and applied for a job with Trans-Canada Airlines, or Air Canada as it was known overseas.

Although he was physically moving around a great deal, George had also decided to settle down. He had met Bernice, the English widow of an RAF pilot who had died in the war when a V2 rocket landed on his air base on the outskirts of London. She was a guest at a friend's house in Montreal, where one night George went to dinner. They played some bridge after the meal and George offered to walk her home. They continued to see each other and in November 1946 they were married.

Flying was George's life and he enjoyed his work with Air Canada, initially on domestic routes in Canada as a first officer on DC 3 Dakotas, then on the transatlantic routes, flying the civilian version of the Lancaster, the Lancastrian. These flights originated in Montreal, with a stopover in Gander for refuelling, another stop in Prestwick, then finally landing in London. The journey could take as long as thirty hours, with seventeen of those spent in the air. Soon the era of big piston engines was over and George became first officer in the cockpit of four-engined turbo prop aircraft like the Vickers Viscount and Vanguard. Later he became the captain, converting to jet aircraft. By the middle of the 1960s he was flying Air

Canada's new four-engined jet liner, the DC 8, direct from Montreal to London, then on to Frankfurt.

George had stayed in touch with Geoff and Curly via the odd letter, but one day in the spring of 1963 he walked up the garden path of a house in Bishop's Stortford in Hertfordshire and rang the bell. The door opened and there stood Geoff King. After a few moments of amazement and disbelief, Geoff burst out laughing and they clapped their arms around each other. It was the first time they had met for almost twenty years.

In 1944, when he came back from leave after the raid on München-Gladbach, Geoff was sent to 5 Group headquarters at Swinderby. After two weeks' further training on the latest radar sets, he was quickly posted back to 57 Squadron at East Kirkby to become an instructor in bombing and radar navigation. He stayed there at his old squadron, training operational crews, but also planning and briefing the aircrew who were flying on mining operations and any other special raids. He had to debrief the crews as well, going over the navigators' charts and log of the flight to work out as accurately as possible where they had laid the mines. When Germany was finally defeated, it would be Britain's responsibility to make sure that any mines that had been laid by their forces were no longer a danger to shipping. Geoff's last briefing in 57 Squadron was on 25 April 1945, when five crews were sent on a long trip to attack the SS barracks at Hitler's stronghold in Berchtesgaden in the Bavarian Alps, and on the same day other Lancasters took part in an operation to mine Oslo fjord.

When VE-Day arrived, East Kirkby became the site for the formation of Tiger Force, a long-range bomber group that the British government wanted to send to the Pacific, where it would take part in the bombing of Japan. The force, composed of ten squadrons of Lancasters, was due to depart for the Far East in November and Geoff was in charge of the navigational training programme. The navigators gained a lot of experience, because while the force was being assembled many of the crews made trips to ferry British troops home from Italy in their Lancasters. Geoff avoided his posting to the Far East with Tiger Force, however, when the B-29 Superfortresses dropped two atomic bombs on Hiroshima and Nagasaki and the war with Japan came to an abrupt end. Bomber Harris's dream of strategic air power proving to be the final winning weapon had finally been realized.

While at East Kirkby Geoff had met a WAAF, Mary, the widow of a rear gunner who had been killed earlier in the war when his Lancaster was shot down. Geoff had offered her a spare set of collar studs one morning to save her from being put on a charge and after this their interest in each other flourished to the extent that after six weeks they were married.

Despite being offered a permanent commission in the post-war RAF, Geoff cut his links with flying and the armed forces and returned to civilian life in March 1946. For some weeks he was like a fish out of water, with no idea what he wanted to do or what he could do. With a wife and a young daughter, who had been born on 25 February that year, the need to find work was pressing. By chance, while he was visiting his family at Manuden, he was offered a job as a farm manager for a company that ran two farms in Essex. He took it and within a few more years the company bought up several adjoining farms to become a large mixed arable farm of over 3,000 acres in Essex and Hertfordshire. It was a successful career, but eventually he again wanted a change. By the time that George and Geoff looked at each other on Geoff's doorstep he had left the farming business and was the manager of a large furnishing company. It was a very different life from flying over Berlin.

The other members of the crew of C Charlie had been scattered to the far corners of the globe for a while. Independently, Geoff and George had each attempted to keep up some contact with them over the years. Flight Lieutenant Roy Davis, Curly the navigator, had left the RAF as soon as he could. When his days in a front-line squadron were over, he decided to return to his old job in ICI. It was a reserved occupation, so he was able to leave the RAF before the war ended. It meant of course that he could stay closer to his wife, Laura. They had two children and he continued to work for ICI in Hyde in Cheshire for many years before moving to the Isle of Man, where he worked for a small car company. His love of fast motorcycles never left him and he was an enthusiastic marshal for the Isle of Man TT races – another reason why he eventually persuaded Laura that they should go to live there.

Jock, Flight Sergeant Robbie Burns, remained in 97 Squadron and took part in the fire-bombing of Dresden on

13 February 1945. His view of the city after the attack impressed him more than anything he had seen over Berlin or on any of the other raids in which he had taken part. He would sometimes describe the sight of 'a whole city in flames' to his family after the war. He was awarded the Distinguished Flying Medal in February 1945, and in May he became an instructor in No. 1645 Heavy Conversion Unit, which was flying Stirlings. He then went to Canada, where he worked in Transport Command as a senior engineer. Finally, he found himself in San Diego, southern California, at the Consolidated Aircraft Company, who were testing a more advanced version of the B-24 Liberator with a single tail and an even longer range than the aircraft that had been the mainstay of the US Eighth Air Force in Britain. Jock was compiling the maintenance manuals for the RAF, which was expecting to use these aircraft in the Pacific. As with Tiger Force, the Royal Air Force abandoned these plans with the Japanese surrender and Jock returned to the UK, where he too was demobilized in 1946. He went to work for Vickers-Armstrong at their Brooklands factory, but then opened up a garage with his brother before moving back home to Kirkcudbright.

Vincent Day, the wireless operator, also stayed in 97 Squadron and continued on operations with Jock. He too took part in the Dresden raid, but a few weeks later he was shot down – not over Germany, but over Coningsby when his Lancaster was preparing to land. A German intruder had infiltrated UK airspace and shot down several bombers on their approach to the airfield. Vin parachuted out of the burning aircraft. He said later that hanging from a parachute in the darkness, looking at several burning air-craft on the ground, not knowing where he was going to land, was something that he never wanted to repeat. He was Mentioned in Dispatches and awarded a Distinguished Flying Medal in April 1945.

Flash, Frank Green, the mid-upper gunner, was awarded a Distinguished Flying Cross in 1945 but was upset that no one from his old crew or family was able to get there for the ceremony. When he returned to Australia, he married Gwen, the girl he had met just before he had left for the UK. He could not settle down, however, and was affected perhaps more than anyone else in the crew of C Charlie by his experiences over Germany. First he tried to work for the Australian post office, opening up a branch near his old family farm in Victoria, but found that he could not deal with the demands of the customers and the hierarchy. He never wanted to talk very much about his war, except to say that the crew had become like a second family for him and that he had enjoyed visits to the farm with Geoff and the regular weekends in Boston on leave. Other than that, he remained quiet, and somewhat withdrawn. Later he moved to Queensland, where he and Gwen bought an orchard, which they enlarged over the years, producing cherries and some other fruit.

George eventually tracked down Flash and paid him a visit. They remained talking for hours in the sun and, according to Gwen, his mood seemed to lighten after this. George made several visits over the years, sometimes with Bernice, as though he knew it was important for Flash to keep in touch with his old crew. However, he would never talk about his time in Bomber Command with anyone other than George, and he died with his family – Gwen and three daughters – mostly unaware of what he had done in his twelve months with 57 and 97 Squadrons.

Tommy, Sidney Thomas, their first rear gunner, died in an air crash soon after the war, and neither George nor Geoff was ever able to get in touch with Dickie Polson again.

In 1988 a museum and heritage centre was set up at the now disused East Kirkby airfield and a Lancaster bomber was stationed there as part of a collection of Second World War aeroplanes. Geoff, George, Curly and Jock attended for a reunion of old 57 Squadron members. The Lancaster, with C for Charlie painted on one side of the fuselage, is kept in working order. Many former wartime bombers and fighters are preserved throughout Britain and America and prove increasingly popular in air displays and museums.

The role of Bomber Command in the war, however, has come under increasing scrutiny, and the morality of mass bomber attacks and their devastating effects on the civilian population is often now strongly criticized. Geoff has sometimes been asked how he can live with his conscience. In old age, knowing with the benefit of hindsight what havoc he was wreaking on the cities he held in his bomb-sight, he says, 'My conscience is sometimes heavy with sadness.' In 1939, and when he started flying in 1943, he felt fully justified in what he was doing. After the raids on Coventry and London, and the occupation of the whole of Europe, he had no qualms about bombing Germany. What, he asks, would have happened if Bomber Command had not mounted the campaign that it did? Would Germany have been defeated? The damage caused by Bomber Command might not have been as great or as crucial as Bomber Harris claimed, but the raids, the very threat that Bomber Command posed, cost Germany enormous resources that it could not devote to the war against Russia, or in the Mediterranean.

George Laing has no doubts about what he did. He enjoyed his time as a bomber pilot, or so he has claimed. In all his flying career, culminating as captain of a Boeing 747, the flying he did in Bomber Command was the most taxing and most demanding of all. 'It was the highlight of my life. I had fun from day one to day ten. I really enjoyed it.'

He also has no qualms about the results. He remembers his father telling him a story about the end of the First World War, when as a soldier he walked from Mons to Cologne, a march that took him three days. He and thousands of other Canadian troops had fought and died for four years in trenches and thick mud. Walking into Cologne, George's father recalled that the lights worked, the streetcars ran and the shops were open. This was not the case at the end of the Second World War. The Allies did not fight in Europe until 1944, but Germany was nevertheless being devastated.

George travelled in Germany and met with many former Luftwaffe officers in the 1950s and 1960s. He believed that the damage caused by the bombing campaign helped shorten the war, and that it did weaken Hitler and the Nazi government. On a visit to Mainz after the war, a minister told him that after an air raid in 1941 the public rallied round to rebuild a church, the only thing in the town that had been damaged by the bombs. In 1943 the church was bombed again during a raid on Frankfurt, but the funds were never found to repair it. 'The people,' says George, 'were getting tired, and disillusioned, and had troubles of their own. Of course the bombing campaign shortened the war.'

The arguments will continue long after all of the participants are gone. At the time of writing, only Geoff and George are left alive out of the eight crew members who served together in 57 and 97 Squadrons. George is seriously ill, and the two of them will never meet again. Of course the grand strategy, the morality, of what they did in Bomber Command was important to them, as were the great swathes of their lives that they spent at work and with their families after the war was won. Separate from all that, however, and what stayed with them until the end, was the friendship, trust and loyalty that they found in a bomber over Berlin.

BIBLIOGRAPHY

Barker, Ralph. *The Thousand Plan*, Chatto and Windus, London, 1965.

Bennett, Air Vice Marshal D. C. T. *Pathfinders*, Frank Muller Ltd, London, 1958.

Bishop, Patrick. *Bomber Boys*, Harper Press, London, 2007.

Blucke, Air Vice Marshal R. S. *Employment of Strategic Forces in Support of Land Ops*, Royal Air Force Museum Collection, London, 1946.

Calder, Angus. *The People's War*, Jonathan Cape, London, 1969.

Cheshire, Group Captain Leonard VC. *Bomber Pilot*, Goodall Publications Ltd, London, 1943.

Cooper, Alan. *Target Leipzig*, Pen and Sword Aviation, Barnsley, 2009.

Frankland, Noble. *The Bombing Offensive Against*

Germany, Faber & Faber, London, 1965.

Gilbert, Martin. *Finest Hour: Winston Churchill 1939–1941*, Heineman, London, 1983.

Hastings, Max. *Bomber Command*, Michael Joseph, London, 1979.

Harris, Air Chief Marshal Sir Arthur. *Despatch on War Operations 23rd Feb 1942 to 8th May 1945*, ed. Sebastian Cox, Frank Cass Studies in Air Power, London, 1995.

Lawrence, W. J. *No 5 Bomber Group RAF*, Faber & Faber, London, 1952.

McKinstry, Leo. *Lancaster*, John Murray, London, 2009.

Middlebrook, Martin. *The Berlin Raids*, Viking, London, 1988.

Peden, Murray. *A Thousand Shall Fall*, Stoddart, Toronto, 1988.

Richards, Denis. *Portal of Hungerford*, Heinemann, London, 1977.

Royal Air Force Centre for Air Power Studies. *The RAF in the Bomber Offensive Against Germany Vol. II: Restricted Bombing Sept 1939–May 1940*, MLRS Books, Buxton, 1953.

Searsby, Sir John. *The Bomber Battle for Berlin*, Airlife Publishing Ltd, London, 1991.

Sereny, Gitta. *Albert Speer: His Battle with Truth*, Knopf, New York, 1995.

Wakelam, Randal T. *The Science of Bombing*, University of Toronto Press, Toronto, 2009.

Wilson, Kevin. *Bomber Boys*, Weidenfeld & Nicolson, London, 2005.

National Archives Publications. *The Rise and Fall of the German Air Force 1933–1945*, 2008.

National Archive Documents on 57 Squadron, 97 Squadron and 5 Group: AIR 27/538, 27/539, 27/768, 14/754, 14/804, 14/827, 14/868, 14/3943, 16/159.

PICTURE ACKNOWLEDGEMENTS

All photos were kindly supplied by Geoff King except where otherwise credited:

Wellington and Tiger Moth at the training school, Desford, Leicstershire: Imperial War Museum CH 7936

Lancaster III bomber: Imperial War Museum CH 12346; RAF engine fitters, 1942: Imperial War Museum CH 6600

Lancasters lined up: Imperial War Museum CL 4214; 'Jane Flags 'em Down': © mirrorpix; factory worker producing MIRROR: Imperial War Museum E(MOS) 1451; German radar device: © ullsteinbild/TopFoto/TopFoto.co.uk; radar scan of a German town: © ullsteinbild/TopFoto/ TopFoto.co.uk; Junkers 88 equipped with radar: Bundesarchiv, Bild 101I-476-2090-02A

Background: night raid on Hanover: Imperial War Museum C 3898; Lancaster bomber: Imperial War Museum CH 11929; Berlin burning, July 1944: Bundesarchiv, Bild 183-J30142; German searchlight: Bundesarchiv, Bild 146-1977-091-13A; Lancaster bomber in German searchlight: © ullsteinbild/TopFoto/TopFoto.co.uk

Background: Lancaster bomber, Lincolnshire Aviation Heritage Centre, East Kirby: photo Charlie Waite

INDEX

Aachen, bombing raids, 157, 251
Aberystwyth, No. 6 Initial Training
    Wing, 93–4
Admiral Scheer, German cruiser, 77
Afrika Korps, 56
Air Canada, 281–2
Air Ministry: awareness of casualties,
    124; criticisms of Harris, 195; Gee
    system, 126; planners, 110;
    Recruitment Office, 41; response
    to bomber losses, 78; strategy, 125
Airspeed Oxford trainer ('Oxbox'),
    89–90, 101
Alster, River, 164
Alvis works, 68, 69
anti-aircraft defences: Berlin, 5, 122,
    198–200; bombed, 149; confused
    by Window, 163; Coventry, 69;
    German, 115–16, 140; Hanover,
    170, 171; Leipzig, 241; London,
    261; radar-controlled, 134, 145–6,
    160, 266; Stuttgart, 183, 277;
    Swedish, 249, 273
Argus aircraft works, 196
Armstrong Whitworth Whitley, *see*
    Whitley bombers

Austen, Flight Sergeant, 152
Avro, designs, 106
Avro Lancaster, *see* Lancaster bombers
Avro Manchester, *see* Manchester
    bombers

B-17 Flying Fortress bombers, 8–9,
    194, 262
B-21 bombers, 9
B-24 Liberator bombers, 194, 262, 285
B-29 Superfortress bombers, 283
Baker, Pilot Officer, 200–1
Battle of Britain, 8, 46, 86
Beaufighter, 56
Belgium: bomber route, 198, 226;
    factories, 166; German air bases,
    71; German invasion, 44, 81
Bennett, Don, 137, 171, 179, 255, 256,
    270
Berlin: Battle of, 211, 240, 242, 272;
    bomb damage, 218–19, 231–2,
    238–9; Bomber Command
    strategy, 185, 193–7, 216–17, 233,
    240, 241–2; British view of raids,
    124; defences, 4, 5, 122, 193,
    198–9, 212–15, 231, 239–40; raid

Berlin: Battle of (*cont.*)
(August 1940), 60–1; raid
(November 1941), 118–19, 121;
raids (November 1943) 196–201,
205, 212; raids (December 1943),
204–11, 212, 216, 219–20; raids
(January 1944), 225–38; raid
(February 1944), 238–40; raids
(March 1944), 241; spoof raid,
232–3; target, 4–5
Bichelonne, Jean, 166
Billancourt, Renault factory, 126–8,
131, 171, 195
Birmingham, German bombing, 67, 69
Blenheim bombers, 47, 48, 76–7, 82,
120, 133
Blitz, 2, 3, 69, 74, 125
Blohm & Voss shipyards, 167
BMW works, 196
Bochum, 157, 174–7
Boden, Peter, 163
Bomber Command: 1 Group, 133, 178;
2 Group, 133; 3 Group, 119, 133,
187; 5 Group, 60–1, 119, 135, 140,
171, 178, 188, 195, 230, 256, 261,
266–7, 275, 276, 282; 6 Group,
187; 8 Group, 255, 256; accuracy
issues, 84, 110–11, 111–15, 127,
265; aircraft numbers, 46, 196–7;
aircraft types, 46–9; Berlin
strategy, 60–1, 193–7; commander-
in-chief, 82, 109, 123, 124; crew
selection, 99–101; criticisms of
war role, 287–9; daylight raids,
262; heavy bombers, 9, 47, 123,
136; HQ, 130, 132, 218, 225, 233;
influence on war, 288–9; morale,
124, 134, 137, 159, 167, 264–5;
Operational Research Section,
159–60, 171, 243; propaganda
leafleting, 79–81; strategy, 2–3,
74–7, 81–6, 109–10, 262, 266,
287–9; target-marking unit, 138,
256–7, 267; training, 45, 48–9;
wartime crises, 58
Boozer device, 229–30
Bosch sparkplug factory, 196
Boulton Paul Defiant aircraft, 173–4

Boulton Paul Overstrand aircraft, 49
Bourdon, Pilot Officer, 152
Bremen: fighter forces, 229; oil refinery
bombing, 83; propaganda leaflets,
79; radar, 117
Bremerhaven, bombing raid, 277
Brighton, RAF training, 93
Bristol Beaufighter, 56
Bristol Blenheim, *see* Blenheim
bombers
Bristol Pegasus engine, 43, 49, 51–2
British Commonwealth Air Training
Plan, 33, 73
British Expeditionary Force, 83
British Field Forces, 261
Brocks flares, 137
Brunsbüttel, battleship bombing raid,
76–7
Brunswick, bombing raid, 257–8
Bruntingthorpe, RAF, 105
Burns, Robert 'Jock', Warrant Officer:
Aachen aborted mission, 251–2;
background, 12, 107; Berlin raids,
197–200, 204–10, 219–24, 225–40;
Bochum raid, 175–7; bomb aimer,
257, 258, 259; Bremerhaven raid,
277; Brunswick raid, 257–8; career
in RAF, 285; Clermont-Ferrand
raid, 244; diary, 177, 186, 223,
224, 277; Distinguished Flying
Medal, 285; Dresden raid, 284–5;
Düsseldorf raid, 186–9;
employment, 285; end of first
tour, 252–3, 254–5; end of second
tour, 279; first Lancaster mission,
14–15, 143, 146–52, 168, 279;
flight engineer, 4, 12, 107, 257;
formation flying, 262–3, 265;
Frankfurt aborted mission, 180–3,
184; Frankfurt raids, 217–18,
245–8; Hagen raid, 177; Hanover
raid, 171–2; Joigny-Laroche
daylight raid, 266; Königsberg
raids, 249–51, 272–5; Lancaster C
Charlie, 189–93; Modane raid,
192–3, 244; München-Gladbach
raid, 277–8; Munich raid, 177–80;
Normandy raids (1944), 260–1;

Pathfinder training, 255–7; postwar life, 285; reunion of 57 Squadron, 287; Ruhr raid, 248; St-Valéry-en-Caux raid, 259; social life, 203, 216; Stuttgart raids, 183–4, 244, 270–1, 277; training, 107; V1 site raids, 267–9
Butt, D. M., 113–14
Butt Report, 113–15

Caen, raid on bridges, 261
Cardington, RAF, 42
Carter, Wing Commander, 259, 260, 263
Castagnola, Pilot Officer, 231–2
casualties: accidents, 51, 174, 263; attitudes to losses, 121–3, 124, 159–60; Bomber Command aircrew in WWII, 6; causes, 116, 159–60; operations against German advance, 82; operations against German warships, 76–7; raids (1941), 118–19, 121; raids (1942), 136; raids (1943), 151–2, 159–60, 163, 176, 188, 200–1, 218, 233; raids (1944), 233, 237, 241, 242
Cessna Crane, 35–6, 37, 89
Chadwick, Harold, 220
Chadwick, Roy, 106
Chamberlain, Neville, 40
Chambers, Flight Lieutenant, 260
Chateau Rault, munitions depot bombing, 261, 270
Chatten, Flight Lieutenant, 258
Cherwell, Frederick Lindemann, Lord, 112–13
Cheshire, Leonard, Group Captain, 255
Church Lawford, RAF, 89–93
Churchill, Winston: attitude to Bomber Command losses, 121–2; Berlin bombing, 60, 194; bomber force funding, 112; bombing strategy concerns, 114–15, 121–2, 194; Luftwaffe strategy against, 71; on thousand-bomber raid, 136; Window strategy, 161

Clements, Flying Officer, 188
Clermont-Ferrand, bombing raid, 244
Cochrane, Ralph, Air Vice Marshal: CO 5 Group, 140, 171; Dambuster strategy, 255; formation flying, 262; Gibson's death, 278–9; Reid's VC award, 189; target-marking issues, 171, 178, 179, 256
Cologne: bomb damage, 288; bombing raids, 118–19, 158, 194; diversionary raid, 186, 187, 189; thousand-bomber raid, 3, 133–6, 158, 185, 211, 238
Coman, Flight Sergeant, 263
Coningsby, 54 Base, 256, 258, 261, 278–9, 285
Consolidated Aircraft Company, 285
Coventry: Blitz damage, 2, 3, 68–70; effects of Blitz on population, 70, 132; Geoff King's view of bombing, 287; Luftwaffe strategy, 67, 69, 124
Culmont-Chalindrey, raid, 265
Curran, Joan, 160–1

D-Day landings, 6, 7, 260, 266
Daily Express, 157
Daily Mirror, 98
Daimler-Benz, 196
Daimler works, 68, 69
Dambusters (617 Squadron), 171, 189, 195, 255, 277
Dams raids, 171, 195, 255, 277
Danzig, Bay of, 248–9
Darmstadt, bombing raids, 276
Davis, Laura, 99, 202–3, 236
Davis, Roy 'Curly', Flight Lieutenant: Aachen aborted mission, 251–2; appearance, 9; background, 9, 98; Berlin raids, 197–200, 204–10, 219–24, 225–40; Bochum raid, 175–7; Bomber Command crew selection, 100–1; Bremerhaven raid, 277; Brunswick raid, 257–8; Clermont-Ferrand raid, 244; Darmstadt raid, 276; Düsseldorf raid, 186–9; at East Kirkby air base, 141; education, 98–9;

Davis, Roy 'Curly' (*cont.*)
employment, 284; end of first
tour, 252–3, 254–5; end of second
tour, 279; first Lancaster mission,
14–15, 145–7, 149–52, 168, 279;
formation flying, 263; Frankfurt
aborted mission, 180–3, 184;
Frankfurt raids, 217–18, 245–8;
girlfriend, 99, 202–3, 236; Hagen
raid, 177; Hanover raid, 171–2;
Joigny-Laroche daylight raid, 266;
Königsberg raids, 249–51, 272–5;
Lancaster C Charlie, 189–93;
marriage, 236, 238, 284; Modane
raid, 192–3, 244; München-
Gladbach raid, 277–8; Munich
raid, 177–80; navigator, 4, 10, 100,
102, 149; Normandy raids (1944),
260–1; Pathfinder training, 255–7;
postwar contact with Geoff and
George, 282, 284; postwar life,
284; reunion of 57 Squadron, 287;
Ruhr raid, 248; St-Valéry-en-Caux
raid, 259; social life, 202–4;
Stuttgart raids, 183–4, 244, 270–1,
277; V1 site raids, 267–9
Day, Vincent 'Vin', Warrant Officer
First Class: Aachen aborted
mission, 251–2; Berlin raids,
197–200, 204–10, 219–24, 225–40;
Bochum raid, 175–7; Bomber
Command crew selection, 100–1;
Bremerhaven raid, 277; Brunswick
raid, 257–8; Clermont-Ferrand
raid, 244; Darmstadt raid, 276;
Distinguished Flying Medal, 286;
Dresden raid, 285; Düsseldorf
raid, 186–9; end of first tour,
252–3, 254–5; end of second tour,
279; first Lancaster mission,
14–15, 146, 149–52, 168, 279;
formation flying, 263; Frankfurt
aborted mission, 180–3, 184;
Frankfurt raids, 217–18, 245–8;
Hagen raid, 177; Hanover raid,
171–2; Joigny-Laroche daylight
raid, 266; Königsberg raids,
249–51, 272–5; Lancaster C

Charlie, 189–93; Modane raid,
192–3, 244; München-Gladbach
raid, 277–8; Munich raid, 177–80;
Normandy raids (1944), 260–1;
Pathfinder training, 255–7; Ruhr
raid, 248; St-Valéry-en-Caux raid,
259; shot down, 285–6; Stuttgart
raids, 183–4, 244, 270–1, 277; V1
site raids, 267–9; wireless operator,
4, 10, 100, 149
DC 3 Dakota aircraft, 281
DC 8 jet liner, 282
de Havilland Gipsy engine, 43
de Havilland Mosquito, *see* Mosquito
aircraft
decorations, 223, 243, 259, 275, 285,
286
decoy fires, 129, 218
Denmark: bomber route, 237, 238, 239,
249; fall, 63; German aircraft, 214,
239; German fleet, 76; German
invasion, 44, 81; propaganda
leaflets, 79
Desford, No. 7 Elementary Flying
Training School, 94–5
Dobbin, George, 99
Dornier: 17 bomber, 59, 62; 217
aircraft, 215; factory, 196
Dortmund, bombing raids, 157
Dortmund–Ems Canal: bombing raid,
171, 255; bombing target, 85
Dresden, fire-bombing, 284–5
Duff, Pilot Officer, 142–3
Duisburg, bombing raids, 157
Dumfries, bomb aimer training, 95–7
Duncan, Flight Lieutenant, 264
Dunkirk, evacuation, 83
Düsseldorf, bombing raids, 158, 186–9

Eaker, Ira, Lieutenant General, 194
East Kirkby air base: arrival, 139–40;
billets, 139–40; crew of Lancaster
E Edward, 8–14; diversion from,
172, 246; fog, 172, 185; Geoff
King's posting, 282; Mannheim
mission, 144; museum and
heritage centre, 287; returning to,
150–2, 173–4, 189, 209, 223,

227–8, 230, 254; Ruhr mission, 248; social life, 202; training, 141–3
Eindhoven, Philips factory, 259
Elizabeth, Queen, 30
Emden, German cruiser, 77
Erbar sugar factory, 121
Essen: bombing raids, 128–9, 131, 156–7, 159, 248; target-finding strategy, 126, 128, 129, 156, 248
Evans, Evan, Group Captain, 264

Fairey Battle bombers, 47, 48, 82
Falck, Wolfgang, Major, 115
Fighter Command, 45–6, 133, 161
First World War, 18, 27, 31, 38, 288
Fisher, Wing Commander, 174
Flensburg, bombing raid, 138
Focke-Wulf 190: aircraft, 213, 250, 273–4; factory, 196
France: Allied invasion, 259–60, 266; British bombing raids, 6, 244, 259–61, 270, 272; British evacuation, 67, 83; British forced landings, 79; factories, 166; fall (1940), 44, 61; German airfields, 70, 71; German forces, 62, 82; German invasion, 44, 61, 81; WWI, 31; WWII, 32, 75
Frankenthal, bombed by mistake, 151
Frankfurt: bombing raids, 180–3, 217–18, 245–6; propaganda leaflets, 80; 'spoof' raid, 196
French aircrew, 44

Gee: Cologne raid, 134; Curly's use of, 149, 261; Essen raids, 128–9; GH system, 187; limitations, 126, 153, 155; Lübeck raid, 131; range, 126, 133, 160, 191, 272; Renault factory raid, 126–7; system, 125–6, 154; use of, 132
Gee, Bill, Flight Lieutenant, 263
Gelsenkirchen: bombing raids, 157; oil plants, 83, 110–11
George VI, King, 30
German-American Petroleum company, 121
GH blind-bombing system, 187

Gibson, Guy, Wing Commander, 277–9
Gobbie, Flight Lieutenant, 200
Goering, Hermann, Reichsmarschall, 67, 115
Gomorrah, Operation, 162
Green, Frank 'Flash', Warrant Officer First Class: Aachen aborted mission, 251–2; background, 10–11, 106–7; Berlin raids, 197–200, 204–10, 219–24, 225–40; Bochum raid, 175–7; Bremerhaven raid, 277; Brunswick raid, 257–8; Clermont-Ferrand raid, 244; Darmstadt raid, 276; DFC, 286; Düsseldorf raid, 186–9; end of first tour, 252–3, 254–5; end of second tour, 279; first Lancaster mission, 14–15, 146–52, 168, 279; formation flying, 263; Frankfurt aborted mission, 180–3, 184; Frankfurt raids, 217–18, 245–8; Hagen raid, 177; Hanover raid, 171–2; Joigny-Laroche daylight raid, 266; Königsberg harbour raid, 249–51; Lancaster C Charlie, 189–93; marriage, 286; mid-upper gunner, 4, 10–11, 107; Modane raid, 192–3, 244; München-Gladbach raid, 277–8; Munich raid, 177–80; Normandy raids (1944), 260–1; Pathfinder training, 255–7; postwar contact with George, 286–7; postwar life, 286–7; Ruhr raid, 248; St-Valéry-en-Caux raid, 259; social life, 235–6; Stuttgart raids, 183–4, 244, 270–1, 277; V1 site raids, 267–9
Guthrie, Archie, 31, 32, 78

H2S ground-mapping radar: Geoff's use of, 185, 190–2, 197–8, 206, 207, 229, 256; German defences, 214–15; Hamburg raids, 162, 163, 167; operation of, 154, 163, 170, 195, 256; Pathfinder Force, 155, 162, 176, 178, 191, 211, 220, 227; secrecy, 167; system, 154, 190–1; testing, 160

Hagen, bombing raid, 177
Halifax bombers: Berlin raids, 205,
    238; Bomber Command, 185;
    Hamburg raid, 162; losses, 159;
    Mannheim diversionary raid, 196;
    mid-upper gun turret, 95;
    operation height, 106; Pathfinder
    Force, 137
Hamborn, bombed by mistake, 129
Hamburg: bombing raids, 161–6, 194,
    212, 213; death toll, 165; fire-
    raising raids, 3, 163–6; oil plant
    bombing, 83, 111; propaganda
    leaflets, 79; RAF bombing
    strategy, 133, 160–1; recovery from
    raids, 167; spoof raid, 226
Hampden bombers: Berlin raids, 60,
    63; design, 47; German fleet
    missions, 76, 77; Hamburg and
    Bremen raids, 83; losses, 51;
    Mannheim-Ludwigshafen raid,
    120; role of observer, 95; training,
    48
Handley Page Halifax, see Halifax
    bombers
Handley Page Hampden, see Hampden
    bombers
Handley Page Harrow, 49
Hanover, 79, 141–2, 168, 170–3, 245
Hargrave, Pilot Officer, 174
Harris, Sir Arthur: attitude to losses,
    159, 161; Berlin bombing, 193,
    196, 233, 240; Bomber Command
    c-in-c, 123, 124–5; bombing
    strategy, 132–3, 136–8, 153–5, 167,
    193–6, 262, 266, 283, 288; Cologne
    raid, 133–6; effectiveness of raids,
    132; Gee system, 125, 128, 129,
    132, 153; Lübeck raid, 130;
    modernization of Bomber
    Command, 3, 125; Oboe system,
    153–5, 160; Pathfinder Force, 171,
    178, 210; target-marking unit, 267;
    Window, 160–1
Heinkel: 111 bomber, 59, 62, 67–8, 70;
    works, 131–2, 196
Heligoland, 77
Heward, Wing Commander, 263–4

High Wycombe, Bomber Command
    HQ, 130, 132, 218, 225, 233
Hiroshima, atomic bomb, 283
Hitler, Adolf, 63–4, 75, 166, 167, 282,
    288
Hogan, Pilot Officer, 152
Holland: bomber route, 134, 187, 205,
    207, 221, 233–4; factories, 166;
    German airfields, 237; German
    invasion, 44, 61, 63, 81; radar
    aerials, 117; V1 launch sites, 267
Horder, Lord, 24–5
Hurricane fighters, 40–1, 45, 53, 62, 63

icing, 48, 79–80, 122
IG Farben, 119, 151
Ile de France (liner), 280
Irish Sea, night exercises, 107
Ivens, Group Captain, 53

Jefferies, Flight Lieutenant, 189
Jespersen, Lieutenant, 260
Joigny-Laroche, raid on marshalling
    yard, 266
Junker: 87 'Stuka' dive bombers, 59,
    62; 88 twin-engine aircraft, 116,
    172, 213, 215, 226, 230, 258, 260

Kain, George, 104–5, 183
Kammhuber, Josef, General, 116
Kassel, bomb damage, 196; bombing
    target, 157
Keitel, Field Marshal, 61
Kestrel engine, see Rolls-Royce Kestrel
Kiel, radar, 117
Killian, Warrant Officer, 53
King, Geoff 'Kingy': Aachen aborted
    mission, 251–2; appearance, 11,
    72; attitude to fear, 168–9;
    background, 4, 17–20, 104–5;
    Berlin raids, 197–200, 204–10,
    219–24, 225–40; Bochum raid,
    175–7; bomb aimer, 11–12, 102,
    148–9, 175, 257; bomb aimer
    training, 96–7; Bomber Command
    crew selection, 100–1; Bomber
    Command posting to Manby,
    45–56, 58, 73–4, 107; Bremerhaven

raid, 277; Brunswick raid, 257–8;
childhood, 17–22; Clermont-
Ferrand raid, 244; close-formation
flying, 263; Culmont-Chalindrey
raid, 265; Darmstadt raid, 276;
DFC, 259; Düsseldorf raid,
186–9; at East Kirkby air base,
139–42, 282–3; education, 20, 23;
emergency pilot, 103–4;
employment, 23–4, 25–6, 39–42,
284; end of first tour, 252–3,
254–5; end of second tour, 279;
first Lancaster mission, 14–15,
143–52, 168, 279; flight mechanic
qualification, 45; Frankfurt
aborted mission, 180–3, 184;
Frankfurt raids, 217–18, 245–8;
girlfriends, 93, 202–3, 236, 271–2;
H2S set, 185, 190–2, 197–8, 206,
207, 229, 256; Hagen raid, 177;
Hanover raid, 171–2; health, 24–5,
94; instructor on bombing and
radar navigation, 282–3; Joigny-
Laroche daylight raid, 266;
Königsberg raids, 249–51, 272–5;
Lancaster C Charlie, 189–93;
length of training, 107; lucky belt,
180, 210; marriage, 283; Modane
raid, 192–3, 244; München-
Gladbach raid, 277–8, 282;
Munich raid, 177–80; Normandy
raids (1944), 260–1; Pathfinder
training, 255–7; pilot officer
commission, 97; pilot training,
94–5, 97, 104; postwar contact
with Curly and George, 282, 284;
postwar life, 283–4; promotion to
flying officer, 107; RAF aircrew
training, 56–7, 73, 93–7; RAF
mechanic training, 42–5, 58; RAF
recruitment, 41–2; retirement, 7–8;
reunion of 57 Squadron, 287;
reunion with George, 282; Ruhr
raid, 248; St-Valéry-en-Caux raid,
259; social life, 202–4, 230–1,
235–6; Stuttgart raids, 183–4, 244,
270–1, 277; V1 site raids, 267–9;
view of Bomber Command

strategy, 287–8; volunteering for
Bomber Command, 3, 14;
weekend leave, 104–5; Wellington
training course, 101–5
Knickebein navigation system, 60, 67,
125

Königsberg, bombing raids, 249–51,
272–5
Krefeld, bomb damage, 157
Krupps works, 126, 128–9, 130, 156–7

Laing, Charles, 27–8, 38
Laing, Elizabeth, 27–30, 37–8
Laing, George, Flight Lieutenant:
Aachen aborted mission, 251–2;
Air Canada career, 281–2; air
training, 33–8, 73; appearance, 9,
38, 203; attitude to fear, 168–9;
background, 9, 27–8; Berlin raids,
197–200, 204–10, 219–24; Bochum
raid, 175–7; Bremerhaven raid,
277; Brunswick raid, 257–8;
character, 28, 103, 180–1, 272;
childhood, 28–30; Clermont-
Ferrand raid, 244; close-formation
flying, 262–3; crew selection,
99–101; Culmont-Chalindrey raid,
265; Darmstadt raid, 276; DFC
and bar, 225, 243, 275; Düsseldorf
raid, 186–9; at East Kirkby air
base, 140–1; education, 28–9, 31,
32–3; employment, 28, 281; end of
first tour, 252–3, 254–5; end of
second tour, 279; first Lancaster
mission, 14–15, 143–52, 168, 279;
Frankfurt aborted mission, 180–3,
184; Frankfurt raids, 217–18,
245–8; Hagen raid, 177; Hanover
raid, 171–2; health, 28; Joigny-
Laroche daylight raid, 266;
Königsberg raids, 249–51, 272–5;
Lancaster C Charlie, 189–93;
Lancaster training, 106–7; length
of training, 107; Manchester
training, 105–6; marriage, 281;
Modane raid, 192–3, 244;
München-Gladbach

King, Geoff 'Kingy' (*cont.*)
raid, 277–8; Munich raid, 177–80;
Normandy raids (1944), 260–1;
Pathfinder training, 255–7;
postwar contact with Curly and
Geoff, 282, 284; postwar life,
281–2; RAF training, 89–93;
return to Canada, 280–1; reunion
of 57 Squadron, 287; reunion with
Geoff, 282; Royal Canadian Air
Force, 33–4, 262, 280–1; Ruhr
raid, 248; St-Valéry-en-Caux raid,
259; skipper, 1, 4, 9, 101–2; social
life, 202, 203, 235–6, 272; sports,
29; Stuttgart raids, 183–4, 244,
270–1, 277; V1 site raids, 267–9;
view of Bomber Command
strategy, 288–9; voyage to Britain,
87–9; weekend leave, 104;
Wellington training course,
101–4

Lancaster bombers: Berlin raids, 185,
205; bomb aimer, 95; bomb
payload, 205; Cologne raids, 135,
186; crew, 95; crew training, 108;
damaged, 216; daylight raids, 262,
265–6; design, 106; engines, 8;
escape hatches, 222; formation
flying, 262–3, 265; gunners, 95;
Hamburg raid, 162; Hanover raid,
141–2; layout, 9–12; losses, 159,
216, 226, 258, 268–9; navigator,
95; operation height, 155;
Pathfinder Force, 137, 178; take-
off, 12–14; Tiger Force, 283
Lancaster C Charlie: Berlin raids,
197–201, 205–10, 219–24, 227,
229, 230–3, 237–40; Boozer device,
229–30; Clermont-Ferrand raid,
243–4; crash landing, 246–8;
damage from Berlin raid, 209–10;
exercises, 216; Frankfurt raids,
217–18, 245–6; H2S set, 190–1;
landing with two engines out,
222–4, 225; Leipzig raid, 240–1;
mining raid, 248–51; Modane
raid, 192; museum piece, 287; new

aircraft, 248; oil pressure problem,
233–4
Lancaster D Dog, 177
Lancaster E Edward, 8, 9–15, 143–52
Lancaster F Freddie, 175–6
Lancaster G George, 187–9
Lancaster H Harry, 170–3
Lancaster I Ink, 178–83, 184, 187
Lancaster S Sugar, 142–3
Lanz machine works, 120–1
Lees, Pilot Officer, 200
Leipzig: diversionary raid, 219–20;
raid, 240–1, 242
Lichtenstein radar sets, 213, 215
Lindemann, Frederick, *see* Cherwell
Link flight simulator, 103, 104
L'Isle-Adam, V1 site raid, 268
Lloyd, Geoffrey, 111
Locke, Squadron Leader, 264
London: Blitz, 2, 3, 64–7, 69, 70–1,
124, 287; bomb damage, 71; City,
59, 70; deaths, 71; East End, 64–6;
Luftwaffe bombing, 59, 60; Surrey
Docks, 64–5
losses, *see* casualties
Lübeck, bombing raid, 130–1, 133
lucky charms, 180, 210, 235
Ludwigshafen, 119–20, 150, 151, 196
Luftwaffe: XII Fliegerkorps, 116; air
defences, 115–18; aircraft
numbers, 45, 46; aircraft types, 48,
59, 62; Battle of Britain, 46; Blitz,
2, 3; bombing raids, 58–9; fighter
forces, 229; KG 100, 67–8, 70;
Knickebein navigation system, 60,
67, 125; London raids, 59, 60,
64–7; losses, 63; navigation
systems, 60, 67–8; night-fighter
force, 159, 163, 198, 212–15, 226,
272; radar, 116–18; Rotterdam
bombing (1940), 83; strategy
(1940), 59, 61–3, 67, 71; strategy
(1941), 71

Magdeburg, bombing raid, 232, 233
Mainz: bomb damage, 288–9; bombed
by mistake, 218
Mammoth radar system, 214

INDEX

Manby, RAF, 45, 48–56, 73–4
Manchester bombers, 105–6, 135
Mandrel system, 214
Mann, Jim, 189
Mannesmann-Röhrenwerke steelworks, 186
Mannheim: bombing raids, 118, 119–20, 144, 150, 168, 196; diversionary raid, 217
Manuden, Lincolnshire, 21–2, 173, 197, 235, 259, 284
Merlin engines, *see* Rolls-Royce Merlin
Messerschmitt aircraft: Me 109, 48, 62–3, 77, 82; Me 110, 62, 115, 116, 213, 215
Messerschmitt factory, 195
Millars engineering factory, 23–4, 25–6, 39, 41–2
Modane, bombing raid, 192–3, 244
Morecambe, Lancashire, 42–3
Morris Motors, 68
Mosquito aircraft: Berlin photo missions, 218; design, 137; diversionary raids, 186, 219, 237; Frankfurt spoof raid, 196; French raid, 265; H2S sets, 160; Hamburg raid, 162; Oboe equipment, 154–6, 177, 248, 261; Essen raid, 156; München-Gladbach raid, 278; shot down, 211; speed and handling, 105, 137; target-marking section, 256; versatility, 215; Window dropping, 183
Mülheim, bombing raids, 157
München-Gladbach, bombing raids, 157, 277–9
Munich, bombing raid, 177–80
Münster, bomb damage, 157
Murrow, Ed, 211

Nagasaki, atomic bomb, 283
navigation: aids, 13, 115, 128, 143, 189, 191, 272; exercises, 96, 101–2; night, 59–60; problems, 84; training, 2, 34, 36, 93, 115, 280–3
Naxos system, 214–15
Neckar, River, 119
Nickel (propaganda leafleting), 79, 84

No 5 Group Tactical Notes, 140
Normandy landings (1944), 6, 7, 260–1, 266
North Luffenham, RAF, 93, 97–9, 105
Nuremberg, bombing raid, 242

Oberhausen, bombing raids, 157
Oboe navigation system, 153–6, 158, 160, 176, 177, 248, 260
Offenbach, bomb damage, 218
Oppau, bombed by mistake, 151

Paris, German occupation, 44
Parliamentary Committee on the German Oil Position, 111
Paterson, Pat, 211
Pathfinder Force: aircraft, 137; Berlin raids, 199, 210, 220, 226, 255; Bochum raid, 176; casualties, 211, 226–7, 255; creation, 137; Essen raids, 156, 248; failures, 171, 178–9, 210, 220, 226; Flensburg raid, 138; Frankfurt raid, 217–18; German monitoring, 214; H2S equipment, 155, 162, 176, 178, 191, 211, 220, 227; Hamburg raids, 162–3; Hanover raids, 170, 171, 172; Leipzig raid, 241; Modane raid, 192–3; Mosquitoes, 137, 154–5; Munich raid, 178–9; Oboe, 154–5, 176; offset marking, 178; problems, 241, 244; role, 138, 155; Stuttgart raids, 244, 270; training, 255–6
Peenemünde V1 plant, RAF raid, 195, 267
Pegasus engines, *see* Bristol Pegasus
Peirse, Sir Richard, 109, 115, 118–19, 121–3
Perkins, Flight Lieutenant, 263
Pforzheim, 183
Pillau, mining raid, 248
Polson, 'Dickie': appearance, 257; Bremerhaven raid, 277; Brunswick raid, 257–8; character, 257; close-formation flying, 263; Darmstadt raid, 276; end of tour, 279; Joigny-Laroche daylight raid, 266;

Polson, 'Dickie' (*cont.*)
Königsberg raid, 272–5;
München-Gladbach raid, 277–8;
Normandy raids (1944), 260–1;
postwar life, 287; rear gunner, 257;
St-Valéry-en-Caux raid, 259;
Stuttgart raids, 270–1, 277; V1 site
raids, 267–9
Portal, Sir Charles, Air Chief Marshal,
82, 84–6, 109–15, 120, 121–3, 137
Pregel, River, 249
propaganda leafleting, 79–81

Queen Elizabeth (liner), 87–9, 280

radar: anti-aircraft sets, 116–18, 134,
145–6, 160, 211, 266; destruction
of German sites, 272;
development 3, 46, 116; German
airborne, 213, 214–15; German
long-range systems, 214, 217;
German radar-controlled night-
fighter zones, 116–18, 134, 160–1,
226, 229; German radio beacons,
219, 229; H2S, 154–5, 160, 190,
194, 220, 257; Lichtenstein, 213,
215; Pathfinder Force, 210; RAF
knowledge of German defensive
system, 140; SN2, 215, 226;
training, 282; Window, 161–3, 212,
213, 215, 232–3
Regensburg, planned raid, 195
Reid, Bill, Flight Lieutenant, 188–9
Remscheid, bomb damage, 157
Renault factory, Billancourt, 126–8,
131, 171, 195
Rheinberg, decoy fires, 129
Rhine, River: banks, 119; Cologne, 135;
estuary, 117; navigation aid, 150
Rolls-Royce Kestrel engine, 43
Rolls-Royce Merlin engines: in fighters,
8, 40, 43; knowledge of, 107, 208;
in Lancasters, 8, 106, 148, 274; in
Mosquitoes, 137; oil pressure, 208
Rolls-Royce Vulture engines, 105, 106
Roosevelt, Franklin D., 75
Rostock, bombing raid, 131–2
Rotterdam, German bombing, 83

Roulton, L. G., Sergeant, 189
Royal Air Force (RAF): 9 Squadron,
31, 200; 57 Squadron, 4, 139–42,
144, 152, 174, 186, 188, 193, 200,
216, 218, 243, 282, 289; 61
Squadron, 188; 76 Squadron, 161;
83 Squadron, 256; 97 Squadron, 5,
256–7, 259, 261, 266, 270, 271,
277, 280, 284–5, 287, 289, 266,
277, 284, 289; 106 Squadron, 256;
207 Squadron, 200; 617 Squadron,
171, 189, 195, 255, 256, 277; 627
Squadron, 256; Advanced Flying
Units, 89, 101; Bomber
Command, *see* Bomber
Command; commander-in-chief,
109; Fighter Command, 45–6;
Heavy Conversion Units, 105, 108,
285; losses (August 1941), 118;
losses (Ruhr campaign 1943), 159;
Operational Training Units
(OTUs), 93, 97, 108, 133, 140,
188, 191, 280; target strategy, 74–6
Royal Australian Air Force, 107, 211
Royal Canadian Air Force: Central
Flying School, 280; flagpole gift,
264; Initial Training School, 34–5;
recruitment of George, 31, 33;
Service Flying Training School,
35–7
Ruhr: bombing raids, 124, 126, 212,
248; defences, 116–18;
identification of targets, 129; RAF
campaign (1943), 157–60, 174–5;
RAF strategy, 74–5, 81, 83, 110,
125; railways, 110, 121; synthetic
oil industry, 83, 110

Sachsenhausen, bomb damage, 218
St Athan, RAF, 43–5
St-Pierre-du-Mont, raid, 259–60
St-Valéry-en-Caux, bombing raid, 259
Sampson target-marking method, 128–9
Saunders-Roe aircraft works,
Southampton, 59
Sayn-Wittgenstein, Heinrich, Major,
226
Schneider Trophy, 54

Schweinfurt, US raid, 195
Schwelm, bombed by mistake, 129
Sea Lion, Operation, 86
Searby, John, Squadron Leader, 211
Second World War, 40, 288
Shaker target-marking method, 127, 128
Shipham, Norfolk, US base, 189
Short Stirling, see Stirling bombers
Shorts Brothers aircraft factory,
    Rochester, 59
Siemens plants, 196
sky-marking, 154–5, 227, 241, 258
Sloman, Sergeant, 50–1
Smith, Bryan, Squadron Leader, 260
SN2 airborne radar, 215, 226
Somme, Battle of the, 18, 27
Southampton, bombing, 59, 132
Speer, Albert, 165–6
Spilsby, RAF, 201
Spitfire fighters, 45, 62, 63
Stainforth, George, Wing Commander,
    54–6
Stansted: airport, 7; US base, 8, 260
Stirling bombers: Canadian training,
    285; Cologne raid, 135;
    diversionary raids, 196; Hamburg
    raid, 162; losses, 159; mid-upper
    gun turret, 95; operation height,
    106, 155; Pathfinder Force, 137;
    withdrawn, 185
Stuttgart: bombing raids, 183–4, 196,
    270–1; Bosch factory, 196
Supermarine S.6B seaplane, 54
Swinderby, RAF, 105–7, 282
Syerston airfield, 246–7

Taft, Group Captain, 193
Tame Sow flights, 213
target-marking: Berlin raids, 201; fire-
    raising, 130–1; flares, 137, 154,
    256–7, 278; improved, 272, 275;
    offset marking, 178, 266–7;
    Pathfinder Force, 137–8, 156,
    210–11; Sampson method, 128–9;
    Shaker technique, 127, 128; sky-
    marking, 154–5, 227, 241, 258; use
    of radar, 257, 278
Thameshaven, oil-storage depot, 59

Thomas, Sidney 'Tommy', Pilot
    Officer: Aachen aborted mission,
    251–2; background, 11; Berlin
    raids, 197–200, 204–10, 219–24,
    225–40; Bochum raid, 175–7;
    Bomber Command crew selection,
    100–1; Clermont-Ferrand raid,
    244; death, 287; Düsseldorf raid,
    186–9; end of first tour, 252–3,
    254–5; first Lancaster mission,
    14–15, 146–52, 168; Frankfurt
    aborted mission, 180–3, 184;
    Frankfurt raids, 217–18, 245–8;
    Hagen raid, 177; Hanover raid,
    171–2; health, 256; Königsberg
    raid, 249–51; Lancaster C Charlie,
    189–93; Modane raid, 192–3, 244;
    Munich raid, 177–80; night vision,
    256; rear gunner, 4, 11, 100, 256;
    Ruhr raid, 248; social life, 203;
    Stuttgart raids, 183–4, 244
Tiger Force, 283, 285
Tiger Moth biplane, 34–5, 94
Trans-Canada Airlines, 281
Transport Command, 285
Trave, River, 130
Trossy-St-Maximin, raid on V1 launch
    site, 267–8

US Eighth Air Force, 164, 194–5, 285
USAAF (United States Army Air
    Force), 8–9, 194–5, 262

V1 'buzz' bombs, 6, 195, 267–8, 270
Van Raalte, Flight Lieutenant, 263
Vickers-Armstrong factory,
    Brooklands, 285
Vickers Wellington bombers, see
    Wellington bombers
VKF factory, 196
Vulture engines, see Rolls-Royce
    Vulture

Wanne-Eickel, oil plant, 111
War Cabinet: attack on German navy,
    77; Bomber Command casualties,
    124; bombing strategy, 86, 111–13,
    130, 160; Ruhr raid, 83

Warboys, Cambridgeshire, 255–6
Wassermann radar system, 214
Waterbeach, Cambridgeshire, 172–3
Wellington bombers: Berlin raids, 60,
    63; bomb load, 46, 47; Canadian
    pilots, 31, 32, 101; Cologne raid,
    134–6; design, 46–7; engines,
    49–50, 51–2; Hamburg raid, 162;
    losses, 77, 78, 136; Lübeck raid,
    131; operation height, 155; raids
    on German warships, 76–8; role of
    observer, 95; training role, 49–53,
    101; withdrawn, 185
West, Lieutenant, 188
Whitley bombers, 47, 48, 79–81, 83,
    120
Wild Sow aircraft, 213, 215
Wilhelmshaven: bombing raid on

warships, 76, 78; port, 32
'Window': development, 160–1; effects,
    162–3, 183, 207, 212; German
    response to, 213, 215; production,
    161; secrecy, 167; use, 161–2, 183,
    232–3
Wolverhampton, German bombing,
    67, 69
Women's Auxiliary Air Force (WAAF),
    54, 142
Women's Land Army, 44
Woodruffe, Wing Commander, 273
Wuppertal, bomb damage, 157
Wyton, RAF, 270

X-beam system, 67–8, 70

Zuider Zee, 117, 234

ABOUT THE AUTHOR

Mike Rossiter is the author of a number of bestselling books on military history – *Ark Royal*, *Sink the Belgrano*, *Target Basra* and *I Sank the Bismarck* (which he co-authored with John Moffat).